Betty Crocker's *best* CHRISTMAS

COOKBOOK

Hungry Minds™

HUNGRY MINDS, INC.

New York, NY ◆ Cleveland, OH ◆ Indianapolis, IN

Hungry Minds, Inc.

909 Third Avenue
New York, NY 10022

 Hungry Minds™ is a trademark of Hungry Minds, Inc.

BETTY CROCKER, Bisquick, Cheerios and Bugles are registered trademarks of General Mills, Inc.

For general information on Hungry Minds' products and services please contact our Customer Care Department within the U.S. at 800-762-2974, outside the U.S. at 317-572-3993 or fax 317-572-4002.

Library of Congress Cataloging-in-Publication Data

Crocker, Betty.
  Betty Crocker's Best Christmas Cookbook.
  p. cm.
    ISBN 0-02-863465-9
    1. Christmas cookery. I. Title.
  TX739.2.C45C7 1999
  641.5'68—dc21   99-35731
                                      CIP

GENERAL MILLS, INC.

Betty Crocker Kitchens
Manager, Publishing: Lois L. Tlusty
Editors: Kelly Kilen, Karen Sorensen
Recipe Development: Karen Linden
Food Stylists: Cindy Lund, Carol Grones,
  Cindy Syme

Nutritionist: Nancy Holmes, R.D.
Photographic Services
Art Director: Emily Oberg
Photographers: Steven B. Olson, Valerie J. Bourassa

Cover Design: Michele Laseau

For consistent baking results, the Betty Crocker Kitchens recommend Gold Medal Flour.

Manufactured in the United States of America

10 9 8 7 6 5 4

First Edition

Cover photo:
1. Melt-in-Your-Mouth Sugar Cookies (p. 204)
2. Sensational Shortbread Cookies (p. 207)
3. Shortbread Buttons (variation of Sensational Shortbread, p. 207)
4. Holiday Spritz (p. 210)
5. Ginger Cookie Cut-Outs (variation of Gingersnaps, p. 220)
6. Laced Gingersnaps (variation of Gingersnaps, p. 220)
7. Almond Bonbons (p. 214)
8. Chocolate Crinkles (p. 224)
9. Peppermint Pinwheels (variation of Slice-it-Easy Cookies, p. 222)

Christmas cheer is contagious!

So I am sharing some of my best ideas with you . . .

These pages are packed full of great things to make for the holiday—from decking your halls to sitting down to your Christmas feast.

Every Christmas category is covered—party appetizers and holiday drinks, merry main dishes and sides, scrumptious desserts and home-made breads, a cascade of cookie and candy recipes plus food gifts and decorations to make any holiday sparkle. And if you're looking for great ideas, this is the place to be—every recipe in the book is photographed so you'll see exactly what you are making.

There's a wonderful blend of treasured traditional recipes and updated classics, making it easy to keep up with family tradition plus create some new ones of your own. You'll also find our Most Requested Recipes in each chapter for all your favorites to make the holiday unforgettable.

Furthermore, enjoy a host of "at a glance" tips and suggestions you'll find on each page that will help make all your festivities shine. So, if you are looking for easy, creative ideas for the holidays, look no further. Let's get started creating some lifelong memories!

Betty Crocker
P.S. Merry Christmas!

CONTENTS

CHAPTER 1

*Simple
Sippers
and
Savory
Nibbles*

6

CHAPTER 2

*Merry
Main
Dishes*

44

CHAPTER 3

*Sensational
Salads
and Sides*

90

CHAPTER 4

*Fabulous
Finales*

126

CHAPTER 5

*Holiday
Breads*

166

CHAPTER 6

*Sweet
Shop
Favorites*

202

CHAPTER 7

*Festive
Family
Fun*

254

CHAPTER 8

*Holiday
Gifts and
Decorations*

282

*Helpful Nutrition and Cooking
Information, 340*
Metric Conversion Guide, 342
Index, 343

*Cucumbers, Carrots and Smoked Salmon Crudités
(page 23), Cranberry-Orange Slush Cocktail (page 12)
and Meatball Merriment (page 30)*

CHAPTER 1

Simple Sippers
and
Savory Nibbles

A sip of merriment and a bite of cheer. What better way to welcome in the holidays with family and friends?

Quick Cranberry Punch

PREP: 5 MIN
24 SERVINGS

2 cans (6 ounces each) frozen lemonade concentrate, thawed

1 1/2 cups cold water

2 bottles (32 ounces each) cranberry juice cocktail, chilled

4 cans (12 ounces each) ginger ale, chilled

Ice ring (see Holiday Hints, below) or ice

Mix lemonade concentrate and water in large pitcher. Stir in cranberry juice cocktail. Just before serving, stir in ginger ale. Pour into large punch bowl. Add ice ring.

1 Serving: Calories 110 (Calories from Fat 0); Fat 0g (Saturated 0g); Cholesterol 0mg; Sodium 10mg; Carbohydrate 27g (Dietary Fiber 0g); Protein 0g
% Daily Value: Vitamin A 0%; Vitamin C 54%; Calcium 0%; Iron 2%
Diet Exchanges: 2 Fruit

New Twist

Add a finishing touch to holiday drinks with these festive beverage additions:

• Garnish holiday drinks with a slice of starfruit on the rim of each glass.

• Freeze fresh mint leaves and cranberries in water in ice-cube trays.

• Make ice cubes with juice instead of water. When the juice cubes melt in the punch, it won't be diluted.

Holiday Hints

Here's an easy way to make a frosty, festive ice ring: Fill a ring mold or bundt cake pan with crushed ice (make sure the mold you choose is smaller than your punch bowl). Cut fruit such as lemons, limes, oranges and starfruit into 1/4-inch slices; arrange in the ice so the fruit sticks up above the top of the ring mold. You can also cut orange peel into star shapes, using tiny cookie cutters. Freeze the mold 15 minutes, then slowly add cold water or fruit juice to fill the mold. Freeze the mold overnight to make sure the ice ring is solid. When you are ready to serve the punch, run hot water over bottom of the mold to loosen the ice ring. Remove the ice ring from the mold, and float it in the punch. Or, with the same technique, use muffin cups to make floating ice disks, which take less time to freeze.

Quick Cranberry Punch

Frosty Citrus Punch

PREP: 10 MIN

15 SERVINGS

2 cans (6 ounces each) frozen limeade or lemonade
concentrate, thawed

3 cups cold water

2 cans (12 ounces each) lemon-lime soda pop
(3 cups), chilled

1/2 pint lime or lemon sherbet (1 cup), softened

Mix limeade concentrate and water in large pitcher. Just
before serving, stir in soda pop. Pour into punch bowl.
Float scoops of sherbet on top.

1 Serving: Calories 95 (Calories from Fat 0); Fat 0g (Saturated 0g);
Cholesterol 0mg; Sodium 10mg; Carbohydrate 24g (Dietary Fiber 0g);
Protein 0g
% Daily Value: Vitamin A 0%; Vitamin C 6%; Calcium 0%; Iron 0%
Diet Exchanges: 1 1/2 Fruit

Party Pointers

Light the way with luminarias! Here's
how:

- Purchase luminaria bags at a party
store. Fill with about 3 inches of
sand or kitty litter. Place a 1-pint
canning jar into the sand and add
a votive candle. Light luminarias
right before the guests arrive.

- Fill a 7-inch balloon with water
until 6 inches in diameter; tie end.
Place filled balloon in a plastic container of similar size for support.
Freeze at least 12 hours or until ice
is about 1/2 inch thick around
inside of balloon. Remove balloon
from around ice ball. Chisel opening in top of ball; drain water.

Place outside, insert a votive candle
and light candle. If you'd like colored luminaria, add a few drops of
food color to the water.

- Or for a super simple idea, use a
1-liter soda pop bottle to make
holes in the snow along a driveway
or walkway. Fill holes with candles
for a glowing path of light.

Frosty Citrus Punch

Cranberry-Orange Slush Cocktail

PREP: 10 MIN; FREEZE: 8 HR
30 SERVINGS

1 bottle (32 ounces) cranberry juice cocktail

2 cups brandy

1 can (12 ounces) frozen cranberry juice concentrate, thawed

1 can (12 ounces) frozen orange juice concentrate, thawed

2 bottles (1 liter each) lemon-lime soda pop or sparkling water

Lime slices, if desired

Mix all ingredients except soda pop and lime slices. Divide among pint containers. Cover and freeze at least 8 hours or until slushy.

For each serving, stir equal amounts of slush mixture and soda pop in glass. Garnish with lime slices.

1 Serving: Calories 85 (Calories from Fat 0); Fat 0g (Saturated 0g); Cholesterol 0mg; Sodium 5mg; Carbohydrate 21g (Dietary Fiber 0g); Protein 0g
% Daily Value: Vitamin A 0%; Vitamin C 60%; Calcium 0%; Iron 0%
Diet Exchanges: 1 1/2 Fruit

Timesaving Tips

This is the perfect drink to have on hand for drop-in guests! The slush freezes quickly when packaged in 1-pint containers and can be used directly from the freezer.

If you'd like to freeze this drink in large quantities for punch, freeze for one or two days until firm. You can make this drink up to two months ahead of time. Covered tightly, it keeps in the freezer and will stay slushy until you're ready to serve it.

Frozen Strawberry Margaritas

PREP: 10 MIN; FREEZE: 24 HR
10 SERVINGS

1 can (6 ounces) frozen limeade concentrate, thawed

1 package (10 ounces) frozen strawberries in syrup, thawed

3 cups water

3/4 cup tequila

1 bottle (1 liter) lemon-lime soda pop, chilled

Place limeade concentrate and strawberries in blender. Cover and blend on medium speed until smooth. Mix strawberry mixture, water and tequila. Pour into 2-quart plastic container. Cover and freeze at least 24 hours or until slushy.

For each serving, stir 2/3 cup slush and 1/3 cup soda pop in glass.

1 Serving: Calories 120 (Calories from Fat 0); Fat 0g (Saturated 0g); Cholesterol 0mg; Sodium 15mg; Carbohydrate 31g (Dietary Fiber 0g); Protein 0g
% Daily Value: Vitamin A 0%; Vitamin C 24%; Calcium 0%; Iron 0%
Diet Exchanges: 2 Fruit

FROZEN RASPBERRY MARGARITAS: Substitute thawed 10-ounce package of frozen raspberries in syrup for the strawberries.

Holiday Hints

Dress up these frosty drinks by dipping the moistened rims of margarita glasses in red and green colored sugar.

Holiday Eggnog

PREP: 10 MIN; COOK: 20 MIN
6 SERVINGS

The holidays give us license to splurge on simple pleasures, such as a cup of creamy, heartwarming cheer. So go ahead and take an extra sip of simple indulgence.

3 eggs, slightly beaten

1/3 cup granulated sugar

Dash of salt

2 1/2 cups milk

1 teaspoon vanilla

1/2 cup rum, if desired

1 cup whipping (heavy) cream

1 tablespoon packed brown sugar

Ground nutmeg

Mix eggs, granulated sugar and salt in heavy 2-quart saucepan. Gradually stir in milk. Cook over low heat 15 to 20 minutes, stirring constantly, just until mixture coats a metal spoon; remove from heat. Stir in vanilla and rum. Keep warm.

Just before serving, beat whipping cream and brown sugar in chilled small bowl with electric mixer on high speed until stiff. Gently stir 1 cup of the whipped cream into eggnog mixture.

Pour eggnog into small heatproof punch bowl. Drop remaining whipped cream into 4 or 5 mounds onto eggnog. Sprinkle nutmeg on whipped cream mounds. Serve immediately. Cover and refrigerate any remaining eggnog.

1 Serving: Calories 260 (Calories from Fat 155); Fat 17g (Saturated 10g); Cholesterol 160mg; Sodium 100mg; Carbohydrate 20g (Dietary Fiber 0g); Protein 7g
% Daily Value: Vitamin A 18%; Vitamin C 2%; Calcium 16%; Iron 2%
Diet Exchanges: 1 Fruit, 1 Skim Milk

Holiday Hints

EGGNOG FOR EVERYONE!

- For the coffee lovers in your family, make **Hot Cappuccino Eggnog**: Substitute coffee liqueur for the rum and add 1 cup hot espresso coffee. Don't worry if you don't have brewed espresso coffee; any strongly brewed cup of coffee (regular or decaf) will work.

- Freeze small dollops of whipped cream by scooping them out onto a cookie sheet and freezing until firm. Keep them handy in a resealable plastic freezer bag. Place one dollop on each drink just before serving, and sprinkle lightly with ground cinnamon or nutmeg.

- Place plain or chocolate-dipped pirouette cookies in a pretty serving piece for guests to use as edible stirring spoons.

- Love the flavor of eggnog but not the calories? Substitute 2 eggs plus 2 egg whites for the 3 eggs and 2 1/4 cups skim milk for the milk. Instead of the beaten whipping cream and brown sugar, use 2 cups frozen (thawed) whipped topping.

- Don't have time to make your own eggnog? Dress up purchased eggnog instead. Place eggnog in punch bowl, scoop dollops of cinnamon or French vanilla ice cream over the nog and sprinkle with ground nutmeg.

Holiday Eggnog and Cinnamon Cider (page 18)

Hot Buttered Rum

PREP: 15 MIN

ABOUT 3 CUPS BATTER (ENOUGH FOR 24 SERVINGS)

Hot Buttered Rum Batter:

  1 cup butter or margarine, softened

  1 cup plus 2 tablespoons packed brown sugar

  1 cup whipping (heavy) cream

  2 cups powdered sugar

  1/8 teaspoon ground cloves

  1/8 teaspoon ground cinnamon

  1/4 teaspoon ground nutmeg

Have ready at serving time:

  2 tablespoons rum

  1/2 cup boiling water

  Ground nutmeg

Beat butter and brown sugar in medium bowl with electric mixer on medium speed about 5 minutes or until light and fluffy. Beat in whipping cream and powdered sugar alternately on low speed until smooth. Stir in cloves, cinnamon and nutmeg.

Use immediately, or spoon into 1-quart freezer container. Cover, label and freeze up to 3 months.

For each serving, place rum and 2 tablespoons Hot Buttered Rum Batter in mug. Stir in boiling water. Sprinkle with nutmeg.

1 Serving: Calories 180 (Calories from Fat 100); Fat 11g (Saturated 7g); Cholesterol 30mg; Sodium 60mg; Carbohydrate 20g (Dietary Fiber 0g); Protein 0g
% Daily Value: Vitamin A 8%; Vitamin C 0%; Calcium 2%; Iron 0%
Diet Exchanges: 1 1/2 Fruit, 2 Fat

Timesaving Tips

A cup of warm cheer is just minutes away! Prepare the batter ahead of time, and tuck it away in your freezer. Or for individual servings, freeze 2 tablespoons batter in each section of ice-cube trays; when frozen, place cubes in freezer bag.

Party Pointers

If you're having a large party, avoid congestion by placing drinks at one table and appetizers at another.

If using disposable dishes, place wastebaskets throughout the house. Or if using regular dishes and glasses, place trays throughout the house and have someone frequently empty them of dirty dishes.

Hot Buttered Rum

Cinnamon Cider

PREP: 10 MIN; COOK: 25 MIN
32 SERVINGS

1 gallon apple cider

2/3 cup sugar

2 teaspoons whole allspice

2 teaspoons whole cloves

2 cinnamon sticks, 3 inches long

2 oranges, studded with cloves

Heat all ingredients except oranges to boiling in Dutch oven; reduce heat. Cover and simmer 20 minutes.

Strain punch. Pour into small heatproof punch bowl. Float oranges in bowl. Serve hot.

1 Serving: Calories 75 (Calories from Fat 0); Fat 0g (Saturated 0g); Cholesterol 0mg; Sodium 5mg; Carbohydrate 19g (Dietary Fiber 0g); Protein 0g
% Daily Value: Vitamin A 0%; Vitamin C 0%; Calcium 0%; Iron 2%
Diet Exchanges: 1 Fruit

Party Pointers

- Pull out the slow cooker to help you with the holidays. When serving hot cider at a holiday buffet, pour heated cider into slow cooker set on low and let guests help themselves.

- If you prefer to keep the hot cider in the kitchen, invite guests into the kitchen to ladle cider into their own mugs. Use an attractive saucepan kept right on the stove top over low heat.

- You can make a glass punch bowl safer for hot beverages by filling it first with hot water and letting it stand about 30 minutes. Pour out water, and slowly add hot punch.

Hot Spiced Wine

PREP: 10 MIN; COOK: 20 MIN
10 SERVINGS

1 cup packed brown sugar

2 1/2 cups orange juice

1 cup water

1/2 teaspoon salt

Peel of 2 oranges, cut into 1/4-inch strips

6 whole cloves

3 whole allspice

1 four-inch stick cinnamon

1 bottle (750 milliliters) dry red wine or nonalcoholic red wine

Orange slices, if desired

Additional whole cloves, if desired

Heat all ingredients except wine, orange slices and additional cloves to boiling in Dutch oven, stirring occasionally; reduce heat. Simmer uncovered 15 minutes.

Remove orange peel and spices. Stir in wine. Heat just until hot (do not boil). Serve hot in mugs or heatproof glasses. Garnish each serving with orange slice studded with additional whole cloves.

1 Serving: Calories 120 (Calories from Fat 0); Fat 0g (Saturated 0g); Cholesterol 0mg; Sodium 135mg; Carbohydrate 29g (Dietary Fiber 0g); Protein 1g
% Daily Value: Vitamin A 0%; Vitamin C 18%; Calcium 2%; Iron 6%
Diet Exchanges: 2 Fruit

Holiday Hints

Citrus fruits and spices such as cinnamon, cloves and allspice are the secret to making delicious spiced wine. You can also use granulated sugar in this recipe, but brown sugar adds a delightful touch of caramel sweetness.

Timesaving Tips

If you like, cover and refrigerate spiced wine up to one week. Just reheat until hot (do not boil) before serving.

Appetizer Cheese Trees

PREP: 30 MIN; CHILL: 4 HR
ABOUT 7 CUPS SPREAD

3 packages (8 ounces each) cream cheese, softened

4 cups shredded Cheddar cheese (16 ounces)

2 tablespoons pesto

1 tablespoon grated onion

1/4 teaspoon ground mustard (dry)

2 or 3 drops red pepper sauce

Have ready at serving time:

1/4 cup finely chopped parsley or cilantro

1/4 cup pine nuts

2 tablespoons chopped red bell pepper

Assorted crackers, if desired

Mix cream cheese and Cheddar cheese; divide in half. Mix pesto into 1 half; mix onion, mustard and pepper sauce into other half. Cover each half and refrigerate about 4 hours or until firm enough to shape.

Place cheese mixtures on cookie sheet. Shape each half into cone shape to look like Christmas tree. Roll trees in parsley, pressing parsley evenly onto trees. Press pine nuts onto trees in string form for garland. Press bell pepper pieces onto trees for ornaments. Top each tree with star shape cut from lemon peel if desired. Serve with crackers.

1/4 Cup: Calories 155 (Calories from Fat 125); Fat 14g (Saturated 9g); Cholesterol 45mg; Sodium 180mg; Carbohydrate 1g (Dietary Fiber 0g); Protein 6g
% Daily Value: Vitamin A 10%; Vitamin C 0%; Calcium 10%; Iron 2%
Diet Exchanges: 1 High-Fat Meat, 1 Fat

Timesaving Tips

This is a great do-ahead appetizer. After shaping cheese mixtures on the cookie sheet, wrap in plastic wrap or aluminum foil, label and freeze up to one month. Twelve hours before serving, remove the trees from the freezer. Thaw in wrapper in the refrigerator. Continue as directed.

New Twist

Here's an idea the kids will love! Instead of trees, make snowmen! Shape the cheese mixture into a **Snowman Cheese Ball** (you'll have enough to make 2 small snowmen or 1 large one). Omit parsley, pine nuts and bell pepper. Mix cream cheese and Cheddar cheese; divide into 3 equal parts. Mix 2 parts to equal two-thirds of mixture; mix in pesto. Mix onion, mustard and pepper sauce into remaining one-third of cheese mixture. Refrigerate as directed. Shape each cheese mixture into 2 balls; roll in 1/3 cup finely chopped blanched almonds. Arrange balls on serving plate with smaller ball on top for head of snowman; press together slightly. Insert pretzel sticks for arms. Decorate as desired with capers, sliced olives, chopped carrots, sliced cucumber, chopped bell peppers and fresh thyme leaves.

Appetizer Cheese Tree and Snowman Cheese Ball (variation)

Cream Cheese Penguins

PREP: 45 MIN
18 APPETIZERS

18 jumbo ripe olives (from 5 3/4-ounce can)

1 package (8 ounces) cream cheese

1 carrot (at least 6 inches long and 1 inch in diameter), cut into 1/4-inch slices

18 small ripe olives

18 frilled toothpicks

Cut a slit in each jumbo olive from top to bottom on one side only. Insert about 1 teaspoon cream cheese into olive to fill cavity.

Cut small notch out of each carrot slice to form feet. Press cutout notch piece into center of small olive to form beak (if necessary, pierce olive with small paring knife or toothpick to make a hole).

Using a frilled toothpick, stack small olive (head), stuffed jumbo olive (body) and carrot slice (feet), adjusting so that beak, cream cheese breast and notch in carrot slice line up. (Penguin will stand better if olives are stacked with larger holes facing downward.)

1 Appetizer: Calories 60 (Calories from Fat 55); Fat 6g (Saturated 3g); Cholesterol 15mg; Sodium 140mg; Carbohydrate 1g (Dietary Fiber 0g); Protein 1g
% Daily Value: Vitamin A 10%; Vitamin C 0%; Calcium 2%; Iron 2%
Diet Exchanges: 1 Fat

Holiday Hints

Set these perky little party penguins in a bed of crushed ice, and they'll look like they've waddled right down from the North Pole.

Use regular toothpicks in place of the frilled picks. Then attach a small piece of pimiento to toothpick on top of the small olive for a stocking cap.

Cucumbers, Carrots and Smoked Salmon Crudités

PREP: 15 MIN
24 APPETIZERS

2 ounces salmon lox, finely chopped

1/2 package (8-ounce size) cream cheese, softened

3/4 teaspoon chopped fresh or 1/4 teaspoon dried
dill weed

1 large cucumber, cut into 1/4-inch slices
(12 slices)

1 large carrot, cut into 1/4-inch slices (12 slices)

Crackers, if desired

Dill weed sprigs, if desired

Mix lox, cream cheese and chopped dill weed. Place lox
mixture in decorating bag fitted with large star tip; pipe
or spoon 1 heaping teaspoonful onto each cucumber and
carrot slice or cracker. Garnish each with dill weed sprig.

1 Appetizer: Calories 25 (Calories from Fat 20); Fat 2g (Saturated
1g); Cholesterol 5mg; Sodium 35mg; Carbohydrate 2g (Dietary
Fiber 0g); Protein 1g
% Daily Value: Vitamin A 2%; Vitamin C 2%; Calcium 0%; Iron 0%
Diet Exchanges: 1/2 Fat

HOLIDAY MENU

Office Bash

- Cinnamon Cider (page 18)
- Cucumbers, Carrots and Smoked Salmon
  Crudités
- Sun-Dried Tomato Dip (page 24) with
  assorted veggies
- Three-Bean Christmas Chili (page 79)
- Christmas Spinach Salad (page 99)
- Garlic Bread Wreath (page 189)
- Almond-Toffee Triangles (page 230)
- Deluxe Christmas Fudge (page 236)

Party Pointers

Need ideas for a smashing bash?
Here are a few tips and menu ideas:

- Post a sign-up sheet and copies of
  the recipes, and ask everyone to vol-
  unteer to bring a prepared dish
  (and serving utensils!), with the
  option to use the provided recipe. If
  you have a large office, have two or
  more people bring the same dish.
  Don't forget beverages, decorations
  and disposable plates, napkins and
  other serving items on the list.

- If you're in an office that shares a
  refrigerator, give coworkers notice
  to "clear out and clean up," so
  there will be plenty of room for
  the party fare.

- Set up a buffet table in a designat-
  ed room, and let coworkers come
  and help themselves. Using gift
  wrap as a "tablecloth" is an inex-
  pensive way to cover any table and
  give the room a festive look!

- To get the party off to a glorious
  start, ask each person to bring a
  holiday mug to share. When it is
  time to ladle out the Cinnamon
  Cider (page 18), everyone picks
  out a different mug than the one he
  or she brought and gets to keep it.

Sun-Dried Tomato Dip

PREP: 20 MIN; CHILL: 2 HR
ABOUT 2 1/4 CUPS DIP

8 sun-dried tomato halves (not oil-packed)

1/4 cup chopped fresh parsley

1 tablespoon chopped fresh or 1 teaspoon freeze-dried chives

1 tablespoon olive or vegetable oil

2 teaspoons lemon juice

1 teaspoon red wine vinegar

1/2 teaspoon salt

1/2 teaspoon pepper

1 clove garlic, finely chopped

3/4 cup plain low-fat yogurt

3/4 cup sour cream

Place tomato halves in 1 inch water in 1 1/2-quart saucepan. Heat to boiling; reduce heat to medium.

Simmer uncovered about 5 minutes or until water has evaporated.

Place tomatoes and remaining ingredients except yogurt and sour cream in blender or food processor. Cover and blend on medium-high speed until smooth.

Place tomato mixture in medium glass or plastic bowl. Stir in yogurt and sour cream. Cover and refrigerate about 2 hours or until chilled.

1 Tablespoon: Calories 15 (Calories from Fat 10); Fat 1g (Saturated 1g); Cholesterol 5mg; Sodium 45mg; Carbohydrate 1g (Dietary Fiber 0g); Protein 0g
% Daily Value: Vitamin A 0%; Vitamin C 2%; Calcium 2%; Iron 0%
Diet Exchanges: Not Recommended

Holiday Hints

When serving dips, don't limit yourself to butter crackers! Offer an assortment of crunchy foods—such as raw veggies, assorted wheat crackers and long breadsticks—for dipping.

- If calorie counts are climbing this holiday season, make a lighter version of this dip by using fat-free yogurt and fat-free sour cream. Set out a plate of colorful, cut-up veggies—try zucchini slices, jicama sticks, radishes or baby corn on the cob. The deli and produce sections of supermarkets have precut veggies just waiting for you. Whatever you choose, keep in mind that dippers should be sturdy enough to scoop up the dip without breaking so you can "skinny dip" all you like.

- Check out the variety of crackers available. Look for different sizes, shapes, colors and flavors. Big pretzel rods, flavored chips and snacks in unusual shapes are also nice additions.

- For a fun way to serve dip, slice off tops of red and green bell peppers, clean peppers and fill with dips. If you're running short of time, purchase dips. Serve purchased dips in peppers, and no one will ever guess they're not homemade.

Cheese Fondue Dip

PREP: 15 MIN; COOK: 10 MIN
8 SERVINGS

2 cans (11 ounces each) condensed Cheddar cheese
    soup

1/4 cup dry white wine or apple juice

2 cups shredded Swiss or Cheddar cheese
    (8 ounces)

4 medium green onions, finely chopped (1/4 cup)

1/4 teaspoon garlic powder

Dash of red pepper sauce

Cut-up raw vegetables, if desired

Bite-size pieces French bread, if desired

Heat soup, wine and cheese in 2-quart saucepan or chafing dish over medium heat, stirring occasionally, until cheese is melted. Stir in onions, garlic powder and pepper sauce. Pour into fondue pot or chafing dish to keep warm.

Spear vegetables and bread pieces with fondue forks, and dip into fondue. (If fondue becomes too thick, stir in a small amount of dry white wine or apple juice.)

1 Serving: Calories 220 (Calories from Fat 125); Fat 14g (Saturated 8g); Cholesterol 35mg; Sodium 760mg; Carbohydrate 8g (Dietary Fiber 0g); Protein 11g
% Daily Value: Vitamin A 22%; Vitamin C 0%; Calcium 32%; Iron 2%
Diet Exchanges: 1/2 Starch, 1 1/2 High-Fat Meat

New Twist

Dare to dip and prepare to share, fondue is back! To make this dynamite dipper even hipper, sprinkle with crumbled blue or Gorgonzola cheese and toasted chopped walnuts. For dipping, add red and green apple slices to the selection of vegetables. You can also offer an assortment of rustic breads, cut into bite-size pieces, and place them in baskets for a bountiful fondue buffet.

Hot Crab Dip

PREP: 15 MIN; BAKE: 20 MIN
2 1/2 CUPS DIP

1 package (8 ounces) cream cheese, softened

1/4 cup grated Parmesan cheese

1/4 cup mayonnaise or salad dressing

1/4 cup dry white wine or apple juice

2 teaspoons sugar

1 teaspoon ground mustard (dry)

4 medium green onions, thinly sliced (1/4 cup)

1 clove garlic, finely chopped

1 can (6 ounces) crabmeat, drained, cartilage removed and flaked*

Assorted crackers or sliced raw vegetables for dipping, if desired

1/3 cup sliced almonds, toasted (page 31), if desired

Heat oven to 375°. Mix all ingredients except crabmeat, crackers and almonds in medium bowl until well blended. Stir in crabmeat.

Spread crabmeat mixture in ungreased pie plate, 9 × 1 1/4 inches, or shallow 1-quart casserole.

Bake uncovered 15 to 20 minutes or until hot and bubbly. Serve on crackers. Sprinkle with almonds.

*6 ounces imitation crabmeat, coarsely chopped, can be substituted for the canned crabmeat.

1 Tablespoon: Calories 50 (Calories from Fat 35); Fat 4g (Saturated 2g); Cholesterol 10mg; Sodium 50mg; Carbohydrate 1g (Dietary Fiber 0g); Protein 2g
% Daily Value: Vitamin A 2%; Vitamin C 0%; Calcium 2%; Iron 4%
Diet Exchanges: 1 Fat

Holiday Hints

Ring in the holidays on the lighter side—use fat-free cream cheese and fat-free mayonnaise, and omit the almonds.

For a finishing touch, sprinkle baked dip with extra sliced green onion in a wreath shape, and make a bow with red bell pepper strips or pimientos. Serve with crackers or sliced raw vegetables for dipping.

Hot Crab Dip

Ginger Shrimp Kabobs

PREP: 30 MIN; CHILL: 1 HR; BROIL: 6 MIN
12 APPETIZERS

12 uncooked large shrimp in shells

1 tablespoon grated gingerroot

2 tablespoons lime juice

2 teaspoons soy sauce

1 teaspoon dark sesame oil

1/4 teaspoon crushed red pepper

3 cloves garlic, finely chopped

2 medium bell peppers

12 small whole mushrooms

6 green onions, cut into 1-inch pieces

Peel shrimp. (If shrimp are frozen, do not thaw; peel in cold water.) Make a shallow cut lengthwise down back of each shrimp; wash out vein.

Mix gingerroot, lime juice, soy sauce, sesame oil, red pepper and garlic in glass or plastic dish. Stir in shrimp until well coated. Cover and refrigerate 1 hour.

Cut bell peppers with small star-shaped cookie cutter, or cut into 1-inch squares.

Set oven to broil. Remove shrimp from marinade; reserve marinade. Alternate bell pepper star, mushroom, shrimp and onion pieces on each of twelve 6-inch skewers. Brush lightly with marinade. Place on rack in broiler pan.

Broil with tops about 4 inches from heat about 6 minutes, turning once, until shrimp are pink and firm and vegetables are crisp-tender. Discard remaining marinade.

1 Appetizer: Calories 25 (Calories from Fat 10); Fat 1g (Saturated 0g); Cholesterol 15mg; Sodium 70mg; Carbohydrate 3g (Dietary Fiber 1g); Protein 2g
% Daily Value: Vitamin A 2%; Vitamin C 16%; Calcium 0%; Iron 2%
Diet Exchanges: 1 Vegetable

Timesaving Tips

You can make these kabobs ahead of time. Cover and refrigerate prepared kabobs up to 24 hours ahead, then they'll be ready to pop under the broiler when your guests arrive.

Party Pointers

If you are having a large group and the guests may not know one another, consider having each guest wear a name tag. This helps people remember each other and puts people at ease if they've forgotten the name of someone they have just met.

Ginger Shrimp Kabobs

Meatball Merriment

PREP: 40 MIN; COOK: 20 MIN
30 APPETIZERS

*The best things come in small packages, and these memorable mouthfuls live up to that promise.
Just the right size to satisfy, these meaty morsels have become an all-time party favorite.*

1 pound ground beef

1 medium onion, chopped (1/2 cup)

1 egg

1/3 cup dry bread crumbs

1/4 cup milk

1/4 teaspoon salt

1/8 teaspoon pepper

1 jar (12 ounces) salsa

2 medium green onions, thinly sliced
(2 tablespoons), if desired

Heat oven to 400°. Mix all ingredients except salsa and green onions. Shape into thirty 1-inch balls. Place in ungreased rectangular pan, 13×9×2 inches. Bake uncovered about 15 minutes or until no longer pink in center.

Place salsa and meatballs in 2-quart saucepan. Heat to boiling, stirring occasionally; reduce heat. Cover and simmer about 15 minutes or until salsa and meatballs are hot. Sprinkle with green onions. Serve hot with toothpicks.

1 Appetizer: Calories 40 (Calories from Fat 20); Fat 2g (Saturated 1g); Cholesterol 15mg; Sodium 70mg; Carbohydrate 2g (Dietary Fiber 0g); Protein 3g
% Daily Value: Vitamin A 0%; Vitamin C 2%; Calcium 0%; Iron 2%
Diet Exchanges: 1/2 Medium-Fat Meat

SWEDISH MEATBALLS: Substitute 1 can (10 3/4 ounces) condensed cream of chicken soup, 1/4 cup milk and 1/2 teaspoon ground nutmeg for the salsa; omit green onions. Sprinkle meatballs with dried dill weed, if desired.

BURGUNDY MEATBALLS: Substitute Burgundy Sauce for the salsa; omit green onions. To make **Burgundy Sauce**, mix 2 tablespoons cornstarch and 1/4 cup cold water in 3-quart saucepan. Gradually stir in 1/2 cup red Burgundy, other dry red wine or beef broth, 1/2 clove garlic, crushed, and 1 can (10 1/2 ounces) condensed beef broth. Heat to boiling, stirring constantly. Boil and stir 1 minute.

CRANBERRY MEATBALLS: Substitute Cranberry Sauce for the salsa; omit green onions. To make **Cranberry Sauce**, mix 1 cup whole berry cranberry sauce, 1/2 cup hoisin sauce, 1/2 teaspoon onion powder, 1/4 teaspoon salt and 1/8 teaspoon pepper in 2-quart saucepan.

SPICY APRICOT MEATBALLS: Substitute Apricot Sauce for the salsa; omit green onions. To make **Apricot Sauce**, mix 1 cup apricot preserves, 2/3 cup stir-fry or sweet-and-sour sauce and 1/2 teaspoon five-spice powder in 2-quart saucepan.

SWEET-AND-SOUR MEATBALLS: Substitute 1 jar (about 9 1/2 ounces) sweet-and-sour sauce for the salsa; omit green onions.

Timesaving Tips

Make and bake these meatballs ahead and freeze them up to 3 months before you plan to serve them. Or, make it super-easy! Purchase frozen meatballs from your supermarket. Heat sauce ingredients to boiling, then stir in ftozen meatballs. Simmer uncovered for about 20 minutes or until meatballs are hot.

Savory Chicken Cheesecake

PREP: 15 MIN; BAKE: 1 1/4 HR; COOL: 15 MIN; CHILL: 4 HR
24 SERVINGS

2 packages (8 ounces each) cream cheese, softened

1 container (8 ounces) sour cream-and-onion dip

1 tablespoon all-purpose flour

1 1/2 teaspoons dried dill weed

3 eggs

1 cup finely chopped cooked chicken

1/2 cup cranberry-orange relish, drained

2 tablespoons chopped walnuts, toasted

Orange peel, if desired

Heat oven to 300°. Lightly grease springform pan, 8×3 inches. Beat cream cheese in large bowl with electric mixer on medium speed until fluffy. Beat in dip, flour and dill weed. Beat in eggs, one at a time. Fold in chicken. Spread in pan.

Bake about 1 1/4 hours or until edge is golden brown and center is firm. Cool 15 minutes. Run metal spatula along side of cheesecake to loosen. Cover tightly and refrigerate at least 4 hours but no longer than 24 hours.

Remove side of pan. Spoon relish onto center of cheesecake. Sprinkle with walnuts. Garnish with orange peel. To serve, cut into wedges.

1 Serving: Calories 85 (Calories from Fat 55); Fat 6g (Saturated 3g); Cholesterol 45mg; Sodium 110mg; Carbohydrate 4g (Dietary Fiber 0g); Protein 4g
% Daily Value: Vitamin A 4%; Vitamin C 0%; Calcium 2%; Iron 2%
Diet Exchanges: 1/2 Very Lean Meat, 1 Vegetable, 1 Fat

Holiday Hints

TOASTING NUTS

Here are several methods; use the one that's most convenient for you (watch carefully so the nuts don't burn):

- **Microwave Method:** Place 1 teaspoon butter or margarine and 1/2 cup nuts in a microwavable pie plate; microwave uncovered on High 2 1/2 to 3 minutes, stirring every 30 seconds, until nuts are light brown.

- **Oven Method:** Spread nuts in a shallow ungreased pan; bake uncovered in a 350° oven 6 to 10 minutes, stirring frequently, until light brown.

- **Skillet Method:** Sprinkle nuts in ungreased heavy skillet. Cook over medium heat 5 to 7 minutes, stirring frequently until nuts begin to brown, then stirring constantly until light brown.

Simple Sippers and Savory Nibbles

Bruschetta Romana

PREP: 15 MIN; BAKE: 8 MIN
12 APPETIZERS

1 jar (7 ounces) roasted red bell peppers, drained and cut into 1/2-inch strips

1 or 2 medium cloves garlic, finely chopped

2 tablespoons chopped fresh parsley or 1 teaspoon parsley flakes

2 tablespoons shredded Parmesan cheese

1 tablespoon olive or vegetable oil

1/4 teaspoon salt

1/4 teaspoon pepper

12 baguette slices, each 1/2 inch thick

Heat oven to 450°. Mix all ingredients except baguette slices. Place baguette slices on ungreased cookie sheet. Spoon bell pepper mixture onto bread. Bake 6 to 8 minutes or until edges are golden brown.

1 Appetizer: Calories 40 (Calories from Fat 20); Fat 2g (Saturated 0g); Cholesterol 0mg; Sodium 105mg; Carbohydrate 4g (Dietary Fiber 0g); Protein 1g
% Daily Value: Vitamin A 4%; Vitamin C 38%; Calcium 2%; Iron 2%
Diet Exchanges: 1 Vegetable, 1/2 Fat

Timesaving Tips

Looking for more easy ideas to dress up your bruschetta? Here are some toppings to spoon onto toasted bread. No need to bake them—just eat and enjoy!

• Mix feta cheese and cream cheese; spread on toasted bread. Top with sliced Kalamata or Greek olives and sliced cherrry tomatoes.

• Spread cream cheese on toasted bread. Top with julienne strips of sun-dried tomatoes packed in oil and herbs, drained. Sprinkle with toasted pine nuts.

• Spread mascarpone cheese on toasted bread. Top with dried cranberries, crumbled dried rosemary leaves and a dash of ground cardamom.

Bruschetta takes its name from the Italian dialect word *bruscare*, meaning "toasted." It is a small open-face sandwich you will find on appetizer menus of many popular restaurants. With these recipes and ideas, you can offer the flavors of Italy in your home—pronto!

Start with baguette slices.

- **Pesto-Brie Bruschetta:** Spread each baguette slice with 1 tablespoon basil pesto. Top with thinly sliced unpeeled red apple and thinly sliced Brie cheese. Bake as directed on page 32.

- **Portabella-Parmesan Bruschetta:** Heat 2 tablespoons olive oil in 10-inch skillet over medium heat. Add 2 cloves garlic, finely chopped, and 2 packages (12 ounces each) portabella mushrooms, chopped. Cook about 10 minutes, stirring occasionally, until light brown. Stir in 1/4 teaspoon salt and 1/8 teaspoon pepper. Spoon mushroom mixture onto baguette slices. Sprinkle with 1 cup shredded Parmesan cheese. Bake as directed on page 32.

- **Star Bruschetta:** Cut baguette slices with star-shape cookie cutter. Mix 1 1/2 cups drained, chopped oil-packed sun-dried tomatoes, 3 tablespoons olive oil and 2 cloves garlic, finely chopped. Spread each star with 1 tablespoon mixture. Bake as directed on page 32. Garnish each star with rosemary sprig, if desired.

Basil Brie in Pastry

PREP: 20 MIN; BAKE: 25 MIN; COOL: 30 MIN
12 SERVINGS

2 tablespoons grated Parmesan cheese

2 tablespoons finely chopped fresh or 2 teaspoons dried basil leaves

1 round (14 ounces) Brie cheese

1/2 package (17 1/4-ounce size) frozen puff pastry (1 sheet), thawed

Assorted crackers or sliced fruit, if desired

Heat oven to 400°. Grease cookie sheet. Mix Parmesan cheese and basil. Cut Brie cheese round horizontally into 2 layers. Sprinkle basil mixture evenly over cut surface of bottom layer. Reassemble cheese round.

Roll pastry into rectangle, 15×9 inches, on lightly floured surface. Cut out 2 circles, one 8 1/2 inches and the other 6 inches. Place cheese round on center of large circle. Bring pastry up and over cheese, pressing to make smooth and even. Brush top edge of pastry lightly with water. Place 6-inch circle on top, pressing gently around edge to seal. Cut decorations from remaining pastry if desired; moisten pastry with water to attach.

Bake about 25 minutes or until golden brown. Cool on cookie sheet on wire rack 30 minutes before serving. Serve with crackers.

1 Serving: Calories 210 (Calories from Fat 145); Fat 16g (Saturated 8g); Cholesterol 50mg; Sodium 340mg; Carbohydrate 9g (Dietary Fiber 0g); Protein 8g
% Daily Value: Vitamin A 8%; Vitamin C 0%; Calcium 4%; Iron 14%
Diet Exchanges: 1/2 Starch, 1 Medium-Fat Meat, 2 Fat

Timesaving Tips

A bundle of savory flavors, this holiday appetizer, also known as *Brie en Croûte,* gets its name from the pastry wrapping that covers the cheese while it bakes. If you don't have time to roll out the pastry, you can spruce up Brie with some simple holiday toppers. Begin by heating the oven to 350°. Lightly brush an ovenproof plate with vegetable oil. Place unpeeled cheese on the center of the plate; bake uncovered 8 to 10 minutes or until cheese is soft and partially melted. Top with:

• Pear-Cranberry Chutney (page 295) and toasted slivered almonds.

• Caramel topping and toasted chopped pecans. Serve with crisp apple slices.

• Sun-dried tomatoes packed in oil and herbs, drained and chopped, and toasted pine nuts. Garnish with chopped fresh basil leaves.

Basil Brie in Pastry

Pesto Pinwheels

PREP: 20 MIN; BAKE 10 MIN
40 APPETIZERS

1 package (17 1/4 ounces) frozen puff pastry, thawed

1 cup pesto

1 egg, slightly beaten

Heat oven to 400°. Roll each sheet of puff pastry on very lightly floured surface into rectangle, 14 × 10 inches.

Spread 1/2 cup of the pesto evenly over each rectangle to within 1/2 inch of long sides. Starting at 10-inch side, loosely fold pastry into roll; brush edge of roll with egg, then pinch into roll to seal.

Cut each roll into 1/2-inch slices, using sharp knife. Place on ungreased cookie sheet. Bake 8 to 10 minutes or until golden brown. Serve warm.

1 Appetizer: Calories 105 (Calories from Fat 70); Fat 8g (Saturated 2g); Cholesterol 20mg; Sodium 80mg; Carbohydrate 6g (Dietary Fiber 0g); Protein 2g
% Daily Value: Vitamin A 0%; Vitamin C 0%; Calcium 2%; Iron 4%
Diet Exchanges: 1/2 Starch, 1 1/2 Fat

HOLIDAY MENU

Red & Green Appetizer Party

- Pesto Pinwheels
- Sun-Dried Tomato Dip (page 24)
- Appetizer Cheese Trees (page 20)
- Bruschetta Romana (page 32)

Party Pointers

Finding it hard to squeeze in time to make both Christmas Eve and Christmas Day dinners? Consider an appetizer alternative instead of the traditional sit-down holiday dinner.

- Invite family and friends to bring an appetizer, and have a meal of little nibbles. If you really want to capture the spirit of the holiday season, make red and green appetizers the focus of your party (see Holiday Menu, above).

- When planning your event, decide not only on the menu but also on what each appetizer will be served in. Set out dishes and serving utensils the night before. If you have a lot of appetizers or are having someone help you, label each bowl with the menu item that should be served in it. Remove the label before placing food in the dish.

Bruschetta Romana (page 32), Sun-Dried Tomato Dip (page 24) and Pesto Pinwheels

Simple Sippers and Savory Nibbles

Gorgonzola and Rosemary Cream Puffs

PREP: 15 MIN; BAKE: 24 MIN; COOL: 5 MIN
25 APPETIZERS

1/2 cup water

1/4 cup butter or margarine

1/2 cup all-purpose flour

1/4 teaspoon salt

1/4 teaspoon dried rosemary leaves, crumbled

1/8 teaspoon coarsely ground pepper

2 eggs

1 cup shredded Gorgonzola cheese (4 ounces)

2 tablespoons chopped pistachio nuts

Heat oven to 425°. Spray large cookie sheet with cooking spray.

Heat water and butter to boiling in 3-quart saucepan over medium heat. Add flour, salt, rosemary and pepper all at once; stir constantly 30 to 60 seconds or until mixture forms ball. Remove from heat. Add eggs, one at a time, beating with electric mixer on medium speed until mixture is well blended.

Drop mixture by heaping teaspoonfuls about 2 inches apart onto cookie sheet. Bake 15 to 20 minutes or until golden brown. Cool 5 minutes.

Gently press center of each puff with tip of spoon to make slight indentation. Sprinkle with cheese and nuts. Bake 2 to 4 minutes or until cheese is melted. Serve warm.

1 Appetizer: Calories 50 (Calories from Fat 35); Fat 4g (Saturated 2g); Cholesterol 25mg; Sodium 60mg; Carbohydrate 2g (Dietary Fiber 0g); Protein 2g
% Daily Value: Vitamin A 2%; Vitamin C 0%; Calcium 2%; Iron 0%
Diet Exchanges: 1 Fat

Timesaving Tips

To make ahead, prepare cream puff dough as directed—except drop mixture by heaping teaspoonfuls onto cookie sheet covered with waxed paper. Freeze until firm. Place drops of dough in airtight container or resealable plastic bag. To bake, place frozen dough on cookie sheet and continue as directed.

Holiday Hints

Searching for a few last-minute appetizers to round out your platter?

• Wrap small slices of honeydew melon with thinly sliced smoked turkey. Or for a new twist, wrap pear slices with prosciutto.

• Heat a round of Brie cheese for 8 to 10 minutes at 350° or until cheese is soft and partially melted. Top with 1/4 cup whole berry cranberry sauce.

• Arrange slices of fresh mozzarella cheese and ripe tomatoes in a circular pattern; sprinkle with chopped fresh basil leaves and drizzle with olive oil.

Gorgonzola and Rosemary Cream Puffs

Caramelized Onion Tartlets

PREP: 30 MIN; BAKE: 15 MIN
ABOUT 24 APPETIZERS

1 package (15 ounces) refrigerated pie crusts

2 tablespoons butter or margarine

3/4 cup coarsely chopped red onion

2 eggs

1/2 cup sour cream

1/4 teaspoon salt

1/8 teaspoon red pepper sauce

3/4 cup finely shredded Cheddar cheese (3 ounces)

Additional chopped red onion, if desired

Let refrigerated pie crusts come to room temperature; cut with 3-inch round biscuit cutter or glass. Press crust circle in each of 24 small muffin cups, 1 3/4 × 1 inch.

Melt butter in 10-inch skillet over medium-high heat. Cook 3/4 cup onion in butter 5 minutes, stirring occasionally; reduce heat to medium. Cook about 15 minutes longer, stirring occasionally, until onion is softened and golden brown; remove from heat.

Heat oven to 400°. Beat eggs in large bowl. Stir in sour cream, salt and pepper sauce. Stir in onion. Stir in 1/4 cup of the cheese. Spoon onion mixture into crusts. Sprinkle with remaining cheese.

Bake 10 to 15 minutes until golden brown and set in center. Serve warm or at room temperature. Garnish with additional onion.

1 Appetizer: Calories 135 (Calories from Fat 80); Fat 9g (Saturated 3g); Cholesterol 25mg; Sodium 180mg; Carbohydrate 10g (Dietary Fiber 0g); Protein 3g
% Daily Value: Vitamin A 2%; Vitamin C 0%; Calcium 2%; Iron 2%
Diet Exchanges: 2 Vegetable, 2 Fat

Holiday Hints

For a sit-down, eat-with-a-fork appetizer, double the filling ingredients (except use 3 eggs) and bake in one pie crust placed in an 11 × 1-inch tart pan or 9-inch pie plate. Bake about 30 minutes or until set; let stand 20 minutes before cutting into wedges.

New Twist

Vary the cheese in these appetizers, and you'll have a whole new appetizer! Pesto-garlic cheese, Monterey Jack cheese with jalapeño peppers or bacon cheese add their own special flavors. If you are short of time, check out the preshredded cheeses in your supermarket—you may be surprised at your options.

Caramelized Onion Tartlets

Cheesy Apple-Polenta Bites

Cheesy Apple-Polenta Bites

Prep: 25 min; Cook: 10 min; Chill: 12 hr; Bake: 20 min
72 appetizers

1 cup yellow cornmeal

1 cup cold water

2 3/4 cups boiling water

1 teaspoon salt

2 tablespoons grated onion

1 tablespoon chopped fresh sage leaves

1 cup shredded Cheddar cheese (4 ounces)

1 small unpeeled apple

Juice of 1 medium lemon (2 to 3 tablespoons)

Fresh sage leaves, if desired

Shaved fully cooked ham, if desired

Line square baking dish, 8 × 8 × 2 inches, with aluminum foil, leaving 1 inch of foil overhanging at 2 opposite sides of pan; grease foil.

Mix cornmeal and cold water in 2-quart saucepan. Stir in boiling water and salt. Cook about 5 minutes, stirring constantly, until mixture boils and thickens; reduce heat to low. Stir in onion, chopped sage and 1/2 cup of the cheese. Cook uncovered 5 minutes, stirring occasionally; remove from heat.

Spread cornmeal mixture (polenta) in baking dish. Cover and refrigerate at least 12 hours or until firm.

Heat oven to 400°. Grease jelly roll pan, 15 1/2 × 10 1/2 × 1 inch.

Remove polenta from baking dish, using foil edges to lift. Cut polenta into 6 rows by 6 rows to make 36 squares. Cut each square diagonally to make 2 triangles; place in jelly roll pan. Bake about 15 minutes until golden brown.

Cut apple into thin slices. Cut slices into quarters. Dip apple pieces into lemon juice to keep them from discoloring. Top each triangle with 1 apple piece. Sprinkle remaining 1/2 cup cheese over apple pieces. Bake about 5 minutes or until cheese is melted. Serve warm, garnished with sage leaves and ham.

1 Appetizer: Calories 30 (Calories from Fat 10); Fat 1g (Saturated 1g); Cholesterol 5mg; Sodium 85mg; Carbohydrate 4g (Dietary Fiber 0g); Protein 1g
% Daily Value: Vitamin A 0%; Vitamin C 0%; Calcium 2%; Iron 0%
Diet Exchanges: 1/2 Starch

Timesaving Tips

If you're short of time, you can use purchased polenta and eliminate the preparation step in this recipe. Prepared polenta is now available in supermarkets in both plain and gourmet flavors. Simply slice polenta, cut slices into fourths and bake as directed.

*Roast Turkey (page 64), Old-Fashioned Stuffing
(page 106) and Traditional Turkey Gravy (page 64)*

CHAPTER 2

Merry Main Dishes

Ring in the season with a crackling fire, Christmas music in the background and a table set with treasured holiday foods to warm the soul.

Rib Roast with Herb Rub

Prep: 20 min; Roast: 2 hr; Stand: 15 min
8 servings

Herb Rub (right)

4-pound beef rib roast

1 clove garlic, cut in half

1/4 cup Dijon mustard

Horseradish Sauce (right), if desired

Heat oven to 325°. Prepare Herb Rub. Place beef, fat side up, on rack in shallow roasting pan. Rub garlic over beef. Spread mustard over top and sides of beef. Spread Herb Rub over top and sides of beef.

Insert meat thermometer so tip is in center of thickest part of beef and does not touch bone. Roast uncovered 1 1/2 to 2 hours or until thermometer reads 155° (medium doneness). Prepare Horseradish Sauce.

Cover beef loosely with aluminum foil tent and let stand about 15 minutes or until thermometer reads 160°. Serve beef with sauce.

1 Serving: Calories 270 (Calories from Fat 155); Fat 17g (Saturated 6g); Cholesterol 80mg; Sodium 170mg; Carbohydrate 1g (Dietary Fiber 0g); Protein 28g
% Daily Value: Vitamin A 2%; Vitamin C 6%; Calcium 2%; Iron 20%
Diet Exchanges: 3 1/2 Medium-Fat Meat

Herb Rub

3/4 cup chopped fresh parsley

1 1/2 tablespoons chopped fresh or 1 1/2 teaspoons dried thyme leaves

1 1/2 tablespoons chopped fresh or 1 1/2 teaspoons dried rosemary leaves

1 tablespoon olive or vegetable oil

2 cloves garlic, finely chopped

Mix all ingredients.

Horseradish Sauce

1 cup sour cream

1 tablespoon plus 1 teaspoon horseradish sauce

1 tablespoon plus 1 teaspoon Dijon mustard

1/4 teaspoon coarsely ground pepper

Mix all ingredients. Cover and refrigerate at least 1 hour to blend flavors.

Holiday Hints

Find yourself always hoping someone else will carve the meat? Here are tips that will make carving a snap.

- Let the roast stand for 15 minutes; the juices will set up, making carving much easier.

- Avoid covering the roast too tightly while it stands, which will create steam and soften the surface of the beef.

- Always use a sharp knife and cut beef across the grain at a slanted angle into slices.

New Twist

Instead of the Horseradish Sauce, your family may prefer beef gravy made from beef drippings. Mix 2 tablespoons beef drippings and 2 tablespoons all-purpose flour in 2-quart saucepan; gradually stir in 1 cup beef broth or water. Heat to boiling, stirring constantly; boil and stir 1 minute.

Rib Roast with Herb Rub and Butternut Squash Soup (page 78)

Marinated Tenderloin of Beef

PREP: 15 MIN; CHILL: 8 HR; ROAST: 45 MIN; STAND: 20 MIN
12 SERVINGS

3-pound beef tenderloin

1/3 cup red wine vinegar

1/3 cup olive or vegetable oil

2 tablespoons chopped fresh or 2 teaspoons dried basil leaves

2 tablespoons chopped fresh or 2 teaspoons dried oregano leaves

2 tablespoons chopped fresh parsley or 2 teaspoons parsley flakes

1/2 teaspoon freshly ground pepper

2 cloves garlic, finely chopped

Place beef in resealable plastic bag or large glass or plastic dish. Mix remaining ingredients; pour over beef. Seal bag or cover dish and refrigerate at least 8 hours but no longer than 24 hours, turning beef several times to coat.

Heat oven to 425°. Remove beef from marinade; discard marinade. Place beef on rack in shallow roasting pan. Insert meat thermometer so tip is in center of thickest part of beef.

Roast uncovered 40 to 45 minutes or until thermometer reads 140° (medium-rare doneness). Cover beef loosely with tent of aluminum foil and let stand 15 to 20 minutes or until thermometer reads 145°. (Temperature will continue to rise about 5° and beef will be easier to carve as juices set up.) Cut beef across grain at slanted angle into thin slices.

1 Serving: Calories 185 (Calories from Fat 110); Fat 12g (Saturated 3g); Cholesterol 50mg; Sodium 45mg; Carbohydrate 1g (Dietary Fiber 0g); Protein 18g
% Daily Value: Vitamin A 0%; Vitamin C 0%; Calcium 0%; Iron 10%
Diet Exchanges: 2 1/2 Medium-Fat Meat

HOLIDAY MENU

Christmas Celebration Dinner

Use only the finest accompaniments to this beef dish! Here are a few suggestions for a stunning Christmas meal:

- Lobster Bisque (page 76)
- Marinated Tenderloin of Beef
- Twice-Baked Potatoes (page 110)
- Pesto Biscuits (page 196)
- Raspberry Trifle (page 157)

Marinated Tenderloin of Beef, Lobster Bisque (page 76) and Twice-Baked Potatoes (page 110)

Curried Coconut Beef with Winter Vegetables

PREP: 25 MIN; BAKE: 1 1/2 HOURS
6 SERVINGS

1 tablespoon vegetable oil

2 pounds beef stew meat

1 large onion, chopped (1 cup)

2 cloves garlic, finely chopped

1 1/2 tablespoons curry powder

1 can (14 ounces) unsweetened coconut milk

1 tablespoon packed brown sugar

2 tablespoons lemon juice

3 medium carrots, chopped (1 1/2 cups)

2 medium parsnips, peeled and chopped (1 cup)

1 1/2 cups chopped peeled sweet potatoes

1 teaspoon salt

1/4 teaspoon pepper

Chopped fresh cilantro, if desired

Heat oven to 350°. Heat oil in ovenproof Dutch oven over medium-high heat. Cook beef in oil, stirring occasionally, until brown.

Stir onion and garlic into beef. Cook 2 to 3 minutes, stirring occasionally, until onion is crisp-tender. Stir in curry powder, coconut milk, brown sugar and lemon juice. Cover and transfer to oven; bake about 1 hour or until beef is tender.

Stir in remaining ingredients except cilantro. Cover and bake about 30 minutes or until vegetables are tender. Garnish with cilantro.

1 Serving: Calories 495 (Calories from Fat 260); Fat 29g (Saturated 16g); Cholesterol 80mg; Sodium 510mg; Carbohydrate 35g (Dietary Fiber 7g); Protein 30g
% Daily Value: Vitamin A 100%; Vitamin C 20%; Calcium 6%; Iron 24%
Diet Exchanges: 2 Starch, 3 High-Fat Meat, 1 Vegetable

HOLIDAY MENU

Cozy Winter Supper

For a winter menu good enough to warm the spirits of family and guests, here's a great one to try!

- Curried Coconut Beef with Winter Vegetables

- Crisp Green Salad

- Savory Mini-Scones (page 198)

- Peanut Brittle Bread Pudding (page 149)

- Hot Coffee, Cider or Tea

Curried Coconut Beef with Winter Vegetables

Burgundy Beef Stew

PREP: 25 MIN; COOK: 1 HR 40 MIN

8 SERVINGS

6 slices bacon, cut into 1-inch pieces

2-pound beef boneless chuck eye, rolled rump or bottom round roast, cut into 1-inch pieces

1/2 cup all-purpose flour

1 1/2 cups dry red wine or beef broth

1 1/2 teaspoons chopped fresh or 1/2 teaspoon dried thyme leaves

1 1/4 teaspoons salt

1 teaspoon beef bouillon granules

1/4 teaspoon pepper

1 clove garlic, chopped

1 bay leaf

2 tablespoons butter or margarine

1 package (8 ounces) sliced mushrooms

4 medium onions, sliced

Chopped fresh parsley, if desired

Cook bacon in Dutch oven over medium heat until crisp; drain, reserving fat in Dutch oven. Drain bacon on paper towels; crumble bacon.

Coat beef with flour. Cook beef in bacon fat over medium heat, stirring occasionally, until brown. Drain excess fat from Dutch oven. Add wine and just enough water to cover beef. Stir in thyme, salt, bouillon granules, pepper, garlic and bay leaf. Heat to boiling; reduce heat. Cover and simmer about 1 1/2 hours or until beef is tender.

Melt butter in 12-inch skillet over medium heat. Cook mushrooms and onions in butter, stirring occasionally, until onions are tender. Stir mushroom mixture and bacon into beef mixture. Cover and simmer 10 minutes. Remove bay leaf. Garnish stew with parsley.

1 Serving: Calories 260 (Calories from Fat 115); Fat 13g (Saturated 5g); Cholesterol 45mg; Sodium 680mg; Carbohydrate 13g (Dietary Fiber 1g); Protein 17g
% Daily Value: Vitamin A 4%; Vitamin C 4%; Calcium 2%; Iron 14%
Diet Exchanges: 2 High-Fat Meat, 2 Vegetable

Timesaving Tips

When schedules are hectic and appetites are hearty, use one of these techniques to get dinner cooking while you take care of other projects:

• Cook recipe in a slow cooker. Follow the manufacturer's directions for your slow cooker for cooking times. Stews usually cook on the low heat setting for 6 to 8 hours.

• Cook stew in a 325° oven in an ovenproof Dutch oven for about 4 hours.

Burgundy Beef Stew

Crown Roast of Pork with Stuffing

PREP: 25 MIN; ROAST: 20 TO 25 MIN PER POUND (MEDIUM),
26 TO 31 MIN PER POUND (WELL); STAND: 20 MIN
12 SERVINGS

7 1/2- to 8-pound pork crown roast (about 20 ribs)

2 teaspoons salt

1 teaspoon pepper

Apple-Cranberry Stuffing (page 106) or
  Old-Fashioned Stuffing (page 106)

Heat oven to 325°. Sprinkle pork with salt and pepper. Place pork, bone ends up, on rack in shallow roasting pan. Wrap bone ends in aluminum foil to prevent excessive browning. Insert meat thermometer so tip is in center of thickest part of meat and does not touch bone or rest in fat. Place a small heatproof bowl or ball of crumpled aluminum foil in crown to hold shape of roast evenly.

For medium doneness, roast uncovered 20 to 25 minutes per pound or until thermometer reads 160°: 7 1/2-pound roast, 2 hours 30 minutes to 3 hours 7 minutes; 8-pound roast, 2 hours 40 minutes to 3 hours 20 minutes. For well done, roast uncovered 26 to 31 minutes per pound or until thermometer reads 170°: 7 1/2-pound roast, 3 hours 15 minutes to 3 hours 52 minutes; 8-pound roast, 3 hours 28 minutes to 4 hours 8 minutes.

Prepare Apple-Cranberry Stuffing. One hour before pork is done, remove bowl or foil and fill center of crown with stuffing. Cover only stuffing with aluminum foil for first 30 minutes. When pork is done, place on warmed large platter and let stand about 20 minutes for easiest carving. Remove foil from bone ends; place paper frills on bone ends. To carve, cut roast between ribs.

1 Serving: Calories 460 (Calories from Fat 235); Fat 26g (Saturated 7g); Cholesterol 110mg; Sodium 960mg; Carbohydrate 17g (Dietary Fiber 2g); Protein 42g
% Daily Value: Vitamin A 16%; Vitamin C 2%; Calcium 4%; Iron 14%
Diet Exchanges: 1 Starch, 5 Medium-Fat Meat

New Twist

Looking to add a delicious flavor twist for the stuffing? Try Mushroom Stuffing (page 106) or Orange-Apple Stuffing (page 106) to complement the pork roast nicely.

Crown Roast of Pork with Stuffing

Apricot-Pistachio Rolled Pork

PREP: 25 MIN; CHILL: 2 HR; ROAST: 2 1/2 HR; STAND: 15 MIN
12 SERVINGS

4-pound pork boneless top loin roast (single uncut roast)

1/2 cup chopped dried apricots

1/2 cup chopped pistachio nuts

2 cloves garlic, finely chopped

1/4 teaspoon salt

1/4 teaspoon pepper

1/4 cup apricot brandy or apricot nectar

Crunchy Topping (right)

1/4 cup apricot preserves

To cut pork roast into a large rectangle that can be filled and rolled, cut side of pork horizontally about 1/2 inch down from top of roast to within 1/2 inch of opposite edge; open flat. Cut horizontally from inside middle edge to outer edge; open flat to form a rectangle (see illustrations, below).

Sprinkle apricots, nuts, garlic, salt and pepper over pork to within 1 inch of edge. Tightly roll up pork, beginning with short side. Secure with toothpicks, or tie with string. Place in glass baking dish. Pierce pork all over with metal skewer. Brush entire surface with brandy. Let stand 15 minutes. Brush again with brandy. Cover and refrigerate at least 2 hours but no longer than 24 hours.

Heat oven to 325°. Place pork, fat side up, on rack in shallow roasting pan. Insert meat thermometer so tip is in center of thickest part of pork roll. Do not add water. Roast uncovered 1 1/2 hours. Remove toothpicks or string.

Prepare Crunchy Topping. Brush preserves over pork. Sprinkle with topping. Roast uncovered 30 to 60 minutes longer or until meat thermometer reads 160°. Cover and let stand 15 minutes before serving.

1 Serving: Calories 245 (Calories from Fat 80); Fat 9g (Saturated 3g); Cholesterol 80mg; Sodium 160mg; Carbohydrate 12g (Dietary Fiber 1g); Protein 30g
% Daily Value: Vitamin A 4%; Vitamin C 0%; Calcium 2%; Iron 12%
Diet Exchanges: 4 Very Lean Meat, 1 Fruit, 1 Fat

Crunchy Topping

1 tablespoon butter or margarine

1/4 cup coarsely crushed cracker crumbs

2 tablespoons chopped pistachio nuts

1/4 teaspoon garlic salt

Melt butter in 2-quart saucepan over medium heat. Stir in remaining ingredients. Cook and stir 1 minute; cool.

a. Cut lengthwise about 1/2 inch from top of pork to within 1/2 inch of opposite edge; open flat.

b. Repeat with other side of pork, cutting loose from inside edge; open flat to form rectangle.

Timesaving Tips

Here are some menu shortcuts to make your dinner preparation simple and stress-free!

- You don't have to cut, fill and roll the pork. Just roast the pork as directed (and forget the fruit filling), and sprinkle with the crunchy topping.

- Use frozen bread dough to make the rolls, or pick up a loaf of French bread at your local bakery.

- Serve the dumplings with caramel topping from a jar instead of making the sauce from scratch.

HOLIDAY MENU

Memorable Christmas Eve Dinner

- Apricot-Pistachio Rolled Pork
- Applesauce Sweet Potato Bake (page 116)
- Red, White and Green Beans (page 123)
- Dinner Rolls (page 188)
- Cranberry-Apple Dumplings with Crimson Sauce (page 154)

Apricot-Pistachio Rolled Pork, Applesauce-Sweet Potato Bake (page 116), Red, White and Green Beans (page 123) and Dinner Rolls (page 188)

Glazed Baked Ham

PREP: 10 MIN; BAKE: 13 TO 17 MIN PER POUND; STAND: 10 MIN
12 TO 16 SERVINGS

6- to 8-pound fully cooked bone-in ham

Whole cloves, if desired

1/4 cup honey

1/2 teaspoon ground mustard (dry)

1/4 teaspoon ground cloves

Heat oven to 325°. Place ham, fat side up, on rack in shallow roasting pan. Insert meat thermometer so tip is in thickest part of ham and does not touch bone or rest in fat. Cover ham and bake 13 to 17 minutes per pound or until thermometer reads 135°: 6-pound ham, 1 hour 18 minutes to 1 hour 42 minutes; 7-pound ham, 1 hour 31 minutes to 2 hours; 8-pound ham, 1 hour 44 minutes to 2 hours 16 minutes.

About 20 minutes before ham is done, remove from oven. Pour drippings from pan. Remove any skin from ham. Cut uniform diamond shapes on fat surface of ham. Insert clove in each diamond. Mix honey, mustard and cloves; brush over ham. Bake uncovered 20 minutes.

Cover ham loosely with aluminum foil tent and let stand about 10 minutes or until thermometer reads 140°.

1 Serving: Calories 175 (Calories from Fat 55); Fat 6g (Saturated 2g); Cholesterol 60mg; Sodium 1310mg; Carbohydrate 7g (Dietary Fiber 0g); Protein 23g
% Daily Value: Vitamin A 0%; Vitamin C 0%; Calcium 0%; Iron 8%
Diet Exchanges: 2 1/2 Lean Meat, 1/2 Fruit

Holiday Hints

CARVING BONE-IN HAM

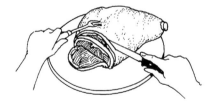

a. Letting the roast stand for 10 minutes allows the juices to set up and makes carving easier. Place ham, fat side up and bone to your right, on carving board. Cut a few slices from the thin side. Turn ham cut side down, so it rests firmly.

b. Make vertical slices down to the leg bone, then cut horizontally along bone to release slices.

Timesaving Tips

If you like the convenience of a presliced ham, ask your meat retailer to cut the ham, reassemble it and tie with cord. You still can use the same wonderful glaze.

New Twist

Looking for a new festive finish for baked ham? Try one of these suggestions:

- **Honey of a Sauce:** Mix 6 tablespoons honey mustard and 1 cup sour cream.

- **Sour Cherry Sauce:** Mix 1/4 cup packed brown sugar, 1 tablespoon cornstarch and 1/2 teaspoon ground mustard (dry) in 1-quart saucepan. Stir in 1/2 cup dried sour cherries, 3/4 cup water, 1/2 teaspoon grated lemon peel and 2 tablespoons lemon juice. Cook over low heat 6 to 8 minutes, stirring constantly, until thickened.

- **Raisin Sauce:** Mix 1/2 cup packed brown sugar, 2 tablespoons cornstarch and 1 teaspoon ground mustard (dry) in 1-quart saucepan. Gradually stir in 1 1/4 cups water and 2 tablespoons lemon juice. Stir in 1 cup raisins. Cook over medium heat, stirring constantly, until mixture boils. Boil and stir 1 minute.

Glazed Baked Ham

Minted Leg of Lamb

PREP: 20 MIN; CHILL: 8 HR; ROAST: 2 1/2 HR
8 SERVINGS

1/2 cup packed brown sugar

1/4 cup chopped fresh mint leaves

1/2 cup vegetable oil

1 teaspoon grated lemon peel

1/4 cup lemon juice

1 tablespoon chopped fresh or 1 teaspoon dried tarragon leaves

3 tablespoons white vinegar

1 teaspoon salt

1 teaspoon ground mustard (dry)

4- to 5-pound leg of lamb

Lamb Gravy (right)

Mix all ingredients except leg of lamb and Lamb Gravy. Heat to boiling; reduce heat. Simmer 5 minutes; cool.

Place lamb in plastic bag or shallow glass dish. Pour cooled marinade over lamb. Fasten bag securely or cover dish with plastic wrap. Refrigerate at least 8 hours but no longer than 24 hours, turning lamb occasionally.

Heat oven to 325°. Place lamb, fat side up, on rack in shallow roasting pan. Insert meat thermometer so tip is in center of thickest part of lamb and does not touch bone or rest in fat. Roast uncovered 2 to 2 1/2 hours or until desired degree of doneness. (Thermometer should read 170° to 180°.) Remove lamb to heated platter; keep warm. Prepare Lamb Gravy; serve with lamb.

1 Serving: Calories 295 (Calories from Fat 155); Fat 17g (Saturated 5g); Cholesterol 100mg; Sodium 150mg; Carbohydrate 5g (Dietary Fiber 0g); Protein 31g
% Daily Value: Vitamin A 0%; Vitamin C 0%; Calcium 0%; Iron 14%
Diet Exchanges: 1 1/2 Medium-Fat Meat, 1 Vegetable

Lamb Gravy

Strain drippings from roasting pan. Remove fat, reserving 2 tablespoons. Add enough water to drippings to measure 2 cups liquid. Stir 2 tablespoons all-purpose flour into reserved fat in 1 1/2-quart saucepan. Cook over low heat, stirring constantly, until smooth and bubbly; remove from heat. Stir in liquid. Heat to boiling, stirring constantly. Boil and stir 1 minute.

Holiday Hints

Cooking leg of lamb for the first time and don't have a clue on how to carve it? Follow these easy instructions and diagram.

Place leg shank bone to your right, on carving board or platter. (Place shank bone to your left if you are left-handed.) Cut a few lengthwise slices from thin side. Turn leg, cut side down, so it rests firmly. Make vertical slices to the leg bone, then cut horizontally along bone to release slices.

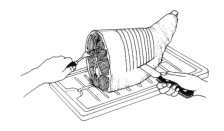

Minted Leg of Lamb

Merry Main Dishes

Chicken with Orange-Pecan Rice

PREP: 10 MIN; BAKE: 45 MIN
4 SERVINGS

1 package (6.25 ounces) fast-cooking long-grain
  and wild rice mix

2 cups orange juice

1/4 cup chopped pecans

1 jar (2 ounces) diced pimientos, drained

4 skinless, boneless chicken breast halves (about 1
  pound)

Chopped fresh parsley, if desired

Orange wedges, if desired

Heat oven to 350°. Grease square pan, 8×8×2 inches.
Mix uncooked rice, contents of seasoning packet, orange
juice, pecans and pimientos in pan. Place chicken on rice
mixture.

Cover and bake 35 to 45 minutes or until liquid is
absorbed and juice of chicken is no longer pink when
centers of thickest pieces are cut. Sprinkle with parsley.
Garnish with orange wedges.

1 Serving: Calories 300 (Calories from Fat 80); Fat 9g (Saturated
2g); Cholesterol 75mg; Sodium 70mg; Carbohydrate 26g (Dietary
Fiber 1g); Protein 29g
% Daily Value: Vitamin A 6%; Vitamin C 46%; Calcium 2%;
Iron 12%
Diet Exchanges: 1 Starch, 3 Lean Meat, 2 Vegetable

HOLIDAY MENU

Dinner Party for Friends

This is a terrific dish for easy entertaining! For a
large crowd, double the recipe and bake it in a
13×9-inch baking dish.

- Cranberry-Pistachio Salad with Champagne
  Vinaigrette (page 92)

- Chicken with Orange-Pecan Rice

- Popovers (page 200)

- Merry Berry Frozen Soufflé (page 165)

Chicken Dijon Casserole

PREP: 30 MIN; BAKE: 30 MIN
6 SERVINGS

3 cups uncooked farfalle (bow-tie) pasta (6 ounces)

2 cups cubed cooked chicken

1/3 cup diced roasted red bell peppers (from 7-ounce jar)

2 cups frozen broccoli cuts (from 16-ounce bag)

1 can (10 3/4 ounces) condensed cream of chicken or cream of mushroom soup

1/3 cup chicken broth

3 tablespoons Dijon mustard

1 tablespoon finely chopped onion

1/2 cup shredded Parmesan cheese

Heat oven to 375°. Grease 2 1/2-quart casserole. Cook and drain pasta as directed on package.

Mix pasta, chicken, bell peppers and broccoli in casserole. Mix soup, broth, mustard and onion; stir into pasta mixture. Sprinkle with cheese.

Cover and bake about 30 minutes or until mixture is hot and cheese is melted.

1 Serving: Calories 400 (Calories from Fat 90); Fat 10g (Saturated 3g); Cholesterol 50mg; Sodium 690mg; Carbohydrate 53g (Dietary Fiber 3g); Protein 27g
% Daily Value: Vitamin A 12%; Vitamin C 20%; Calcium 14%; Iron 20%
Diet Exchanges: 3 Starch, 2 Medium-Fat Meat, 1 Vegetable

Holiday Hints

• Use fresh broccoli instead of frozen; add it to the boiling pasta during the last 2 to 3 minutes of cooking.

• Add a splash of wine! Use 1/3 cup dry white wine instead of the chicken broth.

• Make this recipe your way by using your favorite pasta or the one available in your cupboard.

Roast Turkey

PREP: 25 MIN; ROAST: SEE TIMETABLE (RIGHT)

It's no wonder that this is one of our most requested recipes. Golden-glazed and juicy, this holiday mainstay is a feast for all the senses.

Thaw turkey if frozen (see Tips for a Terrific Turkey, page 65, for how to thaw). If you don't plan on stuffing the turkey, rub cavity lightly with salt if desired.

Stuff turkey just before roasting—do not stuff ahead of time. (Try Old-Fashioned Stuffing, page 106.) Fill wishbone area with stuffing first. Fasten neck skin to back with skewer. Fold wings under back of turkey. Fill body cavity lightly with stuffing. Fill body cavity lightly. (Do not pack—stuffing will expand while cooking.) Tuck drumsticks under band of skin at tail, or tie or skewer drumsticks to tail.

Place turkey, breast side up, on rack in shallow roasting pan. Brush with melted butter or margarine. Insert meat thermometer so tip is in thickest part of inside thigh muscle and does not touch bone. Do not add water. Do not cover.

Roast uncovered in 325° oven. Follow Timetable (page 65) for approximate total roasting time. Place a tent of aluminum foil loosely over turkey when it begins to turn golden. When two-thirds done, cut band of skin or string holding drumsticks.

Turkey is done when thermometer reads 180° and drumsticks move easily when lifted or twisted. (If not using a meat thermometer, test for doneness about 30 minutes before Timetable indicates; roast until juices of turkey are no longer pink when you cut into the center of the thigh.) Prepare Cran-Apple Glaze (right) while turkey is roasting. Remove turkey from oven and let stand 20 minutes for easiest carving. Brush glaze on turkey about 20 minutes before turkey is done. Brush again with glaze before carving. If turkey is stuffed, place tip of thermometer in center of stuffing; it should read 165° after standing time.

Cran-Apple Glaze

1 can (8 ounces) jellied cranberry sauce

1/4 cup apple jelly

1/4 cup light corn syrup

Mix all ingredients in 1-quart saucepan. Cook over medium heat about 5 minutes, stirring occasionally, until melted.

Traditional Turkey Gravy

2 tablespoons turkey drippings (fat and juices)

2 tablespoons all-purpose flour

1 cup liquid (turkey juices, broth or water)

Browning sauce, if desired

Salt and pepper to taste

Pour drippings from roasting pan into bowl, leaving brown particles in pan. Return 2 tablespoons of the drippings to pan. (Measure accurately so gravy is not greasy.) Stir in flour. Cook over low heat, stirring constantly, until smooth and bubbly; remove from heat. Stir in liquid.

Heat to boiling over high heat, stirring constantly. Boil and stir 1 minute. Stir in a few drops browning sauce. Stir in salt and pepper. Makes about 1 cup gravy.

Timetable for Roasting Turkey

READY-TO-COOK APPROXIMATE TOTAL WEIGHT (POUNDS)	ROASTING TIME* (HOURS) AT 325°
Whole Turkey (unstuffed)	
8 to 12	2 3/4 to 3
12 to 14	3 to 3 3/4
14 to 18	3 3/4 to 4 1/4
18 to 20	4 1/4 to 4 1/2
20 to 24	4 1/2 to 5
Whole Turkey (stuffed)	
8 to 12	3 to 3 1/2
12 to 14	3 1/2 to 4
14 to 18	4 to 4 1/4
18 to 20	4 1/4 to 4 3/4
20 to 24	4 3/4 to 5 1/4
Turkey Breast (unstuffed, boneless)	
4 to 6	1 1/2 to 2 1/4
6 to 8	2 1/4 to 3 1/4

* The times in the Timetable are based on chilled or completely thawed turkeys at a temperature of about 40° and placed in preheated ovens. Differences in the shape and tenderness of individual turkeys can also necessitate increasing or decreasing the cooking time slightly. For prestuffed turkeys, follow package directions very carefully; do not use the Timetable.

Holiday Hints

TIPS FOR A TERRIFIC TURKEY

• When buying turkeys, allow 1 pound per serving.

• Select a turkey that is plump and meaty with smooth, moist-looking skin. The skin should be creamy colored. The bone ends should be pink to red in color.

• If the turkey is frozen, thaw it slowly in the refrigerator. A turkey weighing 8 to 12 pounds will thaw in one to two days; 20 to 24 pounds will thaw in four to five days in the refrigerator. A whole frozen turkey can also be safely thawed in cold water. Leave the turkey in its original wrap, free from tears or holes, and place in cold water, allowing 30 minutes per pound for thawing, and changing the water every 30 minutes. Don't be tempted to use warm water—it encourages the growth of bacteria. The cold water actually thaws the bird faster, too. If you need something a bit faster still, thaw the turkey quickly in the microwave following the manufacturer's directions.

• After thawing, remove the package of giblets (gizzard, heart and neck), if present, from the neck cavity of the turkey; reserve for gravy, if desired. Rinse the cavity, or inside of the turkey, with cool water; pat dry with paper towels.

• As soon as possible after serving turkey, remove every bit of stuffing from turkey. Cool stuffing, turkey meat and any gravy promptly; refrigerate separately. Use gravy and stuffing within one or two days; heat thoroughly before serving. Serve cooked turkey meat within two or three days after roasting, or freeze up to three weeks.

Merry Main Dishes

Turkey-Wild Rice Casserole

PREP: 20 MIN; COOK: 55 MIN; BAKE: 45 MIN
12 SERVINGS

Cooked White and Wild Rice (right) or 3 cups
  cooked rice (any variety)

1/2 cup butter or margarine

1/2 cup all-purpose flour

1 1/2 teaspoons salt

1/4 teaspoon pepper

1 1/2 cups chicken broth

2 1/4 cups milk

1 package (8 ounces) sliced mushrooms, or 2 jars
  (4 1/2 ounces each) sliced mushrooms, drained

1 small green bell pepper, chopped (1/2 cup)

1 jar (2 ounces) sliced pimientos, drained

3 cups cubed cooked turkey or chicken

1/2 cup slivered almonds

Chopped fresh parsley, if desired

Prepare Cooked White and Wild Rice. Heat oven to
350°. Grease rectangular baking dish, 13 × 9 × 2 inches.

Melt butter in Dutch oven over medium heat. Stir in
flour, salt and pepper. Cook, stirring constantly, until
smooth and bubbly; remove from heat. Stir in broth and
milk. Heat to boiling, stirring constantly. Boil and stir 1
minute. Stir in cooked rice and remaining ingredients.
Pour into baking dish.

Bake uncovered 40 to 45 minutes or until center is hot.
Sprinkle with parsley.

1 Serving: Calories 265 (Calories from Fat 125); Fat 14g (Saturated
6g); Cholesterol 55mg; Sodium 430mg; Carbohydrate 21g (Dietary
Fiber 2g); Protein 16g
% Daily Value: Vitamin A 10%; Vitamin C 8%; Calcium 8%; Iron 10%
Diet Exchanges: 1 Starch, 1 1/2 Lean Meat, 1 Vegetable, 2 Fat

Cooked White and Wild Rice

1/2 cup uncooked wild rice

1 1/4 cups water

1/2 teaspoon salt

1/2 cup uncooked regular long-grain rice

1 cup water

Heat wild rice, 1 1/4 cups water and salt to boiling in
2-quart saucepan; reduce heat. Cover and simmer 30
minutes. Stir in regular rice and 1 cup water. Heat to
boiling; reduce heat. Cover and simmer 15 minutes.
(Do not lift cover or stir.) Remove from heat. Fluff rice
lightly with fork. Cover and let steam 5 minutes.

Holiday Hints

Want to add that final touch? Try
one of these before serving:

• Make a wreath shape on baked
  casserole with fresh parsley or rosemary sprigs. Add a bow made with
pimientos.

• Sprinkle baked casserole with additional almonds that are toasted.

• Sprinkle baked casserole with
  crushed herb-flavored croutons.

Turkey-Wild Rice Casserole

Hoisin-Cranberry-Turkey Wraps

PREP: 20 MIN; COOK: 10 MIN
6 SERVINGS

1 tablespoon vegetable oil

1 tablespoon grated gingerroot or 1 teaspoon ground ginger

2 cloves garlic, finely chopped

1/2 cup thinly sliced fresh shiitake or regular white mushrooms

1/2 cup thinly sliced snow (Chinese) pea pods

4 medium green onions, thinly sliced (1/4 cup)

1/4 teaspoon crushed red pepper, if desired

1 1/2 cups cubed cooked turkey

1/2 cup shredded carrot (about 1 small)

1/3 cup hoisin sauce

3 tablespoons frozen (thawed) cranberry juice concentrate

1 teaspoon soy sauce

1 can (15 ounces) cooked wild rice, drained

6 whole wheat flour tortillas (8 to 10 inches in diameter)

Heat oil in 12-inch skillet over medium-high heat. Cook gingerroot and garlic in oil about 3 minutes, stirring frequently, until gingerroot is softened and garlic is golden.

Stir in mushrooms, pea pods, onions and red pepper. Cook 3 to 5 minutes, stirring frequently, until vegetables are crisp-tender. Stir in remaining ingredients except tortillas. Cook, stirring frequently, until heated through.

Divide turkey mixture among tortillas. Fold 2 ends of tortilla 1 inch over filling; roll tortilla around filling.

1 Serving: Calories 280 (Calories from Fat 65); Fat 7g (Saturated 1g); Cholesterol 30mg; Sodium 470mg; Carbohydrate 42g (Dietary Fiber 5g); Protein 17g
% Daily Value: Vitamin A 16%; Vitamin C 8%; Calcium 4%; Iron 14%
Diet Exchanges: 2 Lean Meat, 3 Fruit

Holiday Hints

Delight your guests and family by packaging these yummy sandwiches with ribbons of green onion. To make ribbons, heat 10-inch lengths of green onion tops in 1/4 inch water in a large skillet over medium heat for 1 to 2 minutes or until tender and bright green; drain. Run cold water over onions; dry on paper towels. Tie onions around wraps.

For a finishing touch, serve wraps with Pear-Cranberry Chutney (page 295) or a purchased chutney found in the condiment section of your supermarket. Feeling exotic? A hollowed-out passionfruit half makes a great holder for the chutney.

Hoisin-Cranberry-Turkey Wraps

Herbed Cornish Hens

PREP: 20 MIN; ROAST: 1 HR
6 SERVINGS

3 Rock Cornish hens (about 1 pound each)

Salt and pepper to taste

1/4 cup butter or margarine, melted

1/2 teaspoon dried marjoram leaves

1/2 teaspoon dried thyme leaves

1/4 teaspoon paprika

Heat oven to 350°. Rub cavities of hens with salt and pepper. Place hens, breast sides up, on rack in shallow roasting pan.

Mix remaining ingredients; brush hens with part of mixture. Insert meat thermometer so tip is in thickest part of inside thigh muscle and does not touch bone. Roast uncovered about 1 hour, brushing with butter mixture 5 or 6 times, until thermometer reads 180° and juice is no longer pink when center of thigh is cut. Discard any remaining butter mixture.

To serve, cut each hen in half with scissors, cutting along backbone from tail to neck and down center of breast.

1 Serving: Calories 365 (Calories from Fat 260); Fat 29g (Saturated 11g); Cholesterol 170mg; Sodium 125mg; Carbohydrate 0g (Dietary Fiber 0g); Protein 26g
% Daily Value: Vitamin A 10%; Vitamin C 0%; Calcium 2%; Iron 6%
Diet Exchanges: 1 1/2 Medium-Fat Meat, 2 Fat

Holiday Hints

Rock Cornish hens are specially bred chickens that have all white meat. They are usually found in the frozen meat section of your supermarket, although your butcher may be able to special order fresh hens for you.

HOLIDAY MENU

Fireside Supper

Here's a festive menu that's so good, you'll want to use it year-round.

- Herbed Cornish Hens
- Cranberry-Wild Rice Bake (page 108)
- Holiday Marinated Vegetables (page 93)
- Popovers (page 200)
- Winter Poached Pears (page 156)

Herbed Cornish Hens, Cranberry-Wild Rice Bake (page 108) and Holiday Marinated Vegetables (page 93)

71

Roast Goose with Apple Stuffing

PREP: 1 1/2 HR; ROAST: 3 1/2 HR; STAND: 15 MIN
8 SERVINGS

1 goose (8 to 10 pounds)

6 cups soft bread crumbs (about 9 slices bread)

1/4 cup butter or margarine, melted

1 1/2 teaspoons chopped fresh or 1/2 teaspoon
    dried sage leaves

3/4 teaspoon chopped fresh or 1/4 teaspoon dried
    thyme leaves

1/2 teaspoon salt

1/4 teaspoon pepper

3 medium tart cooking apples, chopped (3 cups)

2 medium stalks celery (with leaves), chopped
    (1 cup)

1 medium onion, chopped (1/2 cup)

1/4 cup all-purpose flour, if desired

2 cups water or chicken broth, if desired

Heat oven to 350°. Trim excess fat from goose. Toss remaining ingredients except flour and water. Fill wishbone area of goose with stuffing first. (Do not pack—stuffing will expand while cooking.) Fasten opening with skewers, and lace with string. Pierce skin all over with fork. Fasten neck skin to back with skewer. Fold wings across back with tips touching. Fill body cavity lightly with stuffing.

Place goose, breast side up, on rack in shallow roasting pan. Insert meat thermometer so tip is in thickest part of inside thigh muscle and does not touch bone.

Roast uncovered 3 to 3 1/2 hours, removing excess fat from pan occasionally, until thermometer reads 180° and juice of goose is no longer pink when center of thigh is cut. Place tent of aluminum foil loosely over goose during last hour to prevent excessive browning. Place goose on heated platter. Let stand 15 minutes for easier carving.

Make gravy from drippings if desired. Skim fat from drippings. Pour 1/4 cup drippings into 2-quart saucepan; stir in flour. Gradually stir in water or broth; heat to boiling, stirring constantly. Boil and stir 1 minute; reduce heat to medium. Cook, stirring constantly, until thickened. Serve goose with apple stuffing and gravy.

1 Serving: Calories 535 (Calories from Fat 250); Fat 28g (Saturated 12g); Cholesterol 175mg; Sodium 470mg; Carbohydrate 23g (Dietary Fiber 2g); Protein 50g
% Daily Value: Vitamin A 6%; Vitamin C 4%; Calcium 6%; Iron 32%
Diet Exchanges: 1 Starch, 1 1/2 Medium-Fat Meat, 1/2 Fruit

Party Pointers

Looking for ideas for a fast and fabulous holiday table?

- Use large gold or silver doilies at each place setting for an easy, elegant look. Place doilies underneath the dinner plates on the tablecloth or on each place mat. Sprinkle the table with gold confetti.

- Bedeck the dining table with lots of candles. Don't let the lack of candleholders stop your lighting up. Hollow out a space in the center of apples just large enough to hold candles. Brush the insides of apples with lemon juice to prevent browning. Insert the candles and wrap a rosemary sprig around the base of each candle.

- If candles are sparse, try this glowing table decoration: String small white lights in a basket of greens or in a clear glass bowl of gold or silver ornaments. You may want to use battery-powered lights.

- Give each guest a small memento by their place setting. It can be a small wrapped box with a single piece of premium candy to be unwrapped at the end of the evening. You may like instead to give a holiday decoration with the date inscribed either on the decoration or on ribbons tied to the ornament.

Roast Goose with Apple Stuffing

Merry Main Dishes

Parmesan-Shrimp Pasta Bake

PREP: 20 MIN; BAKE: 40 MIN

8 SERVINGS

1 package (16 ounces) farfalle (bow-tie) pasta

6 tablespoons butter or margarine

3 cloves garlic, finely chopped

6 tablespoons all-purpose flour

1/3 cup dry vermouth or chicken broth

2 3/4 cups half-and-half

1/2 cup clam juice

1 tablespoon tomato paste or ketchup

3/4 teaspoon salt

1/4 teaspoon pepper

1 pound uncooked peeled deveined medium shrimp, thawed if frozen

2 tablespoons chopped fresh or 2 teaspoons dried dill weed

3/4 cup freshly grated Parmesan cheese

Heat oven to 350°. Grease shallow 2-quart casserole. Cook and drain pasta as directed on package.

Melt butter in 2-quart saucepan over medium heat. Cook garlic in butter 1 minute, stirring constantly. Stir in flour. Cook, stirring constantly with wire whisk, until smooth and bubbly.

Stir in vermouth. Stir in half-and-half, clam juice, tomato paste, salt and pepper. Cook over medium heat, stirring constantly, until thickened. Stir in shrimp, dill weed and 1/4 cup of the cheese.

Stir pasta into shrimp mixture. Pour into casserole. Sprinkle with remaining 1/2 cup cheese. Bake uncovered 35 to 40 minutes or until light brown and hot.

1 Serving: Calories 480 (Calories from Fat 100); Fat 22g (Saturated 13g); Cholesterol 115mg; Sodium 560mg; Carbohydrate 53g (Dietary Fiber 2g); Protein 20g
% Daily Value: Vitamin A 18%; Vitamin C 2%; Calcium 22%; Iron 20%
Diet Exchanges: 3 Starch, 1 Medium-Fat Meat, 1 Vegetable, 3 Fat

Party Pointers

Organize a holiday progressive dinner with friends or neighbors. Start with appetizers and cocktails at the first house, have soup, salad and bread at the second stop, the main course and perhaps a vegetable at the next, and dessert and coffee at the last. It's an easy way to share the cooking, plus you get to see everyone's holiday decorations. If those involved are looking to you for menu ideas, here are a few to share:

- Cinnamon Cider (page 18) and Quick Cranberry Punch (page 8)

- Meatball Merriment (page 30), Bruschetta Romana (page 32), Ginger Shrimp Kabobs (page 28) and Basil Brie in Pastry (page 34)

- Butternut Squash Soup (page 78), Christmas Spinach Salad (page 99) and Popovers (page 200)

- Parmesan-Shrimp Pasta Bake and Holiday Marinated Vegetables (page 93)

- Winter Poached Pears (page 156) and White Almond Fondue (page 152)

Parmesan-Shrimp Pasta Bake

Lobster Bisque

PREP: 15 MIN; COOK: 10 MIN
4 SERVINGS

3 tablespoons butter or margarine

1 small onion, finely chopped (1/4 cup)

3 tablespoons all-purpose flour

1 tablespoon chopped fresh parsley

1/2 teaspoon salt

1/8 teaspoon pepper

2 cups milk

1 cup chicken broth

1 1/4 cups chopped fresh or frozen (thawed)
   lobster (about 12 ounces)

Melt butter in 3-quart saucepan over low heat. Cook onion in butter, stirring occasionally, until tender. Stir in flour, parsley, salt and pepper. Cook, stirring constantly, until mixture is bubbly; remove from heat.

Stir in milk and broth. Heat to boiling, stirring constantly. Boil and stir 1 minute. Stir in lobster. Heat to boiling; reduce heat. Simmer about 3 minutes, stirring frequently, until lobster is white.

1 Serving: Calories 205 (Calories from Fat 100); Fat 11g (Saturated 7g); Cholesterol 65mg; Sodium 590mg; Carbohydrate 12g (Dietary Fiber 0g); Protein 14g
% Daily Value: Vitamin A 14%; Vitamin C 2%; Calcium 18%; Iron 2%
Diet Exchanges: 1 High-Fat Meat, 1 Vegetable, 1 Fat, 1/2 Skim Milk

Holiday Hints

• If your family has a favorite fish other than lobster, use it instead. Halibut, orange roughy or haddock make good substitutions.

• Make this bisque extra special by decorating the top with green onion wisps and a carrot slice cut into a decorative shape.

Oyster Stew

PREP: 10 MIN; COOK: 10 MIN
4 SERVINGS

1/4 cup butter or margarine

1 pint shucked oysters, undrained

2 cups milk

1/2 cup half-and-half

1/2 teaspoon salt

Dash of pepper

Italian parsley sprigs, if desired

Red bell pepperstrips, if desired

Melt butter in 1 1/2-quart saucepan over low heat. Stir in oysters. Cook, stirring occasionally, just until edges curl.

Heat milk and half-and-half in 2-quart saucepan over medium-low heat until hot. Stir in salt, pepper and oyster mixture; heat until hot. Garnish with parsley and bell pepper.

1 Serving: Calories 285 (Calories from Fat 180); Fat 20g (Saturated 12g); Cholesterol 115mg; Sodium 700mg; Carbohydrate 12g (Dietary Fiber 0g); Protein 14g
% Daily Value: Vitamin A 22%; Vitamin C 4%; Calcium 24%; Iron 46%
Diet Exchanges: 1 Medium-Fat Meat, 3 Fat, 1 Skim Milk

HOLIDAY MENU

Candlelight Christmas Eve Supper

Oyster stew is a Christmas Eve tradition for many families. This recipe makes about four 1-cup servings; if you're feeding a crowd or using the stew as the main course, you'll want to double the recipe.

You may like these menu suggestions for your Christmas Eve celebration.

- Cranberry-Pistachio Salad with Champagne Vinaigrette (page 92)
- Oyster Stew
- Savory Mini-Scones (page 198)
- Fluffy Peppermint Pie (page 163)

Oyster Stew and Savory Mini-Scones (page 198)

Butternut Squash Soup

PREP: 15 MIN; COOK: 30 MIN
12 SERVINGS

2 tablespoons butter or margarine

1 medium onion, chopped (1/2 cup)

1 can (14 1/2 ounces) ready-to-serve chicken broth

1 pound butternut squash, peeled, seeded and cut into 1-inch cubes

2 medium pears, peeled and sliced

1 teaspoon chopped fresh or 1/4 teaspoon dried thyme leaves

1/4 teaspoon salt

1/4 teaspoon white pepper

1/4 teaspoon ground coriander

1 cup whipping (heavy) cream

1 medium unpeeled pear, sliced

1/2 cup chopped pecans, toasted (page 31)

Melt butter in Dutch oven over medium heat. Cook onion in butter, stirring occasionally, until tender. Stir in broth, squash, 2 sliced pears, thyme, salt, white pepper and coriander. Heat to boiling; reduce heat. Cover and simmer 10 to 15 minutes or until squash is tender.

New Twist

Add a festive touch to your soup presentation with:

• A small dollop of sour cream.

• A touch of cilantro pesto over soup.

• A sprinkle of fresh cilantro and croutons.

Or add a flavor twist to this recipe by using apples instead of pears!

Pour about half of the soup into food processor or blender. Cover and process until smooth; pour into another container. Repeat with remaining soup. Return soup to Dutch oven.

Stir whipping cream into soup. Heat over medium heat, stirring frequently, until hot (do not boil). Garnish with sliced unpeeled pear and pecans.

1 Serving: Calories 155 (Calories from Fat 110); Fat 12g (Saturated 5g); Cholesterol 25mg; Sodium 240mg; Carbohydrate 12g (Dietary Fiber 2g); Protein 2g
% Daily Value: Vitamin A 28%; Vitamin C 6%; Calcium 4%; Iron 2%
Diet Exchanges: 2 Vegetable, 2 Fat

HOLIDAY MENU

Holiday Dinner Party for Friends

Add these trimmings to complete your dinner. If you're serving 8, double the Roasted Vegetable Medley. What's great, you can make the dessert tart as well as the pearl onions a day ahead of time.

• Butternut Squash Soup

• Christmas Spinach Salad (page 99)

• Rib Roast with Herb Rub (page 46)

• Roasted Vegetable Medley (page 121)

• Balsamic-Glazed Pearl Onions (page 296)

• Honey-Wine-Cranberry Tart (page 132)

Three-Bean Christmas Chili

PREP: 15 MIN; COOK: 25 MIN
6 SERVINGS

1 can (28 ounces) whole tomatoes, undrained

1 can (15 to 16 ounces) garbanzo beans, drained

1 can (15 to 16 ounces) kidney beans, drained

1 can (15 to 16 ounces) butter beans, drained

1 can (15 ounces) tomato sauce

3 small red, orange or yellow bell peppers, cut into
  1-inch pieces

1 Anaheim or jalapeño chili, seeded and chopped

1 to 2 tablespoons chili powder

2 teaspoons ground cumin

1/4 teaspoon pepper

1/2 cup sour cream

3 tablespoons salsa

Chopped fresh cilantro, if desired

Mix all ingredients except sour cream and salsa in Dutch oven. Heat to boiling, breaking up tomatoes; reduce heat. Cover and simmer 15 to 20 minutes or until bell peppers are tender.

Mix sour cream and salsa. Serve chili with sour cream mixture. Sprinkle with cilantro.

1 Serving: Calories 265 (Calories from Fat 45); Fat 5g (Saturated 2g); Cholesterol 10mg; Sodium 820mg; Carbohydrate 50g (Dietary Fiber 14g); Protein 16g
% Daily Value: Vitamin A 28%; Vitamin C 72%; Calcium 12%; Iron 34%
Diet Exchanges: 3 Starch, 1 Vegetable

Party Pointers

Invite the gang over for a tree-trimming party. Double the chili recipe, make it in a 6-quart Dutch oven and serve a "make it your way" chili bar. Provide toppings of sour cream, salsa, shredded cheeses, chopped red onion, chopped ripe olives, chopped avocado and, for the bold, red pepper sauce. Have baskets filled with croutons, tortilla chips, crackers, muffins and breadsticks for chili dipping. For an extra treat, offer purchased bread bowls or tortilla bowls (available at your supermarket) to serve the chili in.

Rice and Bean Roll-Ups

PREP: 20 MIN; BAKE: 35 MIN
6 SERVINGS

1 1/2 cups thick-and-chunky salsa

1 cup cooked brown rice

2 medium roma (plum) tomatoes, chopped

1 small bell pepper, cut into 1/2-inch pieces
(1/2 cup)

1 can (15 ounces) black beans with cumin,
undrained

1 can (8 ounces) whole kernel corn, drained

6 jalapeño-flavored or plain flour tortillas
(8 to 10 inches in diameter)

1 cup shredded Mexican-style cheese blend
(4 ounces)

Heat oven to 350°. Spread 1/2 cup of the salsa in
ungreased rectangular baking dish, 13×9×2 inches.

Mix rice, tomatoes, bell pepper, beans and corn. Spread
3/4 cup rice mixture on each tortilla; roll up. Place seam
sides down on salsa in baking dish. Spoon remaining
1 cup salsa over tortillas. Sprinkle with cheese.

Cover and bake 30 to 35 minutes or until heated
through and cheese is melted.

1 Serving: Calories 370 (Calories from Fat 90); Fat 10g (Saturated
5g); Cholesterol 20mg; Sodium 850mg; Carbohydrate 62g (Dietary
Fiber 9g); Protein 17g
% Daily Value: Vitamin A 12%; Vitamin C 26%; Calcium 26%;
Iron 24%
Diet Exchanges: 3 Starch, 3 Vegetable, 1 Fat

Party Pointers

Why not have these roll-ups ready to
pop in the oven after a day on the
ski slopes? For a "warm-me-up"
aprés-ski party, try the following
plan.

• Make and refrigerate the roll-ups
ahead.

• Have some Appetizer Cheese Trees

(page 20) ready with an assortment
of crackers.

• Fill a slow cooker with Hot Spiced
Wine (page 19) or Cinnamon
Cider (page 18) ready to greet
chilled guests.

• When you're ready to bake the
roll-ups, add them to the salsa in

the baking dish and top with the
additional salsa and cheese.

• Serve the roll-ups with a crisp
green salad and warm crusty bread.

• Top off the meal with Heavenly
Cheesecake (page 146).

Rice and Bean Roll-Ups and Hot Spiced Wine (page 19)

Roasted Vegetable Lasagna

PREP: 50 MIN; BAKE: 25 MIN; STAND: 10 MIN
10 SERVINGS

Olive oil-flavored cooking spray

2 medium bell peppers, cut into 1-inch pieces

1 medium onion, cut into 8 wedges and separated
into pieces

2 medium zucchini, sliced (4 cups)

8 ounces mushrooms, sliced (3 cups)

1/2 teaspoon salt

1/4 teaspoon pepper

Tomato Sauce (right) or 1 jar (32 ounces) spaghetti
sauce

12 uncooked lasagna noodles

4 cups shredded mozzarella cheese (16 ounces)

1 cup shredded Parmesan cheese (4 ounces)

Heat oven to 450°. Spray jelly roll pan, 15 1/2 × 10 1/2 ×
1 inch, with cooking spray. Place bell peppers, onion,
zucchini and mushrooms in single layer in pan. Spray
vegetables with cooking spray; sprinkle with salt and
pepper. Bake uncovered 20 to 25 minutes, turning vegetables once, until vegetables are tender.

While vegetables are roasting, prepare Tomato Sauce.
Cook and drain noodles as directed on package. Rinse
noodles with cold water; drain. Mix cheeses; set aside.

Reduce oven temperature to 400°. Spray rectangular baking dish, 13 × 9 × 2 inches, with cooking spray. Spread
1/4 cup of the sauce in dish; top with 3 noodles. Layer
with 3/4 cup sauce, 1 1/4 cups vegetables and
1 cup cheese mixture. Repeat layers 3 more times with
remaining noodles, sauce, vegetables and cheese mixture.

Bake uncovered 20 to 25 minutes or until hot. Let stand
10 minutes before cutting.

1 Serving: Calories 305 (Calories from Fat 110); Fat 12g (Saturated
7g); Cholesterol 30mg; Sodium 780mg; Carbohydrate 31g (Dietary
Fiber 4g); Protein 22g
% Daily Value: Vitamin A 16%; Vitamin C 32%; Calcium 52%; Iron 12%
Diet Exchanges: 1 Starch, 2 Very Lean Meat, 3 Vegetable, 2 Fat

Tomato Sauce

1 large onion, chopped (1 cup)

2 tablespoons finely chopped garlic

1 can (28 ounces) crushed tomatoes, undrained

3 tablespoons chopped fresh or 1 tablespoon dried
basil leaves

3 tablespoons chopped fresh or 1 tablespoon dried
oregano leaves

1 teaspoon sugar

1/2 teaspoon salt

1/2 teaspoon crushed red pepper

Spray 2-quart saucepan with cooking spray. Cook onion
and garlic in saucepan over medium heat 2 minutes, stirring occasionally. Stir in remaining ingredients. Heat to
boiling; reduce heat. Simmer uncovered 15 to 20 minutes or until slightly thickened.

Timesaving Tips

Cover unbaked lasagna tightly with aluminum foil and
refrigerate up to 24 hours. If you prefer, freeze up to two
months. To bake from refrigerator, bake 25 to 35 minutes or until hot. To bake frozen lasagna, thaw in refrigerator overnight; bake 25 to 35 minutes or until hot.

Roasted Vegetable Lasagna

Baked Polenta and Peperonata Casserole

PREP: 15 MIN; BAKE: 40 MIN; STAND 10 MIN
6 SERVINGS

Peperonata Sauce (right)

1 tube (16 ounces) refrigerated polenta

1 1/2 cups grated Romano or Parmesan cheese

Heat oven to 350°. Grease 2-quart casserole or square baking dish, 8×8×2 inches. Prepare Peperonata Sauce.

Cut polenta into twelve 1/2-inch slices. Arrange 6 slices polenta on bottom of casserole. Spread half of the sauce over polenta. Sprinkle with 3/4 cup of the cheese. Repeat with remaining polenta, sauce and cheese.

Bake uncovered 35 to 40 minutes or until heated through and cheese is light brown. Let stand 10 minutes before serving.

1 Serving: Calories 285 (Calories from Fat 135); Fat 15g (Saturated 5g); Cholesterol 15mg; Sodium 1210mg; Carbohydrate 29g (Dietary Fiber 5g); Protein 13g
% Daily Value: Vitamin A 30%; Vitamin C 88%; Calcium 34%; Iron 20%
Diet Exchanges: 2 Starch, 1 1/2 High-Fat Meat

Peperonata Sauce

3 tablespoons olive or vegetable oil

3 medium onions, chopped (1 1/2 cups)

1 clove garlic, finely chopped

3/4 cup chopped pitted Kalamata or ripe olives

1 tablespoon chopped fresh or 1 teaspoon dried basil leaves

1/2 teaspoon salt

1/4 teaspoon pepper

1 can (28 ounces) diced tomatoes, drained

1 jar (12 ounces) roasted red bell peppers, drained and chopped

Heat oil in 3-quart saucepan over medium heat. Cook onions and garlic in oil 2 to 3 minutes, stirring occasionally, until onions are crisp-tender. Stir in remaining ingredients. Simmer uncovered about 8 minutes or until slightly thickened.

Timesaving Tips

If you're short of time, you may like to substitute a 32-ounce jar of your favorite thick-and-chunky-style spaghetti sauce—try to find one flavored with ripe olives—for the Peperonata Sauce. You can also make this colorful casserole ahead of time. Cover and refrigerate it up to 24 hours and just plan on an extra 10 to 15 minutes of baking time.

Baked Polenta and Peperonata Casserole

Cheesy Apple-Bacon Strata

PREP: 25 MIN; CHILL: 2 HR; BAKE: 45 MIN; STAND: 10 MIN
12 SERVINGS

3 tablespoons butter or margarine

3 medium Granny Smith apples, peeled and coarsely chopped (3 cups)

3 tablespoons packed brown sugar

4 cups cubed firm bread (7 slices)

1 pound bacon, crisply cooked and coarsely chopped

2 cups shredded sharp Cheddar cheese (8 ounces)

2 1/2 cups milk

1 teaspoon ground mustard (dry)

2 teaspoons Worcestershire sauce

1/4 teaspoon salt

1/8 teaspoon pepper

5 eggs

Grease 2-quart casserole. Melt butter in 10-inch skillet over medium heat. Cook apples in butter 2 to 3 minutes, stirring occasionally, until crisp-tender. Stir in brown sugar; reduce heat to low. Cook 5 to 6 minutes, stirring occasionally, until apples are tender.

Layer half each of the bread, bacon, apples and cheese in casserole. Repeat with remaining bread, bacon, apples and cheese.

Mix remaining ingredients; pour over cheese. Cover tightly and refrigerate at least 2 hours but no longer than 24 hours.

Heat oven to 350°. Bake uncovered 40 to 45 minutes or until knife inserted in center comes out clean. Let stand 10 minutes before serving.

1 Serving: Calories 320 (Calories from Fat 170); Fat 19g (Saturated 9g); Cholesterol 130mg; Sodium 550mg; Carbohydrate 24g (Dietary Fiber 1g); Protein 14g
% Daily Value: Vitamin A 12%; Vitamin C 2%; Calcium 20%; Iron 8%
Diet Exchanges: 1 Starch, 1 High-Fat Meat, 1/2 Fruit, 2 1/2 Fat

HOLIDAY MENU
Easy Holiday Brunch

Start a new tradition by hosting a holiday brunch! Serve this easy make-ahead strata with plenty of fresh fruits, a variety of warm muffins and steaming-hot coffee. Try this stress-busting menu for a reprieve from last-minute baking and cooking duties.

- Heavenly Fruit Salad (page 102)
- Cheesy Apple-Bacon Strata
- Holiday Hash Browns (page 114)
- Merry Muffins (page 172)

Cheesy Apple-Bacon Strata

Morning Glory Oven French Toast

Morning Glory Oven French Toast

PREP: 25 MIN; BAKE: 12 MIN
6 SERVINGS

Cranberry-Raspberry Topping (right)

3 eggs

3/4 cup milk

1 tablespoon granulated sugar

1/4 teaspoon salt

1/4 teaspoon ground cinnamon

18 slices French bread, 1/2 inch thick

Powdered sugar, if desired

Prepare Cranberry-Raspberry Topping. Heat oven to 500°.

Beat eggs, milk, granulated sugar, salt and cinnamon in small bowl with fork.

Dip bread into egg mixture; place on plate. Lightly grease cookie sheet. Heat cookie sheet in oven 1 minute; remove from oven. Place dipped bread on hot cookie sheet.

Bake 5 to 8 minutes or until bottoms are golden brown. Turn bread; bake 2 to 4 minutes longer or until golden brown. Sprinkle with powdered sugar. Serve with topping.

1 Serving: Calories 340 (Calories from Fat45); Fat 5g (Saturated 2g); Cholesterol 110mg; Sodium 370mg; Carbohydrate 10g (Dietary Fiber 4g); Protein 8g
% Daily Value: Vitamin A 4%; Vitamin C 8%; Calcium 8%; Iron 10%
Diet Exchanges: 2 Starch, 2 1/2 Fruit, 1 Fat

Cranberry-Raspberry Topping

1 package (10 ounces) frozen raspberries, thawed

1 cup sugar

1 cup fresh or frozen cranberries

Drain raspberries, reserving 1/2 cup juice. Mix juice and sugar in 2-quart saucepan. Heat to boiling; boil 5 minutes. Stir in raspberries and cranberries; reduce heat. Simmer about 3 minutes, stirring occasionally, until cranberries are tender but do not burst. Serve warm or cool.

Party Pointers

Want to host a holiday brunch but don't know where to start? The guest list is up to you, but here are a few tips to make the event enjoyable:

- Cover a table or countertop with holiday gift wrap, or cut holiday shapes from gift wrap (using cookie cutters as patterns) to scatter on a tablecloth. Add candles for a formal setting.

- Make an easy centerpiece by filling a basket or copper bowl with small evergreen branches, pinecones, whole oranges and grapefruit, unshelled nuts and cinnamon sticks.

- Arrange foods buffet style, and let guests serve themselves.

- Stack plates on the far left, followed by entrées, fruits and veggies, breads and finally silverware. Roll silverware in napkins to make it easier for guests to grab.

Heavenly Fruit Salad (page 103)

CHAPTER 3

Sensational Salads and Sides

It's simple and satisfying

companions to the starring

main dish that sweeten the memory

of a glorious holiday feast.

Cranberry-Pistachio Salad with Champagne Vinaigrette

PREP: 15 MIN

8 SERVINGS

Champagne Vinaigrette (right)

1 small bunch romaine, torn into bite-size pieces (about 10 cups)

1 jar (7 ounces) roasted red bell peppers, drained and cut into 1/2-inch strips

1/2 cup dried cranberries

1/3 cup chopped pistachio nuts

Prepare Champagne Vinaigrette. Toss vinaigrette and remaining ingredients.

1 Serving: Calories 140 (Calories from Fat 90); Fat 10g (Saturated 1g); Cholesterol 0mg; Sodium 70mg; Carbohydrate 14g (Dietary Fiber 4g); Protein 2g
% Daily Value: Vitamin A 18%; Vitamin C 86%; Calcium 2%; Iron 4%
Diet Exchanges: 1 Fruit, 2 Fat

Champagne Vinaigrette

1/2 cup champagne vinegar or cider vinegar

1/4 cup vegetable oil

1 tablespoon sugar

1 tablespoon Dijon mustard

Shake all ingredients in tightly covered container.

New Twist

Breeze through the holidays with this versatile festive salad:

• Purchase any bag of salad greens from the produce section of the supermarket.

• Use dried cherries or fresh raspberries instead of the dried cranberries.

• Use toasted slivered almonds or toasted pecans for the pistachios.

• Scan the gourmet section of your supermarket to select a fancy bottled dressing.

Holiday Marinated Vegetables

PREP: 10 MIN; CHILL: 3 HR
4 SERVINGS

1/2 cup oil-and-vinegar dressing

2 cups cooked Brussels sprouts, broccoli or asparagus

1 cup cherry tomatoes, cut in half

1 1/2 cups mushroom halves or fourths (4 ounces)

Lettuce leaves, if desired

Pour dressing over Brussels sprouts and tomatoes in large glass or plastic bowl. Cover and refrigerate at least 3 hours but no longer than 24 hours.

Add mushrooms to vegetables; toss until well coated. Drain before serving. Serve vegetables on lettuce.

1 Serving: Calories 80 (Calories from Fat 36); Fat 4g (Saturated 1g); Cholesterol 0mg; Sodium 80mg; Carbohydrate 11g (Dietary Fiber 4g); Protein 4g
% Daily Value: Vitamin A 6%; Vitamin C 74%; Calcium 2%; Iron 6%
Diet Exchanges: 2 Vegetable, 1 Fat

Holiday Hints

Serve these festive marinated vegetables on individual serving plates that you've lined with kale leaves or red leaf lettuce. Sprinkle with toasted pine nuts for extra pizzazz.

Frozen Asian Cabbage Salad

PREP: 25 MIN; FREEZE: 8 HR

6 SERVINGS

1 package (3 ounces) ramen noodle soup mix
(any flavor)

1/2 cup slivered almonds

2 tablespoons butter or margarine

3/4 cup sugar

1/2 cup cider vinegar

1 tablespoon plus 1 1/2 teaspoons soy sauce

1 teaspoon sesame oil

1 bag (16 ounces) coleslaw mix

1 small red or green bell pepper, chopped (1/2 cup)

2 medium green onions, chopped (2 tablespoons)

1 teaspoon grated gingerroot or 1 teaspoon ground
ginger

Break block of ramen noodles into 10-inch skillet
(reserve seasoning packet for another use). Add almonds
and butter. Cook over medium heat, stirring frequently,
until butter is melted and almonds and noodles are light
brown; cool.

Heat sugar, vinegar and soy sauce to boiling in 2-quart
saucepan, stirring frequently. Boil and stir 1 minute;
remove from heat. Stir in sesame oil.

Mix coleslaw mix, bell pepper, onions and gingerroot in
large bowl. Pour vinegar mixture over coleslaw mixture;
toss to coat. Place in freezer bag or container; seal bag or
cover container tightly. Place noodle mixture in freezer
bag; seal bag. Freeze coleslaw and noodle mixtures at
least 8 hours or up to 1 week.

Thaw coleslaw mixture in refrigerator 30 minutes.
Sprinkle with frozen noodle mixture. Serve salad when
slightly frozen. Serve within 8 hours before salad
becomes limp.

1 Serving: Calories 225 (Calories from Fat 90); Fat 10g (Saturated
3g); Cholesterol 5mg; Sodium 705mg; Carbohydrate 32g (Dietary
Fiber 3g); Protein 3g
% Daily Value: Vitamin A 10%; Vitamin C 74%; Calcium 8%;
Iron 10%
Diet Exchanges: 2 Vegetable, 1 Fruit, 2 Fat

Timesaving Tips

Packaged coleslaw mix is available in the produce section
of most supermarkets. If you prefer, shred your own cabbage mixture. For this recipe you'll need 7 to 8 cups or
1 medium head green cabbage (2 pounds), shredded.
You'll find that using a food processor is a real timesaver.

Frozen Asian Cabbage Salad

Zesty Pasta Salad

PREP: 15 MIN; COOK: 20 MIN
6 SERVINGS

1 package (16 ounces) long fusilli (corkscrew) pasta
  or spaghetti

1 pound asparagus, cut into 2-inch pieces

1/2 cup Italian dressing

1/4 cup chopped fresh or 1 tablespoon dried basil
  leaves

2 teaspoons crushed red pepper

3 medium bell peppers, cut into bite-size pieces

1/3 cup oil-packed sun-dried tomatoes, drained
  and chopped

1/4 cup pine nuts, toasted (page 31), if desired

Heat 4 quarts water (salted if desired) to boiling in
6-quart Dutch oven. Cook pasta in boiling water 11
minutes. Add asparagus to boiling water; cook about

3 minutes or until asparagus is crisp-tender. Drain pasta
and asparagus. Rinse with cold water; drain.

Mix dressing, basil and red pepper in large bowl. Add
pasta, asparagus and remaining ingredients; toss.

1 Serving: Calories 405 (Calories from Fat 100); Fat 11g (Saturated
2g); Cholesterol 5mg; Sodium 180mg; Carbohydrate 70g (Dietary
Fiber 5g); Protein 12g
% Daily Value: Vitamin A 10%; Vitamin C 100%; Calcium 4%; Iron 20%
Diet Exchanges: 4 Starch, 2 Vegetable, 1 Fat

Holiday Hints

Extra pasta salad? Serve it as an entrée tossed with 1 cup
chopped cooked turkey or chicken. Complete the meal
with a cup of vegetable soup and a basket of Pesto
Biscuits (page 196).

Gifts for Giving

Create a gift worth giving! Fill a pretty enamel colander
with a package of premium pasta, a fancy jar of sun-
dried tomatoes, a jar of pine nuts and a gourmet bottle
of Italian dressing. If you're giving the gift right away,
you might want to add colorful bell peppers. Include a
wooden pasta server and, of course, the Zesty Pasta Salad
recipe.

Tortellini-Broccoli Salad

PREP: 20 MIN; CHILL: 1 HR
4 SERVINGS

1 package (7 ounces) cheese-filled tortellini

Balsamic Vinaigrette (right)

1 medium carrot, sliced (1/2 cup)

2 cups broccoli flowerets

2 medium green onions, sliced (2 tablespoons)

Cook and drain tortellini as directed on package. Rinse with cold water; drain. Prepare Balsamic Vinaigrette.

Mix carrot, broccoli, onions and vinaigrette in large glass or plastic bowl. Add tortellini; toss until evenly coated. Cover and refrigerate at least 1 hour to blend flavors.

1 Serving: Calories 160 (Calories from Fat 90); Fat 10g (Saturated 2g); Cholesterol 40mg; Sodium 110mg; Carbohydrate 14g (Dietary Fiber 2g); Protein 5g
% Daily Value: Vitamin A 30%; Vitamin C 60%; Calcium 6%; Iron 6%
Diet Exchanges: 1 Starch, 2 Fat

Balsamic Vinaigrette

1/4 cup balsamic or cider vinegar

1 tablespoon chopped fresh or 1 teaspoon dried basil leaves

2 tablespoons olive or vegetable oil

1/4 teaspoon paprika

1/8 teaspoon salt

1 clove garlic, finely chopped

Shake all ingredients in tightly covered container.

Timesaving Tips

- Supermarket salad bars can be a real time-saver. Rather than chopping the vegetables yourself, why not buy the pre-sliced carrots, broccoli and onions from the salad bar?

- To save more time, use 1/3 cup purchased balsamic vinaigrette dressing or another vinaigrette dressing of your choice.

- If you have leftover holiday ham, chop it and add it to make a main-meal salad!

Christmas Couscous Salad

PREP: 15 MIN; COOK: 5 MIN
6 SERVINGS

1 cup uncooked couscous

1 tablespoon olive or vegetable oil

2 medium zucchini, cut into 1/4-inch slices
(4 cups)

1 large red bell pepper, cut into 1-inch pieces

1/2 medium red onion, cut into 8 wedges

1 container (7 ounces) refrigerated pesto with sun-
dried tomatoes or basil pesto

2 tablespoons balsamic or cider vinegar

Prepare couscous as directed on package.

Heat oil in 10-inch nonstick skillet over medium-high
heat. Cook zucchini, bell pepper and onion in oil about
5 minutes, stirring frequently, until crisp-tender.

Toss couscous, vegetable mixture, pesto and vinegar in
large bowl. Serve warm or cold.

1 Serving: Calories 310 (Calories from Fat 180); Fat 20g (Saturated
4g); Cholesterol 5mg; Sodium 270mg; Carbohydrate 29g (Dietary
Fiber 4g); Protein 7g
% Daily Value: Vitamin A 20%; Vitamin C 50%; Calcium 12%; Iron 8%
Diet Exchanges: 1 Starch, 2 Vegetable, 4 Fat

Gifts for Giving

Make the gift of a salad bowl extra special by including
the recipe for Christmas Couscous Salad printed on a
recipe card and attached to a serving spoon. Fill the bowl
with a package of couscous, a jar of pesto, a gourmet
bottle of balsamic vinegar and a special bottle of olive
oil. Wrap the bowl in holiday cellophane, and tie with a
large bow.

Holiday Hints

Pesto comes in lots of flavors and is found in the refrigerated and condiment sections of your supermarket.
Experiment to see which one you like best, or make your
own.

Christmas Spinach Salad

PREP: 20 MIN
12 SERVINGS

Ginger-Honey Dressing (below)

12 cups bite-size pieces spinach

2 cups sliced strawberries

2 cups honeydew melon balls

2/3 cup chopped pecans, toasted (page 31)

2/3 cup julienne strips Gouda or Edam cheese
(about 2 ounces)

Prepare Ginger-Honey Dressing. Toss dressing and
remaining ingredients.

1 Serving: Calories 140 (Calories from Fat 80); Fat 9g (Saturated
2g); Cholesterol 5mg; Sodium 100mg; Carbohydrate 13g (Dietary
Fiber 2g); Protein 4g
% Daily Value: Vitamin A 26%; Vitamin C 52%; Calcium 8%; Iron 6%
Diet Exchanges: 1 Vegetable, 1/2 Fruit, 2 Fat

Ginger-Honey Dressing

1/4 cup lime juice

1/4 cup honey

2 tablespoons vegetable oil

1 teaspoon grated gingerroot or 1/2 teaspoon
ground ginger

Shake all ingredients in tightly covered container.

New Twist

Go ahead and make this salad your
way.

- Use your favorite greens combo.
The variety of salad greens now
available in supermarkets is greater
than ever before. If you're not fond

of spinach, you may like to try a
red leaf lettuce or a rosy radicchio.

- If strawberries aren't your choice,
try dried cranberries, pomegranate
seeds or fresh raspberries.

- Instead of honeydew, try green
grapes, apple or pear slices (dipped
in lemon juice to keep from
browning) or kiwifruit slices.

Winter Wheat Berry Salad

PREP: 25 MIN
6 SERVINGS

Sweet Red Onion Dressing (right)

3 cups cooked wheat berries

1 cup cooked brown rice

1 cup cooked barley

1/2 cup dried cherries or cranberries

1/4 cup diced carrot

1/4 cup diced celery

1/4 cup chopped fresh parsley, if desired

1 medium unpeeled eating apple, chopped (1 cup)

4 medium green onions, chopped (1/4 cup)

Prepare Sweet Red Onion Dressing. Mix remaining ingredients in large bowl. Pour dressing over salad. Cover and refrigerate until ready to serve.

1 Serving: Calories 480 (Calories from Fat 260); Fat 29g (Saturated 4g); Cholesterol 0mg; Sodium 50mg; Carbohydrate 67g (Dietary Fiber 19g); Protein 7g
% Daily Value: Vitamin A 8%; Vitamin C 24%; Calcium 4%; Iron 22%
Diet Exchanges: 2 Starch, 1 Vegetable, 2 Fruit, 6 Fat

Sweet Red Onion Dressing

1/2 cup sugar

3/4 cup vegetable oil

1/2 cup cider vinegar

3 tablespoons grated red onion

1 tablespoon Worcestershire sauce

2 cloves garlic, finely chopped

Mix all ingredients.

Timesaving Tips

Here are a few tips for "holiday harmony":

• Use purchased salad dressings rather than homemade.

• Take advantage of precut salad fixins from the deli and produce sections of your supermarket.

• Think red and green! Often the addition of red bell pepper, red pimiento, red radishes or red cranberries, raspberries or strawberries is all you need to make your favorite green salad "holiday special."

• For a take-along salad, consider using holiday serving trays available at party stores and supermarkets.

Holiday Hints

Use this handy guide to help you prepare this recipe. If you find yourself short of one of these ingredients, feel free to add more of one of the others:

• For 1 cup cooked brown rice, you'll need 1/3 cup uncooked.

• For 1 cup cooked barley, you'll need 1/2 cup uncooked.

• For 3 cups cooked wheat berries, you'll need 1 cup uncooked.

Winter Wheat Berry Salad

Heavenly Fruit Salad

PREP: 20 MIN
6 SERVINGS

Orange-Honey Dressing (right)

1 medium jicama, peeled and cut into 1/4-inch slices

3 oranges, peeled and sliced

3 kiwifruit, peeled and sliced

1/4 cup pomegranate seeds or dried cranberries

Prepare Orange-Honey Dressing. Cut jicama slices with star-shaped cookie cutter.

Mix jicama, oranges and kiwifruit in serving bowl. Toss with dressing. Sprinkle with pomegranate seeds.

1 Serving: Calories 110 (Calories from Fat 0); Fat 0g (Saturated 0g); Cholesterol 0mg; Sodium 5mg; Carbohydrate 32g (Dietary Fiber 6g); Protein 2g
% Daily Value: Vitamin A 2%; Vitamin C 100%; Calcium 4%; Iron 4%
Diet Exchanges: 2 Fruit

Orange-Honey Dressing

1/4 cup orange juice

1/4 cup honey

1/2 teaspoon ground cinnamon

Shake all ingredients in tightly covered container.

Holiday Hints

POMEGRANATE POINTERS

Bright red pomegranate seeds add a holiday finishing touch to any salad. Pomegranates are larger than apples and have a leathery, deep red to purplish red rind. Though not beautiful on the outside, they have a spectacular interior packed full of sparkling, juicy, ruby-colored seeds that are slightly sweet and refreshingly tart.

To remove the seeds, cut the knobby end off the pomegranate, and score the rind lengthwise four to six times. Place the pomegranate in a bowl and cover with cool water; let stand 5 minutes. Holding the pomegranate under the water, break it apart into sections, separating the seeds from the pithy white membrane. The edible seeds will sink to the bottom of the bowl, and the bitter, inedible membrane will float to the top. Discard the membrane and the rind. Drain the seeds in a colander, then gently pat dry with paper towels. Be careful when doing this process because the juice can stain permanently.

Heavenly Fruit Salad

Classic Cranberry Mold

PREP: 20 MIN; CHILL: 6 HR
8 SERVINGS

Crammed with cranberries and bursting with flavor, this Christmastime classic has stood the test of time. We've offered up some new twists to make sure this recipe stays a favorite for years to come.

2 cups water

3/4 cup sugar

3 cups fresh or frozen cranberries

1 package (6-serving size) raspberry-flavored gelatin

1 can (8 ounces) crushed pineapple in syrup, undrained

1 medium stalk celery, chopped (1/2 cup), if desired

1/2 cup chopped walnuts, if desired

Salad greens, if desired

Heat water and sugar to boiling in 2-quart saucepan, stirring occasionally; boil 1 minute. Stir in cranberries.

Heat to boiling; boil 5 minutes, stirring occasionally. Stir in gelatin until dissolved. Stir in pineapple, celery and walnuts.

Pour into ungreased 6-cup mold, 8 individual molds or stemmed goblets. Cover and refrigerate at least 6 hours until firm. Unmold onto salad greens. Garnish with celery leaves and additional cranberries, if desired.

1 Serving: Calories 170 (Calories from Fat 0); Fat 0g (Saturated 0g); Cholesterol 0mg; Sodium 60mg; Carbohydrate 43g (Dietary Fiber 2g); Protein 2g
% Daily Value: Vitamin A 0%; Vitamin C 8%; Calcium 0%; Iron 0%
Diet Exchanges: 3 Fruit

New Twist

Give this classic creation a contemporary flavor by adding one of these:

• 1 can (11 ounces) mandarin orange segments, drained

• 1 cup sliced fresh strawberries

• 1/2 cup white wine (add with the gelatin; decrease water to 1 1/2 cups)

• 1/2 cup pistachio nuts instead of the walnuts

• 1 kiwifruit, peeled and sliced

Holiday Hints

Embellish this shimmering salad by:

• Placing on colorful kale leaves.

• Filling center of gelatin ring with mixture of 1 tub (4 ounces) fruit-flavored whipped cream cheese and

1 cup whipped topping or cherries and fresh berries or try a mixture of 1 cup whipped cream, 1/2 cup lemon yogurt and 1/2 cup sour cream.

• Garnishing with Candied Cranberries (page 165) and salad greens cut to resemble holly leaves.

Classic Cranberry Mold

Old-Fashioned Stuffing

PREP: 20 MIN

9 CUPS STUFFING (ENOUGH FOR A 12-POUND TURKEY)

Old-fashioned stuffing is a common holiday request. Whether you prefer your stuffing dotted with cranberries or chock-full of chestnuts, you're sure to find a tasty takeoff on this traditional favorite.

1 cup butter or margarine

2 large stalks celery (with leaves), chopped (1 1/2 cups)

3/4 cup finely chopped onion

9 cups soft bread cubes (about 14 slices bread)

2 tablespoons chopped fresh or 1 1/2 teaspoons dried sage leaves

1 tablespoon chopped fresh or 1 teaspoon dried thyme leaves

1 1/2 teaspoons salt

1/2 teaspoon pepper

Melt butter in Dutch oven over medium-high heat. Cook celery and onion in butter, stirring occasionally, until tender; remove from heat.

Toss celery mixture and remaining ingredients. Stuff turkey just before roasting.

1 Cup: Calories 300 (Calories from Fat 200); Fat 22g (Saturated 13g); Cholesterol 55mg; Sodium 770mg; Carbohydrate 23g (Dietary Fiber 2g); Protein 4g
% Daily Value: Vitamin A 16%; Vitamin C 2%; Calcium 6%; Iron 8%
Diet Exchanges: 1 Starch, 3 Vegetable, 4 Fat

Holiday Hints

If you don't want to mess with stuffing the turkey, bake your favorite stuffing separately.

Place it in a greased 3-quart casserole or rectangular baking dish, 13×9×2 inches. Cover and bake in a 325° oven for 30 minutes; uncover and bake 15 minutes longer.

APPLE-CRANBERRY STUFFING: Add 3 cups finely chopped apples and 1 cup fresh or frozen cranberries with the bread cubes.

CHESTNUT STUFFING: Add 1 pound chestnuts, cooked and chopped, with the bread cubes. To prepare chestnuts, cut an X on rounded side of each chestnut. Heat chestnuts and enough water to cover to boiling. Boil uncovered 10 minutes; drain. Remove shells and skins. Heat shelled chestnuts and enough water to cover to boiling. Boil uncovered 10 minutes; drain and chop.

CORN BREAD STUFFING: Substitute corn bread cubes for the soft bread cubes.

MUSHROOM STUFFING: Cook 2 cups sliced mushrooms (about 5 ounces) with the celery and onion.

ORANGE-APPLE STUFFING: Add 1 cup diced orange sections or mandarin orange segments and 1 cup finely chopped apples with the bread cubes.

OYSTER STUFFING: Add 2 cans (8 ounces each) oysters, drained and chopped, or 2 cups shucked oysters, drained and chopped, with the bread cubes.

SAUSAGE STUFFING: Omit salt. Cook 1 pound bulk pork sausage until no longer pink; drain, reserving drippings. Substitute drippings for part of the butter. Add cooked sausage with the bread cubes.

Orange-Apple Stuffing (variation)

Cranberry-Wild Rice Bake

PREP: 45 MIN; BAKE: 1 HR 35 MIN
8 SERVINGS

1 cup uncooked wild rice

2 1/2 cups water

1 tablespoon butter or margarine

1 medium onion, chopped (1/2 cup)

1 cup sliced mushrooms

2 1/2 cups chicken broth, heated

1/4 teaspoon salt

2 cloves garlic, finely chopped

1 cup dried cranberries

Heat oven to 350°. Grease square baking dish, 8×8×2 inches. Place wild rice in wire strainer. Run cold water through rice, lifting rice with fingers to clean thoroughly.

Heat wild rice and water to boiling in 2-quart saucepan, stirring occasionally; reduce heat to low. Cover and simmer 30 minutes; drain.

Melt butter in 10-inch skillet over medium heat. Cook onion and mushrooms in butter, stirring occasionally, until onion is tender.

Mix wild rice and onion mixture in baking dish. Mix broth, salt and garlic; pour over rice mixture.

Cover and bake 1 1/4 hours. Stir in cranberries. Cover and bake 15 to 20 minutes or until liquid is absorbed.

1 Serving: Calories 155 (Calories from Fat 20); Fat 2g (Saturated 1g); Cholesterol 5mg; Sodium 410mg; Carbohydrate 35g (Dietary Fiber 7g); Protein 6g
% Daily Value: Vitamin A 2%; Vitamin C 14%; Calcium 2%; Iron 6%
Diet Exchanges: 2 Starch, 1 Vegetable

Timesaving Tips

To make this dish super easy, purchase sliced mushrooms, pick up chopped onion at the salad bar, use finely chopped garlic from a jar and use precooked wild rice from a can.

Holiday Hints

Make this your next dish to take along and share. If you're anticipating feeding a crowd, double the recipe and bake in a 13×9-inch rectangular baking dish or 3-quart casserole.

Do-Ahead Mashed Potatoes

PREP: 35 MIN; CHILL: UP TO 24 HR; BAKE: 45 MIN
8 SERVINGS

3 pounds potatoes (about 9 medium), peeled and
    cut into pieces

3/4 cup milk

1/2 cup whipping (heavy) cream

1/2 cup butter or margarine

1 teaspoon salt

Dash of pepper

Place potatoes in 3-quart saucepan; add enough water
(salted if desired) to cover. Cover and heat to boiling;
reduce heat. Simmer covered 20 to 25 minutes or until
tender; drain. Shake pan with potatoes over low heat to
dry. Mash potatoes in pan with potato masher or electric
mixer until no lumps remain.

Heat milk, whipping cream, butter, salt and pepper over
medium-low heat, stirring occasionally, until butter is
melted; reserve and refrigerate 1/4 cup mixture. Add
remaining milk mixture in small amounts to potatoes,
mashing after each addition, until potatoes are light and
fluffy. (Amount of milk needed to make potatoes smooth
and fluffy depends on kind of potatoes.)

Grease 2-quart casserole. Spoon potatoes into casserole;
cover and refrigerate up to 24 hours.

Heat oven to 350°. Pour reserved milk mixture over
potatoes. Bake uncovered 40 to 45 minutes or until hot.
Stir potatoes before serving.

1 Serving: Calories 285 (Calories from Fat 155); Fat 17g (Saturated
10g); Cholesterol 50mg; Sodium 400mg; Carbohydrate 32g (Dietary
Fiber 3g); Protein 4g
% Daily Value: Vitamin A 14%; Vitamin C 8%; Calcium 4%;
Iron 2%
Diet Exchanges: 2 Starch, 3 Fat

New Twist

- We all have fallen in love with garlic mashed potatoes!
  To make them easily, use the above recipe except leave
  the peels on the potatoes after scrubbing well. While
  mashing potatoes, add 1 to 2 cloves garlic, finely
  chopped.

- For a heavenly rich mashed potato casserole, omit the
  milk, whipping cream and butter in this recipe.
  Instead, beat 1 package (8 ounces) cream cheese, softened, and 1 container (8 ounces) sour cream into potatoes before spooning into casserole. Cover and
  refrigerate up to 24 hours. Pour 1/4 cup melted butter
  over potatoes in casserole dish, and bake as directed.

Twice-Baked Potatoes

PREP: 20 MIN; BAKE: 1 HR 50 MIN

4 SERVINGS

4 large baking potatoes

1/4 to 1/2 cup milk

1/4 cup butter or margarine, softened

1/4 teaspoon salt

Dash of pepper

1 cup shredded Cheddar cheese (4 ounces)

1 tablespoon chopped fresh chives

Heat oven to 350°. Prick potatoes several times with fork to allow steam to escape. Bake 1 1/4 to 1 1/2 hours or until tender.

Cut thin slice from top of each potato; scoop out inside, leaving a thin shell. Mash potatoes in medium bowl with potato masher or electric mixer until no lumps remain. Add small amounts of milk, mashing after each addition.

(Amount of milk needed to make potatoes smooth and fluffy depends on kind of potatoes.) Add butter, salt and pepper; mash vigorously until potatoes are light and fluffy. Stir in cheese and chives. Fill potato shells with mashed potatoes. Place on ungreased cookie sheet.

Increase oven temperature to 400°. Bake about 20 minutes or until hot. Garnish with additional fresh chives if desired.

1 Serving: Calories 355 (Calories from Fat 190); Fat 21g (Saturated 13g); Cholesterol 60mg; Sodium 410mg; Carbohydrate 32g (Dietary Fiber 2g); Protein 11g
% Daily Value: Vitamin A 16%; Vitamin C 16%; Calcium 18%; Iron 4%
Diet Exchanges: 2 Starch, 1 Medium-Fat Meat, 3 Fat

Timesaving Tips

If you want speedy Twice-Baked Potatoes, try microwaving the potatoes.

- For the first step, prick potatoes several times with fork to allow steam to escape. Arrange potatoes about 1 inch apart in circle on microwavable paper towel in microwave oven. Microwave uncovered on High 12 to 14 minutes, turning potatoes over after 6 minutes, until tender. Let stand 5 minutes. Mash potatoes as directed.

- To heat for serving, arrange filled potatoes in circle on microwavable plate. Cover loosely and microwave on High 8 to 10 minutes, rotating plate a half turn after 5 minutes, until hot.

To save some more time, make Twice-Baked Potatoes ahead.

- Refrigerate filled potatoes tightly covered no longer than 48 hours or freeze up to 2 months. To reheat, heat oven to 400°. Uncover and bake on ungreased cookie sheet about 30 minutes (or 40 minutes if frozen) or until hot. To reheat in microwave, arrange refrigerated potatoes in circle on 10-inch microwavable plate. Cover loosely with plastic wrap and microwave on High 12 to 15 minutes (a few minutes longer if frozen), rotating plate a half turn after 5 minutes, until hot.

- Freeze filled potatoes in airtight freezer container no longer than 2 months. To reheat, heat oven to 400°. Bake uncovered on ungreased cookie sheet about 40 minutes or until hot.

Twice-Baked Potatoes

Cheesy Potatoes

PREP: 20 MIN; BAKE: 1 HR
6 SERVINGS

2 pounds potatoes (about 6 medium), peeled and cut into 1/4-inch slices

8 ounces process sharp American cheese loaf, diced (2 cups)

1 small onion, chopped (1/4 cup)

1 teaspoon salt

3 tablespoons chopped fresh parsley or 1 tablespoon parsley flakes

Dash of pepper

3 tablespoons butter or margarine

3/4 cup milk

Heat oven to 350°. Grease 2-quart casserole. Layer one-third each of the potatoes, cheese, onion, salt, parsley and pepper in casserole. Repeat layers twice. Dot with butter. Pour milk over top.

Cover and bake 40 minutes. Uncover and bake about 20 minutes longer or until potatoes are tender.

1 Serving: Calories 320 (Calories from Fat 160); Fat 18g (Saturated 11g); Cholesterol 55mg; Sodium 1000mg; Carbohydrate 30g (Dietary Fiber 3g); Protein 12g
% Daily Value: Vitamin A 16%; Vitamin C 10%; Calcium 24%; Iron 4%
Diet Exchanges: 2 Starch, 1 Medium-Fat Meat, 2 Fat

Timesaving Tips

• No time to peel potatoes? No problem! Just use a 32-ounce bag of frozen hash brown potatoes instead.

• For easy entertaining, prepare these potatoes the day before and refrigerate, then pop them in the oven the next day.

Cheesy Potatoes

Holiday Hash Browns

PREP: 15 MIN; BAKE: 45 MIN

6 SERVINGS

1 bag (1 pound 4 ounces) refrigerated Southwest-
or home-style shredded hash brown potatoes

1 medium bell pepper, finely chopped (1 cup)

1 medium onion, finely chopped (1/2 cup)

2 tablespoons grated Parmesan cheese

1/2 teaspoon salt

1/4 teaspoon pepper

1 tablespoon butter or margarine, melted

1 tablespoon vegetable oil

Additional grated Parmesan cheese, if desired

Heat oven to 325°. Toss potatoes, bell pepper, onion,
2 tablespoons cheese, the salt and pepper. Pour butter
and oil into rectangular pan, 13×9×2 inches; tilt pan to
cover bottom. Spread potato mixture in pan.

Bake uncovered about 45 minutes, stirring once, until
golden brown. Sprinkle with additional cheese before
serving.

1 Serving: Calories 190 (Calories from Fat 45); Fat 5g (Saturated
2g); Cholesterol 5mg; Sodium 560mg; Carbohydrate 36g (Dietary
Fiber 4g); Protein 4g
% Daily Value: Vitamin A 2%; Vitamin C 26%; Calcium 4%; Iron 4%
Diet Exchanges: 2 Starch, 1 Vegetable

Holiday Hints

"Holidazzle" your potatoes with these finishing tips:

• Use a combination of red and green bell peppers for a
holiday feel. Drizzle with sun-dried tomato pesto.

• Bake in a round casserole dish, and garnish with a
wreath made from fresh rosemary sprigs and a bow
made from a pimiento strip.

Timesaving Tips

Call this recipe a "make-ahead," "do-ahead" or just plain
"sanity saver." The ultimate result is the extra winks you
get before rising to prepare for the holiday breakfast. Just
mix it, spread it, cover it and refrigerate it for up to 24
hours before baking.

Holiday Hash Browns

Applesauce-Sweet Potato Bake

PREP: 45 MIN; BAKE: 30 MIN

6 SERVINGS

1 pound sweet potatoes or yams (about 3 medium)

1 cup applesauce

1/3 cup packed brown sugar

1/4 cup chopped nuts

1/2 teaspoon ground cinnamon

2 tablespoons butter or margarine

Place sweet potatoes in 3-quart saucepan; add enough water (salted if desired) to cover. Heat to boiling; reduce heat. Cover and simmer 30 to 35 minutes or until tender; drain. Remove skins; cut each sweet potato lengthwise in half.

Heat oven to 375°. Place sweet potatoes, cut sides up, in ungreased 2-quart casserole or square baking dish, 8×8×2 inches. Spread applesauce over sweet potatoes. Mix brown sugar, nuts and cinnamon; sprinkle over applesauce. Dot with butter. Cover and bake about 30 minutes or until hot.

1 Serving: Calories 185 (Calories from Fat 65); Fat 7g (Saturated 3g); Cholesterol 10mg; Sodium 75mg; Carbohydrate 32g (Dietary Fiber 3g); Protein 2g
% Daily Value: Vitamin A 100%; Vitamin C 12%; Calcium 4%; Iron 4%
Diet Exchanges: 1 Starch, 1 Fruit, 1 Fat

Holiday Hints

Why not try some sweet potato sprinkles?

• Dried cranberries

• Miniature marshmallows

• Canned sliced peaches or pineapple

• Toasted pecans or almonds

• French-fried onion rings or crushed croutons

Timesaving Tips

Looking for a shortcut? Use 1 can (18 ounces) vacuum-packed sweet potatoes, cut lengthwise in half, for the fresh sweet potatoes.

Applesauce-Sweet Potato Bake

Leek-Apple-Yam Gratin

PREP: 30 MIN; BAKE: 45 MIN; STAND: 10 MIN

6 SERVINGS

1 1/4 cups whipping (heavy) cream

2 large leeks, sliced (2 cups)

2 tablespoons chopped fresh or 2 teaspoons dried thyme leaves

1 teaspoon salt

1/4 teaspoon pepper

1/4 teaspoon ground nutmeg

2 medium yams (about 3/4 pound), peeled and thinly sliced (2 cups)

4 medium parsnips, peeled and thinly sliced (2 cups)

2 cups grated white Cheddar cheese (8 ounces)

1 large cooking apple, thinly sliced (1 1/2 cups)

Heat oven to 375°. Grease 3-quart casserole.

Cook whipping cream, leeks, thyme, salt, pepper and nutmeg in heavy 2-quart saucepan over low heat, stirring occasionally, until mixture begins to simmer. Stir in yams and parsnips. Cover and simmer about 10 minutes or until vegetables are slightly tender.

Layer half of the vegetable mixture and half of the cheese in casserole. Top with apple. Repeat layers of vegetables and cheese.

Bake uncovered about 45 minutes or until golden brown and bubbly. Let stand 10 minutes before serving.

1 Serving: Calories 410 (Calories from Fat 250); Fat 28g (Saturated 17g); Cholesterol 95mg; Sodium 660mg; Carbohydrate 32g (Dietary Fiber 6g); Protein 13g
% Daily Value: Vitamin A 100%; Vitamin C 22%; Calcium 28%; Iron 8%
Diet Exchanges: 2 Starch, 1 High-Fat Meat, 3 1/2 Fat

Holiday Hints

A snowy wintery day just begs for this veggie casserole. To add a special touch, sprinkle baked casserole with one of these toppings:

• Crushed seasoned croutons

• French-fried onions

• Toasted nuts

• Finely chopped ham or bacon bits

Leek-Apple-Yam Gratin

Cinnamon Squash Rings

PREP: 25 MIN; BAKE: 35 MIN

6 SERVINGS

2 tablespoons packed brown sugar

2 tablespoons milk

1 egg

3/4 cup soft bread crumbs (about 1 slice bread)

1/4 cup cornmeal

2 teaspoons ground cinnamon

1 medium acorn squash (1 1/2 pounds), cut cross-wise into 1/2-inch slices and seeded

1/3 cup butter or margarine, melted

Heat oven to 400°. Mix brown sugar, milk and egg. Mix bread crumbs, cornmeal and cinnamon. Dip squash slices into egg mixture, then coat with bread crumb mixture.

Place squash in ungreased rectangular pan, 13×9×2 inches. Drizzle with butter. Bake uncovered 30 to 35 minutes or until tender.

1 Serving: Calories 230 (Calories from Fat 110); Fat 12g (Saturated 7g); Cholesterol 65mg; Sodium 200mg; Carbohydrate 30g (Dietary Fiber 4g); Protein 4g
% Daily Value: Vitamin A 12%; Vitamin C 6%; Calcium 8%; Iron 12%
Diet Exchanges: 1 Starch, 1 Fruit, 2 Fat

Holiday Hints

For a prettier center, use a scalloped-edge round cookie cutter to cut out the centers of the squash rings. Add toasted pecans to this picture-perfect dish for a crunchy treat.

Timesaving Tips

Feeling a bit frazzled with company coming? You can cut and seed the squash up to two days ahead of time, then cover and refrigerate.

Roasted Vegetable Medley

PREP: 25 MIN; BAKE: 30 MIN
4 SERVINGS

1/4 cup butter or margarine

1 tablespoon chopped fresh or 1 teaspoon dried
sage leaves

1 clove garlic, finely chopped

1/2 pound Brussels sprouts, cut in half

1/2 pound parsnips, peeled and cut into 2-inch
pieces

1/4 pound baby cut carrots

1 small butternut squash (2 pounds), peeled,
seeded and cut into 1-inch pieces

Heat oven to 375°. Melt butter in 1-quart saucepan over
medium heat; stir in sage and garlic. Place remaining
ingredients in ungreased rectangular pan, 13×9×2
inches. Pour butter mixture over vegetables; stir to coat.

Cover and bake 25 to 30 minutes, stirring occasionally,
until vegetables are crisp-tender.

1 Serving: Calories 170 (Calories from Fat 110); Fat 12g (Saturated
7g); Cholesterol 30mg; Sodium 130mg; Carbohydrate 17g (Dietary
Fiber 6g); Protein 5g
% Daily Value: Vitamin A 100%; Vitamin C 88%; Calcium 12%; Iron 24%
Diet Exchanges: 3 Vegetable, 2 Fat

Holiday Hints

Winter squash, such as butternut, is much easier to peel
and cut if you microwave it first to soften the skin and
the flesh just underneath it. To soften slightly, place
whole squash in microwave oven. Microwave on High 2
to 4 minutes or until tip of knife can pierce skin easily.
Cool slightly before peeling.

Red Cabbage with Apples

PREP: 20 MIN; COOK: 45 MIN
6 SERVINGS

3 tablespoons butter or margarine

2 medium unpeeled tart cooking apples, sliced

1 medium head red cabbage, coarsely shredded (8 cups)

1/4 cup water

1/4 cup red wine vinegar

2 tablespoons sugar

1 teaspoon salt

1/4 teaspoon pepper

Melt butter in Dutch oven over medium heat. Cook apples in butter 5 minutes, stirring occasionally.

Stir in remaining ingredients. Heat to boiling; reduce heat. Cover and simmer 35 to 40 minutes or until cabbage is tender.

1 Serving: Calories 120 (Calories from Fat 55); Fat 6g (Saturated 4g); Cholesterol 15mg; Sodium 460mg; Carbohydrate 19g (Dietary Fiber 4g); Protein 2g
% Daily Value: Vitamin A 6%; Vitamin C 38%; Calcium 6%; Iron 4%
Diet Exchanges: 1 Vegetable, 1 Fruit, 1 Fat

New Twist

Jazz up this classic cabbage dish by adding 1/2 to 1 teaspoon of either caraway seed, celery seed or fennel seed.

For a spicy sweet note, add 1/4 teaspoon each of ground cinnamon, ground cloves and ground nutmeg.

Timesaving Tips

Purchase preshredded cabbage in the produce section or deli at your supermarket. If you choose to shred your own cabbage, you can do so using a food processor up to one week before, and refrigerate it in a plastic bag.

Red, White and Green Beans

PREP: 15 MIN; COOK: 15 MIN
4 SERVINGS

1 pound green beans, cut into 1- to 1 1/2-inch pieces

1 can (15 to 16 ounces) great northern or navy beans, rinsed and drained

1/4 cup chopped drained roasted red bell peppers (from 7-ounce jar) or 2 jars (2 ounces each) sliced pimientos, drained

2 tablespoons butter or margarine, melted

1 tablespoon lemon juice

2 teaspoons Dijon mustard

2 teaspoons honey

1/2 teaspoon lemon pepper

1/4 teaspoon salt

Add 1 inch water (salted if desired) to 3-quart saucepan; add green beans. Heat to boiling. Boil uncovered 6 to 8 minutes or until crisp-tender; drain.

Stir in remaining ingredients. Cook over medium heat about 5 minutes, stirring occasionally, until hot.

1 Serving: Calories 220 (Calories from Fat 65); Fat 7g (Saturated 4g); Cholesterol 15mg; Sodium 680mg; Carbohydrate 38g (Dietary Fiber 10g); Protein 11g
% Daily Value: Vitamin A 12%; Vitamin C 16%; Calcium 12%; Iron 20%
Diet Exchanges: 1 Starch, 4 Vegetable, 1 Fat

Holiday Hints

Those fun plastic trays in Santa and snowman shapes and pretty gift tins also work great as serving dishes for foods other than cookies and candies! You may wish to line the tins with aluminum foil before adding food.

New Twist

Here are some great ideas to make your green beans look extra festive:

• Squeeze lemon juice over cooked beans, and sprinkle with sliced almonds.

• Sprinkle dried cranberries over cooked green beans.

• Toss in 1/2 cup thinly sliced radishes.

Broccoli-Corn Casserole

Broccoli-Corn Casserole

PREP: 15 MIN; BAKE: 1 HR
8 SERVINGS

2 bags (16 ounces each) frozen broccoli flowerets, thawed and drained

2 cans (14 3/4 ounces each) cream-style corn

2 eggs, slightly beaten

2 tablespoons butter or margarine, melted

3/4 cup herb-seasoned stuffing crumbs

Heat oven to 350°. Mix broccoli, corn and eggs in ungreased 3-quart casserole or rectangular baking dish, 13×9×2 inches. Mix butter and stuffing; sprinkle evenly over vegetable mixture.

Bake uncovered about 1 hour or until stuffing is golden and vegetables are hot.

1 Serving: Calories 200 (Calories from Fat 55); Fat 6g (Saturated 3g); Cholesterol 60mg; Sodium 670mg; Carbohydrate 33g (Dietary Fiber 5g); Protein 9g
% Daily Value: Vitamin A 24%; Vitamin C 40%; Calcium 8%; Iron 12%
Diet Exchanges: 1 Starch, 3 Vegetable, 1 Fat

Gifts for Giving

Broccoli-Corn Casserole in a new casserole dish makes a delicious and unique gift for a nearby neighbor or friend. Prepare the recipe in the casserole dish to give, but save the baking for the gift recipient. Cover the casserole tightly with plastic wrap, and include the instructions for baking (you can even include the entire recipe, if you like). Wrap it with a bow, and your gift is ready to go!

Sensational Salads and Sides

Angel Meringue Torte (page 148)
and Christmas Cassata (page 138)

CHAPTER 4

Fabulous Finales

Nowhere is life so sweet as

in the magical world of Christmas

with dustings of powdered-sugar snow

and chocolate-drizzled icicles.

Pumpkin Pie

PREP: 30 MIN; BAKE: 1 HR; COOL: 15 MIN; CHILL: 4 HR

8 SERVINGS

Pastry for 9-Inch One-Crust Pie (right)

2 eggs

1/2 cup sugar

1 can (15 ounces) pumpkin

1 can (12 ounces) evaporated milk

1 teaspoon ground cinnamon

1/2 teaspoon salt

1/2 teaspoon ground ginger

1/8 teaspoon ground cloves

Whipped cream, if desired

Heat oven to 425°. Prepare pastry. Beat eggs slightly in medium bowl with hand beater or wire whisk. Beat in remaining ingredients. To prevent spilling, place pastry-lined pie plate on oven rack before adding filling. Carefully pour filling into pie plate. Bake 15 minutes.

Reduce oven temperature to 350°. Bake about 45 minutes longer or until knife inserted in center comes out clean. Cool 15 minutes. Cover and refrigerate about 4 hours or until chilled. Serve pie with whipped cream. Cover and refrigerate any remaining pie.

1 Serving: Calories 280 (Calories from Fat 125); Fat 14g (Saturated 4g); Cholesterol 60mg; Sodium 370mg; Carbohydrate 34g (Dietary Fiber 2g); Protein 7g
% Daily Value: Vitamin A 100%; Vitamin C 2%; Calcium 16%; Iron 10%
Diet Exchanges: 1 Very Lean Meat, 1 Vegetable, 2 Fruit, 2 Fat

Pastry for 9-Inch One-Crust Pie

1/3 cup plus 1 tablespoon shortening

1 cup all-purpose flour

1/4 teaspoon salt

2 to 3 tablespoons cold water

Cut shortening into flour and salt in medium bowl, using pastry blender or crisscrossing 2 knives, until particles are size of small peas. Sprinkle with cold water, 1 tablespoon at a time, tossing with fork until all flour is moistened and pastry almost cleans side of bowl (1 to 2 teaspoons more water can be added if necessary).

Gather pastry into a ball. Shape into flattened round on lightly floured cloth-covered board. Roll pastry into circle 2 inches larger than upside-down pie plate, 9 × 1 1/4 inches, with floured cloth-covered rolling pin. Fold pastry into fourths; place in pie plate. Unfold and ease into plate, pressing firmly against bottom and side.

Trim overhanging edge of pastry 1 inch from rim of pie plate. Fold and roll pastry under, even with plate; press with tines of fork or flute if desired.

Timesaving Tips

Prepare the pastry the day before; cover tightly with plastic wrap and refrigerate. Uncover and pour in filling when ready to bake. Or, use refrigerated or frozen pie crusts.

Holiday Hints

Add a personal touch with a few of these special additions:

- Top dollops of whipped cream with pecans, crushed gingersnaps or chocolate-covered coffee beans.

- Decorate slices of pie with holiday cutouts. Using small-size cookie cutters, cut leftover rolled pastry. Place on a cookie sheet. Sprinkle cutouts with ground cinnamon and sugar. Bake in 350° oven 8 to 10 minutes or until lightly brown.

Pumpkin Pie and Pecan Pie (page 130)

Fabulous Finales

Pecan Pie

PREP: 20 MIN; BAKE: 50 MIN
8 SERVINGS

Dazzling desserts often take center stage during the holidays, but it's the comforting classics that are so fondly remembered. Touched by tradition and bursting with rich, nutty goodness, this simple and homey pie has become a family favorite.

Pastry for 9-Inch One-Crust Pie (page 128)

2/3 cup sugar

1/3 cup butter or margarine, melted

1 cup corn syrup

1/2 teaspoon salt

3 eggs

1 cup pecan halves or broken pecans

Whipped cream, if desired

Chopped pecans, if desired

Heat oven to 375°. Prepare pastry. Beat sugar, butter, corn syrup, salt and eggs in medium bowl with wire whisk or hand beater until well blended. Stir in pecan halves. Pour into pastry-lined pie plate.

Bake 40 to 50 minutes or until center is set. Serve pie with whipped cream and chopped pecans.

1 Serving: Calories 530 (Calories From Fat 260); Fat 29g (Saturated 9g); Cholesterol 100mg; Sodium 420mg; Carbohydrate 63g (Dietary Fiber 1); Protein 5g
% Daily Value: Vitamin A 8%; Vitamin C 0%; Calcium 2%; Iron 6%
Diet Exchanges: Not Recommended

BRANDY-PECAN PIE: Decrease corn syrup to 3/4 cup and beat in 1/4 cup brandy.

CHOCOLATE-PECAN PIE: Melt 2 ounces unsweetened baking chocolate with the butter.

CRANBERRY-PECAN PIE: Add 1 cup dried cranberries to the filling before baking.

HONEY-PECAN PIE: Substitute 1/2 cup honey for 1/2 cup of the corn syrup.

ORANGE-PECAN PIE: Mix 1 tablespoon grated orange peel with the crust ingredients. Add 1 tablespoon orange liqueur to the filling ingredients.

PEANUT-CHOCOLATE CHIP PIE: Substitute 1 cup salted peanuts for the pecans. After baking, sprinkle with 1/2 cup semisweet chocolate chips.

Timesaving Tips

By making this pie ahead of time, you can have it ready at a moment's notice. After baking, refrigerate pie 2 hours. Freeze uncovered at least 3 hours. Wrap and return to freezer. Store no longer than one month. When ready to serve, unwrap pie and thaw in refrigerator 20 minutes beforehand.

Holiday Hints

For a pie crust with a twist, braid the edges. Loosely braid three 1/4-inch pastry strips, making the braid long enough to fit the edge of the pie. Moisten edge of pie and place braid on top, pressing lightly to seal.

Mincemeat-Pear Pie

PREP: 25 MIN; BAKE: 50 MIN
8 SERVINGS

Pastry for 9-Inch One-Crust Pie (page 128)

1/4 cup all-purpose flour

1/3 cup sugar

1/8 teaspoon salt

1 tablespoon butter or margarine

1/4 cup water

2 tablespoons red cinnamon candies

1 jar (20 1/2 ounces) prepared mincemeat (about
  2 cups)

3 medium pears or apples

Heat oven to 425°. Prepare pastry. Sprinkle 2 tablespoons of the flour in pastry-lined pie plate. Mix remaining flour, sugar, salt and butter until crumbly; set aside. Heat water and cinnamon candies over medium heat, stirring constantly, until candies are dissolved; remove from heat.

Spread mincemeat over pastry in pie plate. Peel pears; cut into fourths. Cut fourths into wedges, 1/2 inch thick at outer side. Arrange pear wedges on mincemeat,

overlapping wedges in 2 circles. Sprinkle with sugar mixture. Spoon cinnamon syrup over top, moistening as much of sugar mixture as possible.

Cover edge of pastry with 2- to 3-inch strip of aluminum foil to prevent excessive browning; remove foil during last 15 minutes of baking. Bake 40 to 50 minutes or until crust is golden brown.

1 Serving: Calories 295 (Calories from Fat 110); Fat 12g (Saturated 3g); Cholesterol 5mg; Sodium 510mg; Carbohydrate 45g (Dietary Fiber 2g); Protein 4g
% Daily Value: Vitamin A 0%; Vitamin C 2%; Calcium 0%; Iron 6%
Diet Exchanges: 1 Starch, 2 Fruit, 2 Fat

New Twist

With a little pizzazz, your pie crusts can look as wonderful as they taste.

• Rim a pie with leaves cut from pastry, using miniature cookie cutters or a knife. For extra detail, use a knife to form veins in leaves. Make extra cutouts and bake them separately. Top baked pie with cutouts.

• Cover a pie with miniature holiday-shaped pastries. Pastry cutouts can be colored with Egg Yolk Paint (page 206) before baking.

Honey-Wine-Cranberry Tart

PREP: 45 MIN; BAKE: 20 MIN; CHILL: 4 HR
8 SERVINGS

Cookie Crust (right)

1/3 cup orange marmalade

1/2 cup coarsely chopped walnuts

1 envelope unflavored gelatin

1/4 cup cold water

1 cup dry white wine or apple juice

1/2 cup honey

3 cups fresh or frozen cranberries

Whipped cream, if desired

Heat oven to 375°. Prepare Cookie Crust. Press dough in bottom and 1 1/2 inches up side of ungreased spring-form pan, 9×3 inches. Bake 18 to 20 minutes or until crust is set and light brown. Cool 10 minutes. Spread marmalade on bottom of crust. Sprinkle with walnuts.

Sprinkle gelatin on cold water in 3-quart saucepan. Let stand about 5 minutes or until gelatin is softened. Stir in wine, honey and cranberries. Heat to boiling, stirring occasionally; reduce heat slightly. Boil uncovered 5 minutes, stirring occasionally; remove from heat. Let stand 30 minutes to cool.

Pour cranberry mixture over walnuts in crust. Cover and refrigerate at least 4 hours until chilled. Run metal spatula around side of tart to loosen; remove side of pan. Serve tart with whipped cream.

1 Serving: Calories 455 (Calories from Fat 200); Fat 22g (Saturated 11g); Cholesterol 45mg; Sodium 125mg; Carbohydrate 62g (Dietary Fiber 3g); Protein 5g
% Daily Value: Vitamin A 14%; Vitamin C 6%; Calcium 2%; Iron 10%
Dietary Exchanges Not Recommended

Cookie Crust

1 3/4 cups all-purpose flour

3/4 cup butter or margarine, softened

1/2 cup powdered sugar

Mix all ingredients until dough forms.

Holiday Hints

Wow your guests or family with the presentation of this tart.

- Press leftover orange marmalade through a sieve, then place in a resealable plastic bag. Snip off a tiny corner of the bag, and squeeze marmalade in a zigzag pattern onto serving plates. Place slices of the tart on the decorated plates, and top with whipped cream.

- For a simple embellishment, center a round paper doily, smaller than the diameter of the tart, on top of the tart; dust with powdered sugar. Lift off the paper doily, and you'll have a beautifully decorated tart.

- If you want a sweet finish, beat 1 cup whipping cream with 1 tablespoon honey and 1 teaspoon grated orange peel. Garnish each dollop of whipped cream with a long, curled orange peel.

Honey-Wine-Cranberry Tart

Fudge Truffle Tart

PREP: 25 MIN; BAKE: 35 MIN
10 SERVINGS

5 ounces bittersweet baking chocolate, chopped

1/2 cup butter or margarine

1 1/2 cups sugar

3/4 cup all-purpose flour

4 eggs, beaten

Chocolate Glaze (right)

2 ounces white baking bar (from 6-ounce package), chopped

1 tablespoon whipping (heavy) cream

Creamy Almond Sauce (right)

Heat oven to 350°. Grease tart pan with removable bottom, 11 × 1 inch.

Melt chocolate and butter in 1-quart saucepan over low heat, stirring occasionally; cool slightly.

Mix sugar, flour and eggs in large bowl until well blended. Stir in chocolate mixture; pour into tart pan. Bake 30 to 35 minutes or until set around edge. Cool completely on wire rack.

Prepare Chocolate Glaze. Reserve 2 tablespoons for plate design, if desired. Spread remaining warm glaze over tart.

Heat chopped white baking bar and whipping cream over low heat, stirring occasionally, until baking bar is melted; drizzle over warm glaze. Pull knife through glaze for marbled design. Let stand until glaze is set. Prepare Creamy Almond Sauce. Remove side of pan. Serve tart with sauce.

1 Serving: Calories 430 (Calories from Fat 180); Fat 20g (Saturated 11g); Cholesterol 160mg; Sodium 125mg; Carbohydrate 57g (Dietary Fiber 1g); Protein 7g
% Daily Value: Vitamin A 14%; Vitamin C 0%; Calcium 8%; Iron 6%
Diet Exchanges: Not Recommended

Chocolate Glaze

1 ounce unsweetened baking chocolate

1 teaspoon butter or margarine

1 cup powdered sugar

5 teaspoons boiling water

Heat chocolate and butter in 2-quart saucepan over low heat, stirring occasionally, until melted. Stir in powdered sugar and water until smooth. Stir in more boiling water, 1/2 teaspoon at a time, until thin enough to drizzle.

Creamy Almond Sauce

1/4 cup sugar

1 tablespoon cornstarch

1 1/2 cups milk

2 eggs, beaten

1/4 teaspoon almond extract

Mix sugar and cornstarch in 2-quart saucepan. Gradually stir in milk. Cook over medium heat, stirring constantly, until mixture thickens. Gradually stir at least half the hot mixture into eggs, then stir back into hot mixture in saucepan. Boil and stir 1 minute; remove from heat. Stir in almond extract. Serve warm or chilled. Cover and refrigerate any remaining sauce up to 1 week.

Holiday Hints

This dessert will look in the spirit of the holiday when you follow these serving tricks:

- Pour a pool of Creamy Almond Sauce onto the serving plates. Place Chocolate Glaze in resealable plastic bag.

- Cut tiny corner from bag and squeeze drops of melted chocolate onto sauce. Pull a toothpick through chocolate to form squiggles or heart shapes. (See photo above).

- Squeeze semicircular lines of Chocolate Glaze across the plate about 1/2 inch apart. Starting at the smallest semicircle, pull a toothpick across lines outward toward the edge of the plate (above).

- Squeeze dots of Chocolate Glaze in a circle 1/2 inch from edge of sauce and in smaller circle in center. Pull a toothpick through the middle of the dots to make heart shapes (above).

Golden Pound Cake

PREP: 15 MIN; BAKE: 1 HR 20 MIN; COOL: 1 HR
16 SERVINGS

3 cups all-purpose flour

1 teaspoon baking powder

1/4 teaspoon salt

2 3/4 cups sugar

1 1/4 cups butter or margarine, softened

1 teaspoon vanilla

5 eggs

1 cup evaporated milk

Heat oven to 350°. Grease and flour 12-cup bundt cake pan or angel food cake pan (tube pan), 10 × 4 inches. Mix flour, baking powder and salt; set aside.

Beat sugar, butter, vanilla and eggs in large bowl with electric mixer on low speed 30 seconds, scraping bowl constantly. Beat on high speed 5 minutes, scraping bowl occasionally. Beat in flour mixture alternately with milk on low speed. Pour into pan.

Bake 1 hour 10 minutes to 1 hour 20 minutes or until toothpick inserted in center comes out clean. Cool 20 minutes. Remove from pan to wire rack; cool completely.

1 Serving: Calories 390 (Calories from Fat 155); Fat 17g (Saturated 10g); Cholesterol 105mg; Sodium 200mg; Carbohydrate 54g (Dietary Fiber 1g); Protein 6g
% Daily Value: Vitamin A 14%; Vitamin C 0%; Calcium 8%; Iron 8%
Diet Exchanges: Not Recommended

Holiday Hints

For a truly elegant pound cake presentation, brush baked cake with 2/3 cup apricot jam, melted. Decorate with whole, dried apricot halves and white chocolate leaves.

ALMOND POUND CAKE: Substitute 1 teaspoon almond extract for the vanilla.

LEMON POUND CAKE: Substitute 1 teaspoon lemon extract for the vanilla, and fold 2 to 3 teaspoons grated lemon peel into batter.

ORANGE-COCONUT POUND CAKE: Fold 1 can (3 1/2 ounces) flaked coconut (1 1/3 cups) and 2 to 3 tablespoons shredded orange peel into batter.

TRIPLE GINGER POUND CAKE: Add 1 tablespoon grated gingerroot, 2 teaspoons ground ginger and 1/2 cup finely chopped crystallized ginger with the flour mixture.

New Twist

Jazz up your homemade or store-bought pound cake.

- Top it . . . with soft cream cheese with strawberries, and sprinkle with miniature chocolate chips.

- Drizzle it . . . with caramel and hot fudge toppings, and sprinkle with chopped pecans.

- Cut it . . . into 3 horizontal layers. Layer cake with whipped cream and crushed hard peppermint candies.

Christmas Cassata

PREP: 25 MIN; CHILL: 2 3/4 HR
16 SERVINGS

1/3 cup currants or raisins

1 can (17 ounces) pitted dark sweet cherries,
drained and syrup reserved

1 container (15 ounces) ricotta cheese

1/2 cup frozen (thawed) whipped topping

6 tablespoons sweet Marsala wine or orange juice

1 loaf (16 ounces) pound cake

1 package (12 ounces) semisweet chocolate chips
(2 cups)

1 cup firm butter or margarine, cut into pieces

Place currants and 3 tablespoons of reserved cherry juice
in small bowl; reserve 1/2 cup cherry juice. Let stand
about 15 minutes or until currants are softened; drain.
Coarsely chop cherries; set aside.

Place ricotta cheese, whipped topping and 3 tablespoons
of the wine in food processor or blender. Cover and
process until smooth. Transfer to medium bowl; fold in
cherries and currants.

Cut pound cake horizontally into 3 layers. Place bottom
layer on serving dish. Spread with half of the ricotta mixture. Add middle cake layer. Spread with remaining
ricotta mixture. Add top cake layer. Cover with plastic
wrap and refrigerate about 2 hours or until ricotta mixture is firm.

Melt chocolate chips in 2-quart saucepan over low heat,
stirring frequently. Stir in remaining 3 tablespoons wine
and reserved 1/2 cup cherry juice until smooth; remove
from heat. Beat in butter, a few pieces at a time, using
wire whisk, until melted. Refrigerate about 45 minutes
or until thick enough to spread.

Spread chocolate mixture over top and sides of dessert.
Cover and refrigerate any remaining dessert.

1 Serving: Calories 420 (Calories from Fat 260); Fat 29g (Saturated
16g); Cholesterol 70mg; Sodium 140mg; Carbohydrate 38g (Dietary
Fiber 2g); Protein 6g
% Daily Value: Vitamin A 13%; Vitamin C 2%; Calcium 10%; Iron 8%
Diet Exchanges: Not Recommended

Gifts for Giving

Offer a "Dessert of the Month" gift
to someone who has a big sweet
tooth! Name all twelve desserts you
will provide, using special paper. To
make it easy, announce the delivery
dates as the same date for each
month on the gift card. Try these
dessert showstoppers:

- *Heavenly Cheesecake* (page 146)—
January

- *Honey-Wine-Cranberry Tart* (page
132)—February

- *White Almond Fondue* (page
152)—March

- *Golden Pound Cake* (page 136)—
April

- *Angel Meringue Torte* (page 148)—
May

- *Meringue-Swirled Chocolate Cake*
(page 144)—June

- *Easy Tiramisu Dessert* (page 158)—
July

- *Fudge Truffle Tart* (page 134)—
August

- *Cranberry-Apple Dumplings with
Crimson Sauce* (page 154)—
September

- *Gingerbread with Lemon Sauce*
(page 142)—October

- *Pumpkin Pie* (page 128)—
November

- *Christmas Cassata* (above)—
December

P.S. Sweet dreams to the lucky recipient!

Wild Rice-Nut Cake

PREP: 20 MIN; BAKE: 1 HR; COOL: 1 HR
24 SERVINGS

2 1/2 cups all-purpose flour

2 cups packed brown sugar

3/4 cup butter or margarine, softened

1 cup buttermilk

1 teaspoon baking powder

1 teaspoon baking soda

1 teaspoon vanilla

1/2 teaspoon salt

1/2 teaspoon ground nutmeg

1/2 teaspoon maple extract

3 eggs

2 cups cooled cooked wild rice, well drained

2 cups chopped nuts, toasted (page 31), if desired

Powdered sugar, if desired

Maple Whipped Cream (right)

Move oven rack to lowest position. Heat oven to 350°. Generously grease and flour 12-cup bundt cake pan or angel food cake pan (tube pan), 10×4 inches.

Beat all ingredients except wild rice, nuts and Maple Whipped Cream in large bowl with electric mixer on low speed 30 seconds, scraping bowl constantly. Beat on high speed 3 minutes, scraping bowl occasionally. Stir in wild rice and nuts. Pour into pan.

Bake 55 to 60 minutes or until toothpick inserted in center comes out clean. Cool 20 minutes. Remove from pan to wire rack; cool completely. Sprinkle with powdered sugar. Serve cake with Maple Whipped Cream.

1 Serving: Calories 195 (Calories from Fat 65); Fat 7g (Saturated 4g); Cholesterol 40mg; Sodium 180mg; Carbohydrate 31g (Dietary Fiber 1g); Protein 3g
% Daily Value: Vitamin A 6%; Vitamin C 0%; Calcium 4%; Iron 6%
Diet Exchanges: 2 Starch, 1 Fat

Maple Whipped Cream

2 cups whipping (heavy) cream

1/4 cup packed brown sugar

1/2 teaspoon maple extract

Beat all ingredients in chilled medium bowl with electric mixer on medium speed until soft peaks form.

Jeweled Fruitcake

PREP: 20 MIN; BAKE: 1 3/4 HR; COOL: 1 HR
16 SERVINGS

2 cups dried apricot halves

2 cups pitted whole dates (not sugar coated)

1 1/2 cups Brazil nuts

1 cup red or green candied pineapple, chopped

1 cup red or green whole maraschino cherries,
   drained

3/4 cup all-purpose flour

3/4 cup sugar

1/2 teaspoon baking powder

1/2 teaspoon salt

1 1/2 teaspoons vanilla

3 eggs

1 tablespoon corn syrup, if desired

Heat oven to 300°. Line loaf pan, 9×5×3 or 8 1/2×
4 1/2×2 1/2 inches, with aluminum foil; grease foil.
Mix all ingredients except corn syrup. Spread in pan.

Bake about 1 3/4 hours or until toothpick inserted in
center comes out clean. If necessary, cover with aluminum foil during last 30 minutes of baking to prevent
excessive browning. Remove from pan to wire rack.

For a glossy top, brush top with corn syrup. Cool completely. Wrap in plastic wrap; store in refrigerator.

1 Serving: Calories 290 (Calories from Fat 90); Fat 10g (Saturated
2g); Cholesterol 40mg; Sodium 110mg; Carbohydrate 50g (Dietary
Fiber 5g); Protein 5g
% Daily Value: Vitamin A 18%; Vitamin C 0%; Calcium 6%; Iron 12%
Diet Exchanges: 1 Starch, 2 1/2 Fruit, 1 Fat

Gifts for Giving

Over the years, fruitcake in America
has taken its share of bad jokes, but
along the way, some wonderful
recipes—like this one—have evolved,
full of fruits and nuts bound together with a sweet batter. If you plan on
giving fruitcake as a gift or as part of
a gift basket, you may like to try
Petite Fruitcakes or Mini-Loaves.

Petite Fruitcakes: Place paper or foil
baking cup in each of 24 medium
muffin cups, 2 1/2×1 1/4 inches.
Divide batter evenly among cups
(about 1/3 cup each). Bake 35 to 40
minutes or until toothpick inserted
in center comes out clean. Remove
from pan to wire rack. Makes 24
servings.

Mini-Loaves: Generously grease 7 or
8 miniature loaf pans, 4 1/2×2 3/4
×1 1/4 inches, or line with aluminum foil and grease. Divide batter
evenly among pans (about 1 cup
each). Bake about 1 hour or until
toothpick inserted in center comes
out clean. Remove from pans to wire
rack. Makes 7 or 8 mini-loaves.

Jeweled Fruitcake (Petite Fruitcakes and Mini-Loaves—variations)

Fabulous Finales

Gingerbread with Lemon Sauce

PREP: 20 MIN; BAKE: 50 MIN
9 SERVINGS

2 1/4 cups all-purpose flour

1/3 cup sugar

1/2 cup shortening

1 cup full-flavor molasses

3/4 cup hot water

1 teaspoon baking soda

1 teaspoon ground ginger

1 teaspoon ground cinnamon

3/4 teaspoon salt

1 egg

Lemon Sauce (right)

Heat oven to 325°. Grease and flour square pan, 9×9×2 inches. Beat all ingredients except Lemon Sauce in large bowl with electric mixer on low speed 30 seconds, scraping bowl constantly. Beat on medium speed 3 minutes, scraping bowl occasionally. Pour into pan.

Bake about 50 minutes or until toothpick inserted in center comes out clean. Prepare Lemon Sauce. Serve warm gingerbread with sauce.

1 Serving: Calories 525 (Calories from Fat 205); Fat 23g (Saturated 10g); Cholesterol 75mg; Sodium 240mg; Carbohydrate 76g (Dietary Fiber 1g); Protein 5g
% Daily Value: Vitamin A 10%; Vitamin C 0%; Calcium 32%; Iron 44%
Diet Exchanges: Not Recommended

Lemon Sauce

1 cup sugar

1/2 cup butter or margarine

1/4 cup water

1 tablespoon grated lemon peel

3 tablespoons lemon juice

1 egg, well beaten

Mix all ingredients in 2-quart saucepan. Heat to boiling over medium heat, stirring constantly. Serve warm or chilled. Store in refrigerator up to 2 weeks.

Holiday Hints

If lemon isn't to your liking, try one of these suggestions:

- Spread 1/2 cup warmed apricot preserves over top of cooled gingerbread.

- Serve warm gingerbread with praline or peach ice cream. Top it off with purchased peach sauce or try

Hot Buttered Rum Sauce (page 149).

- For a lacy-looking gingerbread, bake in a round pan, 9×1 1/2 inches. Cool in pan 10 minutes, then turn upside down onto wire rack and remove pan. When cooled, place paper doily or stencil

on top; dust with powdered sugar. Remove doily.

- Spread purchased cream cheese frosting over top of gingerbread, and sprinkle top with 1/2 cup finely chopped crystallized ginger.

Gingerbread with Lemon Sauce

Meringue-Swirled Chocolate Cake

PREP: 20 MIN; BAKE: 1 1/2 HR; COOL: 1 HR
10 SERVINGS

1 package (1 pound 2.25 ounces) chocolate fudge
cake mix

1 1/3 cups water

1/2 cup vegetable oil

3 eggs

3 egg whites

3/4 cup sugar

Heat oven to 325°. Generously grease and flour spring-form pan, 9×3 inches. Prepare batter for cake mix as directed on package, using water, oil and 3 eggs.

Beat 3 egg whites in medium bowl with electric mixer on high speed until soft peaks form. Beat in sugar, 1 table-spoon at a time; continue beating until stiff and glossy.

Spread two-thirds of the meringue three-quarters of the way up side of pan (do not spread on bottom of pan). Pour cake batter into pan; top with remaining meringue. Cut through meringue and cake batter using tip of knife to swirl meringue through batter.

Bake about 1 1/2 hours or until toothpick inserted in center comes out almost clean. Cool 10 minutes on wire rack. Run metal spatula along side of cake to loosen; open side of pan. Cool cake completely. Store loosely covered at room temperature.

1 Serving: Calories 205 (Calories from Fat 65); Fat 7g (Saturated 2g); Cholesterol 30mg; Sodium 260mg; Carbohydrate 33g (Dietary Fiber 1g); Protein 3g
% Daily Value: Vitamin A 0%; Vitamin C 0%; Calcium 4%; Iron 4%
Diet Exchanges: 2 Starch, 1 Fat

Holiday Hints

Heavenly by itself and divine with a raspberry sauce, this dessert cake is simply beautiful garnished with fresh mint leaves and fresh raspberries.

If you don't have a springform pan, don't worry! You can bake the cake in a greased and floured 13×9×2-inch rectangular pan. Spread two-thirds of the meringue three-quarters of the way up sides of pan (do not spread on bottom of pan). Pour cake batter into pan; top with remaining meringue. Cut through meringue and cake batter to swirl as directed. Bake for 40 to 45 minutes or until toothpick inserted in center comes out clean.

Meringue-Swirled Chocolate Cake

Heavenly Cheesecake

PREP: 40 MIN; BAKE: 1 HR; COOL: 15 MIN; CHILL: 8 HR

16 SERVINGS

1 cup vanilla or chocolate wafer cookie or ginger-
snap cookie crumbs

2 tablespoons butter or margarine, melted

3 packages (8 ounces each) cream cheese, softened

1/2 cup sugar

3 eggs

1 teaspoon vanilla

1 package (12 ounces) white baking chips (2 cups),
melted

1/2 cup half-and-half

Cut-up fresh strawberries, if desired

Fresh mint leaves, if desired

Heat oven to 325°. Mix cookie crumbs and butter. Press evenly in bottom of springform pan, 10×3 or 9×3 inches. Refrigerate while preparing filling.

Beat cream cheese in large bowl with electric mixer on medium speed until smooth. Gradually beat in sugar until smooth. Beat in eggs, one at a time. Beat in vanilla, melted baking chips and half-and-half until blended. Pour over crust; smooth top.

Bake 55 to 60 minutes or until center is set; cool 15 minutes. Run metal spatula around side of cheesecake to loosen. Cover and refrigerate at least 8 hours, but no longer than 48 hours. Remove side of pan. Top cheesecake with strawberries. Garnish with mint leaves. Cover and refrigerate any remaining cheesecake.

1 Serving: Calories 380 (Calories from Fat 235); Fat 26g (Saturated 15g); Cholesterol 95mg; Sodium 190mg; Carbohydrate 32g (Dietary Fiber 1g); Protein 6g
% Daily Value: Vitamin A 16%; Vitamin C 10%; Calcium 8%; Iron 6%
Diet Exchanges: Not Recommended

New Twist

If you're the kind of baker who likes to add your own touch, try stirring in 1/2 cup of these favorites:

- Miniature semisweet chocolate chips

- Chopped candied fruits

- Choppped dried cranberries or dried cherries

- Chopped hazelnuts or pecans

- Crushed hard peppermint candies

Holiday Hints

It's easy to add a personal touch to your cheesecake, whether you make one from scratch or pick one up.

- Flatten large green gumdrops by rolling in sugar, using rolling pin. Cut to resemble holly leaves; arrange on cheesecake. Add red cinnamon candies to look like holly berries.

- On each dessert plate, write a holiday message, such as "Noel" or "Cheers," with melted chocolate placed in a squeeze bottle or with decorating frosting purchased in squeeze tubes. Garnish with fresh strawberry slices and purchased chocolate decorations.

- Spread purchased lemon or lime curd over cheesecake, and garnish with a lemon twist and fresh mint leaves.

Fabulous Finales

Angel Meringue Torte

PREP: 20 MIN; BAKE: 1 1/2 HR; COOL: 2 HR; CHILL: 4 HR
12 SERVINGS

6 egg whites

1/2 teaspoon cream of tartar

1/4 teaspoon salt

1 1/2 cups sugar

1/2 teaspoon vanilla

1/2 teaspoon almond extract

1 cup whipping (heavy) cream

Cranberries Jubilee (right)

Heat oven to 275°. Butter bottom only of springform pan, 9×3 inches, or angel food cake pan (tube pan), 10×4 inches.

Beat egg whites, cream of tartar and salt in large bowl with electric mixer on medium speed until foamy. Beat in sugar, 2 tablespoons at a time, on high speed; continue beating until stiff and glossy. Do not underbeat. Beat in vanilla and almond extract. Spread evenly in pan.

Bake 1 1/2 hours. Turn off oven; leave pan in oven with door closed 1 hour. Finish cooling at room temperature on wire rack.

Run knife around side of torte to loosen; turn upside down onto serving plate. Beat whipping cream in chilled medium bowl with electric mixer on high speed until stiff. Frost torte with whipped cream. Refrigerate at least 4 hours, but no longer than 48 hours. Cut into wedges. Serve with Cranberries Jubilee.

1 Serving: Calories 310 (Calories from Fat 5); Fat 6g (Saturated 4g); Cholesterol 20mg; Sodium 85mg; Carbohydrate 63g (Dietary Fiber 1g); Protein 2g
% Daily Value: Vitamin A 4%; Vitamin C 4%; Calcium 2%; Iron 0%
Diet Exchanges: Not Recommended

Cranberries Jubilee

3/4 teaspoon grated orange peel

1/2 cup orange juice

1/2 cup water

2 cups sugar

2 cups cranberries

2 tablespoons water

2 teaspoons cornstarch

1/4 cup brandy, if desired*

Mix orange peel, orange juice, 1/2 cup water and the sugar in 2-quart saucepan. Heat to boiling; boil 5 minutes. Stir in cranberries. Heat to boiling; boil rapidly 5 minutes, stirring occasionally. Mix 2 tablespoons water and the cornstarch; stir into cranberry mixture. Cook, stirring constantly, until mixture thickens and boils. Boil and stir 1 minute; keep warm. Heat brandy in small, long-handled pan or metal ladle just until warm. Carefully ignite with long, wooden safety match; pour flaming brandy over cranberry mixture. Serve hot after flame dies.

* Brandy is needed to flame this dessert; however, you can substitute 1/4 cup water and 1/4 teaspoon brandy extract for the brandy, skip the flaming step and pour over cranberry mixture.

Peanut Brittle Bread Pudding

PREP: 20 MIN; BAKE: 30 MIN

6 SERVINGS

4 cups soft bread cubes (4 to 5 slices bread)

1/2 cup coarsely broken peanut brittle

1 egg

1/2 cup milk

1/2 cup packed brown sugar

1/4 cup butter or margarine, melted

Hot Buttered Rum Sauce (right)

Whipped cream, if desired

Heat oven to 350°. Grease 1-quart casserole. Place 2 cups of the bread cubes in casserole. Sprinkle with half of the peanut brittle; repeat with remaining bread cubes and peanut brittle.

Beat egg in small bowl. Stir in milk, brown sugar and butter; pour over bread mixture.

Bake uncovered 25 to 30 minutes or until golden brown. Prepare Hot Buttered Rum Sauce. Serve warm pudding with sauce and whipped cream.

1 Serving: Calories 565 (Calories from Fat 325); Fat 36g (Saturated 21g); Cholesterol 130mg; Sodium 3300mg; Carbohydrate 55g (Dietary Fiber 1g); Protein 6g
% Daily Value: Vitamin A 26%; Vitamin C 0%; Calcium 10%; Iron 8%
Diet Exchanges: Not Recommended

Holiday Hints

Warm their hearts with this homey dessert. Instead of making the rum sauce, drizzle purchased chocolate syrup over warm pudding, and sprinkle with extra crushed peanut brittle.

Pour on the decadence! This wonderful rum sauce is also delicious served on ice cream or drizzled over Golden Pound Cake (page 136). Stir in toasted pecans or chopped toffee bits for a crunchy topping.

Hot Buttered Rum Sauce

1/2 cup packed brown sugar

1/2 cup butter or margarine, softened

2/3 cup whipping (heavy) cream

1/4 cup rum or 3 tablespoons water plus 2 teaspoons rum extract

Mix all ingredients in 2-quart saucepan. Heat to boiling over high heat, stirring constantly. Boil 3 to 4 minutes, stirring constantly, until slightly thickened. Serve warm. Store covered in refrigerator up to 1 week. Sauce may separate during storage; stir before serving.

Fabulous Finales

Christmas Steamed Pudding

PREP: 15 MIN; STEAM: 2 HR; STAND: 5 MIN
8 SERVINGS

1 cup boiling water

1 cup chopped raisins

2 tablespoons shortening

1 1/2 cups all-purpose flour

1/2 cup sugar

1 teaspoon baking soda

1 teaspoon salt

1/2 cup molasses

1 egg

Creamy Sauce or Rum Hard Sauce (right)

Generously grease 6-cup mold. Pour 1 cup boiling water over raisins; stir in shortening until melted. Mix flour, sugar, baking soda and salt in medium bowl. Stir in raisin mixture, molasses and egg. Pour into mold.

Cover mold tightly with aluminum foil. Place mold on rack in Dutch oven or steamer. Pour enough boiling water into Dutch oven until halfway up mold. Cover Dutch oven. Keep water boiling over low heat about 2 hours or until toothpick inserted in center of pudding comes out clean. Prepare Creamy Sauce.

Remove mold from Dutch oven. Let stand 5 minutes; unmold. Serve warm with sauce.

1 Serving: Calories 410 (Calories from Fat 180); Fat 20g (Saturated 11g); Cholesterol 75mg; Sodium 550mg; Carbohydrate 54g (Dietary Fiber 1g); Protein 4g
% Daily Value: Vitamin A 14%; Vitamin C 2%; Calcium 6%; Iron 12%
Diet Exchanges: Not recommended

Creamy Sauce

1/2 cup powdered sugar

1/2 cup butter or margarine, softened

1/2 cup whipping (heavy) cream

Mix powdered sugar and butter in 1-quart saucepan until smooth and creamy. Stir in whipping cream. Heat to boiling, stirring occasionally. Serve warm.

Rum Hard Sauce

1/2 cup butter or margarine, softened

1 cup powdered sugar

1 tablespoon rum or 2 teaspoons rum extract

Beat butter in small bowl with electric mixer on high speed about 5 minutes or until smooth. Gradually beat in powdered sugar and rum. Cover and refrigerate 1 hour.

Holiday Hints

A custom still observed in parts of England is to hide a silver charm or a coin wrapped in foil in the batter before the pudding is steamed (just tell your guests to be on the lookout for it!). Whoever finds the treasure will have good luck in the coming year. Another custom requires that every family member take a turn stirring the batter, always in a clockwise direction, while making a secret wish.

Surround your pudding with a platter of sugared fruit. Brush small-sized fruits (such as grapes, cranberries, kumquats) with 1 beaten egg white. Sprinkle with sugar. Remember, these pretty sugared fruits are just to look at, not to eat.

Christmas Steamed Pudding

White Almond Fondue

PREP: 15 MIN
6 TO 8 SERVINGS

12 ounces vanilla-flavored candy coating (almond bark)

1/3 cup half-and-half

1 to 3 tablespoons almond-flavored liqueur or 2 teaspoons almond extract

1/4 teaspoon ground cinnamon

Dippers:

Apple wedges*	Melon pieces
Angel food cake cubes	Miniature doughnuts
Banana slices*	Papaya wedges*
Dried apricots	Pear slices
Grapes	Pineapple chunks
Kiwifruit slices	Pound cake cubes
Maraschino cherries	Pretzels
Mandarin orange segments	Strawberries
	Vanilla wafers

Heat candy coating and half-and-half in heavy 3-quart saucepan over low heat, stirring constantly, until coating is melted and mixture is smooth; remove from heat. Stir in liqueur and cinnamon.

Pour into fondue pot or chafing dish. Keep warm over low flame. To serve, spear Dippers with fondue forks and dip into fondue. If fondue becomes too thick, stir in small amount of half-and-half.

*Dip in lemon or pineapple juice to prevent discoloration of fruit.

1 Serving: Calories 340 (Calories from Fat 180); Fat 20g (Saturated 12g); Cholesterol 15mg; Sodium 55mg; Carbohydrate 36g (Dietary Fiber 0g); Protein 4g
% Daily Value: Vitamin A 2%; Vitamin C 0%; Calcium 12%; Iron 0%
Diet Exchanges: Not Recommended

Party Pointers

Fondues are such a fun, informal way to entertain! Gather a crowd after holiday caroling and make it easy by having each guest bring his or her favorite dipper.

- Make several pots of warm fondue. To vary the flavors of your fondues, use 12 ounces milk chocolate instead of vanilla candy coating for one, and use 12 ounces semisweet chocolate instead of vanilla candy coating for another; just increase the half-and-half to 3/4 cup.

- Don't worry if you don't have enough fondue pots. A small heavy saucepan or heatproof dish will do.

If you don't have fondue forks, just use bamboo skewers available at your supermarket.

- You may like to have bowls of granola, chopped nuts, coconut or candy decorations for guests to dip coated foods into as final toppers.

White Almond Fondue

Cranberry-Apple Dumplings with Crimson Sauce

PREP: 30 MIN; BAKE: 30 MIN

6 SERVINGS

1 can (16 ounces) whole berry cranberry sauce

1/4 cup orange juice or water

2 tablespoons red cinnamon candies

Pastry (right)

4 small cooking apples (each about 3 inches in diameter), peeled and cored

4 teaspoons sugar

1 egg, slightly beaten

Sugar, if desired

Heat oven to 400°. Lightly grease jelly roll pan, 15 1/2 × 10 1/2 × 1 inch, or large cookie sheet. Heat cranberry sauce, orange juice and cinnamon candies over medium heat, stirring occasionally, until hot and candies are melted; set aside.

Prepare Pastry. Roll pastry into rectangle, 10 × 8 inches. Cut pastry into four 4-inch squares, using pastry cutter or knife. Cut leaves from remaining 2-inch piece of pastry, using small leaf-shape cutter or knife.

Place apple on each pastry square. Spoon 1 tablespoon cranberry sauce mixture into center of each apple. Sprinkle each apple with 1 teaspoon of the sugar. Moisten corners of pastry squares. Bring 2 opposite corners of pastry up over apple; pinch to seal. Repeat with remaining corners; pinch edges of pastry to seal. Decorate with pastry leaves. Place dumplings in pan. Brush with egg; sprinkle with additional sugar.

Bake about 30 minutes or until crust is golden brown and apples are tender. Serve warm with remaining sauce mixture.

1 Serving: Calories 590 (Calories from Fat 260); Fat 29g (Saturated 7g); Cholesterol 35mg; Sodium 430mg; Carbohydrate 79g (Dietary Fiber 3g); Protein 6g
% Daily Value: Vitamin A 2%; Vitamin C 6%; Calcium 2%; Iron 12%
Diet Exchanges: Not Recommended

Pastry

2/3 cup plus 2 tablespoons shortening

2 cups all-purpose flour

1/2 teaspoon salt

4 to 5 tablespoons cold water

Cut shortening into flour and salt in medium bowl, using pastry blender or crisscrossing 2 knives, until particles are size of small peas. Sprinkle with cold water, 1 tablespoon at a time, tossing with fork until all flour is moistened and pastry almost cleans side of bowl (1 to 2 teaspoons more water can be added if necessary).

Holiday Hints

Garnish each dumpling with fresh mint leaves and a fresh cranberry. For an extra touch, sprinkle powdered sugar over entire dessert plate before placing the dumpling on top.

Timesaving Tips

If you want to make this treat as easy as pie, use refrigerated pie crusts; you'll save yourself some time and still have a great dessert!

Cranberry-Apple Dumplings with Crimson Sauce

Winter Poached Pears

PREP: 10 MIN; COOK: 45 MIN
4 SERVINGS

4 firm ripe pears

2 cups water

3 tea bags red zesty herbal tea flavored with hibiscus, rosehips and lemongrass

2 cups cranberry-raspberry juice

2 tablespoons red cinnamon candies

Peel pears, leaving stems intact; set aside. Heat water to boiling in 3-quart saucepan; remove from heat. Add tea bags; let steep 10 minutes. Squeeze tea from tea bags; discard bags. Stir juice and candies into tea. Heat over medium heat, stirring occasionally, until candies are melted.

Arrange pears upright and close together in saucepan. Heat to boiling; reduce heat. Cover and simmer about 20 minutes, spooning sauce over pears occasionally, until pears are tender when pierced with tip of sharp knife.

Remove pears from syrup. Cook syrup over medium-high heat about 25 minutes, stirring constantly, until thickened. Serve sauce over pears.

1 Serving: Calories 195 (Calories from Fat 10); Fat 1g (Saturated 0g); Cholesterol 0mg; Sodium 5mg; Carbohydrate 49g (Dietary Fiber 4g); Protein 1g
% Daily Value: Vitamin A 0%; Vitamin C 40%; Calcium 2%; Iron 4%
Diet Exchanges: 3 Fruit

Holiday Hints

These rosy red pears are the perfect ending to any holiday meal, and they're not laden with fat and calories. For a special touch, dust dessert plates with powdered sugar before serving. Serve pears with low-fat vanilla ice cream, and garnish with fresh raspberries and mint leaves.

Do your pesky pears keep falling over?. Try this trick: Cut a very thin slice from the bottom of each pear to make a flat surface and they won't topple over on the serving plates again!

Raspberry Trifle

PREP: 25 MIN; CHILL: 3 HR
10 SERVINGS

1/2 cup sugar

3 tablespoons cornstarch

1/4 teaspoon salt

3 cups milk

1/2 cup dry sherry or white wine or 1/3 cup orange juice plus 2 tablespoons sherry flavoring

3 egg yolks, beaten

3 tablespoons butter or margarine

1 tablespoon vanilla

2 packages (3 ounces each) ladyfingers

1/2 cup raspberry preserves

3 cups fresh raspberries or 2 packages (12 ounces each) frozen raspberries, thawed and drained

1 cup whipping (heavy) cream

2 tablespoons sugar

2 tablespoons slivered almonds, toasted (page 31)

Additional fresh raspberries, if desired

Fresh mint leaves, if desired

Mix 1/2 cup sugar, the cornstarch and salt in 3-quart saucepan. Gradually stir in milk and sherry. Heat to boiling over medium heat, stirring constantly. Boil and stir 1 minute. Gradually stir at least half of the hot mixture into egg yolks, then stir back into hot mixture in saucepan. Boil and stir 1 minute; remove from heat. Stir in butter and vanilla. Cover and refrigerate at least 3 hours, but no longer than 24 hours.

Split ladyfingers horizontally in half; spread each half with raspberry preserves. Layer one-fourth of the ladyfingers, cut sides up, 1 1/2 cups of the raspberries and half of the pudding in 2-quart serving bowl. Repeat layers once using remaining 1 1/2 cups raspberries. Arrange remaining ladyfingers around edge of bowl in upright position with cut sides toward center. (It may be necessary to gently ease ladyfingers down into pudding about 1 inch so they remain upright.)

Beat whipping cream and 2 tablespoons sugar in chilled medium bowl with electric mixer on high speed until stiff; spread over dessert. Sprinkle with almonds. Cover and refrigerate until serving time. Garnish with additional raspberries and mint leaves. Cover and refrigerate any remaining dessert.

1 Serving: Calories 370 (Calories from Fat 145); Fat 16g (Saturated 9g); Cholesterol 110mg; Sodium 180mg; Carbohydrate 53g (Dietary Fiber 2g); Protein 6g
% Daily Value: Vitamin A 14%; Vitamin C 12%; Calcium 12%; Iron 6%
Diet Exchanges: Not Recommended

Easy Tiramisu Dessert

PREP: 15 MIN; CHILL: 1 HR

12 SERVINGS

1 package (10.75 ounces) frozen pound cake, thawed and cut into 9 slices or 9 slices Golden Pound Cake (page 136)

3/4 cup strong-brewed coffee (room temperature)

1 cup sugar

1/2 cup chocolate-flavored syrup

1 package (8 ounces) mascarpone cheese or cream cheese, softened

2 cups whipping (heavy) cream

2 bars (1.4 ounces each) chocolate-covered toffee candy, chopped

Arrange cake slices in bottom of rectangular baking dish, 11×7×1 1/2 inches, cutting cake slices if necessary to cover bottom of dish. Drizzle coffee over cake.

Beat sugar, chocolate syrup and mascarpone cheese in large bowl with electric mixer on medium speed until smooth. Add whipping cream. Beat on medium speed until light and fluffy. Spread over cake. Sprinkle with candy.

Cover and refrigerate at least 1 hour but no longer than 24 hours to set dessert and blend flavors.

1 Serving: Calories 430 (Calories from Fat 250); Fat 28g (Saturated 16g); Cholesterol 95mg; Sodium 130mg; Carbohydrate 42g (Dietary Fiber 1g); Protein 4g
% Daily Value: Vitamin A 16%; Vitamin C 0%; Calcium 6%; Iron 6%
Diet Exchanges: Not Recommended

Party Pointers

Start a new tradition by hosting a Dessert Open House. Ask guests to bring a favorite dessert to share and make sure this tiramisu treat is on the menu! Here are a few party pointers to help you set the table and set the mood:

• You may want to consider using your dining table as well as two or three smaller tables. This allows guests to gather and mingle in more than one area.

• Create an atmosphere. Use lots of twinkling lights and candles. Have a warm fire in the fireplace to welcome guests.

• Nuts and cheeses are perfect alongside decadent desserts. Check out your deli for cheeses such as Camembert, Liederkranz, Brie, Stilton, blue and Cheddar. Serve with platters of fresh apple and pear slices.

• For coffee lovers, serve this dessert with freshly brewed Italian roast coffee and an assortment of fun coffee toppings, such as: whipped cream, eggnog, chocolate shavings, raw sugar, ground cinnamon and flavored liqueurs, such as almond, hazelnut, orange or coffee

Easy Tiramisu Dessert

Chocolate Mousse in Chocolate Cups

PREP: 40 MIN; CHILL: 2 HR

8 SERVINGS

4 egg yolks

1/4 cup sugar

1 cup whipping (heavy) cream

1 package (6 ounces) semisweet chocolate chips (1 cup)

Chocolate Cups (right)

1 1/2 cups whipping (heavy) cream

Sliced strawberries, if desired

Beat egg yolks in small bowl with electric mixer on high speed about 3 minutes or until thick and lemon colored. Gradually beat in sugar.

Heat 1 cup whipping cream in 2-quart saucepan over medium heat just until hot. Gradually stir at least half of the cream into egg yolk mixture, then stir back into hot cream in saucepan. Cook over low heat about 5 minutes, stirring constantly, until mixture thickens (do not boil).

Stir chocolate chips into cream mixture until melted. Cover and refrigerate about 2 hours, stirring occasionally, just until chilled. Prepare Chocolate Cups.

Beat 1 1/2 cups whipping cream in chilled medium bowl with electric mixer on high speed until stiff. Fold refrig-erated mixture into whipped cream. Pipe or spoon mousse into chocolate cups. Garnish with strawberries. Cover and refrigerate any remaining dessert.

1 Serving: Calories 515 (Calories from Fat 360); Fat 40g (Saturated 24g); Cholesterol 190mg; Sodium 35mg; Carbohydrate 39g (Dietary Fiber 3g); Protein 5g
% Daily Value: Vitamin A 20%; Vitamin C 0%; Calcium 8%; Iron 10%
Diet Exchanges: Not Recommended

Chocolate Cups

1 1/3 cups semisweet chocolate chips or white baking chips

Mold aluminum foil to the outsides of eight 6-ounce custard cups. Place upside down on cookie sheet. Melt chocolate chips in heavy 1-quart saucepan over low heat, stirring constantly; remove from heat. Spread about 1 1/2 tablespoons melted chocolate over foil on bottom and about 1 1/2 inches up side of each cup.

Refrigerate about 30 minutes or until chocolate is firm. Carefully remove foil from custard cups, then remove foil from chocolate cups. Store chocolate cups in refrigerator.

New Twist

Here's a chance to go all out on flavor! Stir 2 tablespoons flavored liqueur—such as almond, cherry, coffee, hazelnut or raspberry—into the 1 1/2 cups whipping cream before beating it.

Timesaving Tips

Skip the chocolate cups if you're in a hurry. Serve the mousse in fancy dessert goblets placed on gold-rimmed dessert plates or gold doilies. Garnish with chocolate curls or a purchased rectangular chocolate mint, or top with an easy sprinkle of red or green sugar or nonpareils.

Chocolate Mousse in Chocolate Cups

Christmas Tortoni

PREP: 15 MIN; FREEZE: 4 HR
8 SERVINGS

2/3 cup macaroon cookie or vanilla wafer cookie crumbs (about 12 cookies)

1/2 cup chopped salted blanched almonds

1/4 cup chopped red candied cherries

1 quart vanilla ice cream, slightly softened

Red and green candied cherries, if desired

Place paper or foil baking cup in each of 8 medium muffin cups, 2 1/2 × 1 1/4 inches. Mix cookie crumbs, almonds and 1/4 cup candied cherries; fold into ice cream.

Divide ice-cream mixture among muffin cups. Decorate with red and green candied cherries. Freeze about 4 hours or until firm.

1 Serving: Calories 360 (Calories from Fat 180); Fat 20g (Saturated 7g); Cholesterol 30mg; Sodium 230mg; Carbohydrate 41g (Dietary Fiber 2g); Protein 6g
% Daily Value: Vitamin A 6%; Vitamin C 0%; Calcium 10%; Iron 10%
Diet Exchanges: Not Recommended

Holiday Hints

This easy dessert is perfect to make ahead and keep in the freezer to be ready for drop-in guests. A drizzle of chocolate sauce on the dessert plate will make it even more special.

Put your guests in a winter wonderland mood by presenting tortoni on clear glass plates sprinkled with coarse decorating sugar. Use silver, gold or other decorative cupcake liners available in supermarkets and party stores.

Christmas Tortoni and Fluffy Peppermint Pie (page 163)

Fluffy Peppermint Pie

PREP: 30 MIN; CHILL: 25 MIN; FREEZE: 5 HR
8 SERVINGS

1 1/2 cups chocolate wafer cookie crumbs

2 tablespoons sugar

1/4 cup butter or margarine, melted

30 large marshmallows

1 can (14 ounces) sweetened condensed milk

2 cups whipping (heavy) cream

3 drops red food color

2 teaspoons peppermint extract

1/4 cup crushed hard peppermint candies

Mix cookie crumbs, sugar and butter. Press evenly in bottom and up side of ungreased pie plate, 9 × 1 1/2 inches.

Place marshmallows and milk in large microwavable bowl. Microwave uncovered on High about 3 minutes, stirring once, until marshmallows are melted. Refrigerate about 25 minutes or until mixture mounds slightly when dropped from a spoon.

Beat whipping cream, food color and peppermint extract in chilled medium bowl with electric mixer on high speed until stiff. Stir marshmallow mixture until blended; fold into whipped cream. Fold in crushed candies. Mound mixture into crust. Cover and freeze about 5 hours or until frozen. Cover and freeze any remaining pie.

1 Serving: Calories 655 (Calories from Fat 300); Fat 33g (Saturated 20g); Cholesterol 105mg; Sodium 280mg; Carbohydrate 81g (Dietary Fiber 1g); Protein 9g
% Daily Value: Vitamin A 22%; Vitamin C 2%; Calcium 24%; Iron 6%
Diet Exchanges: Not Recommended

Timesaving Tips

You can have a merry dessert in minutes by filling the crust for this recipe with your favorite softened ice cream and freezing. You may like to try one of these ice cream flavors: eggnog, peppermint bonbon, rocky road or pistachio. Serve with hot fudge sauce if desired.

Holiday Hints

Add a finishing touch to this pie by serving with a hard peppermint candy or a candy cane on each plate! Go all out by dipping the candy in melted chocolate.

Merry Berry Frozen Soufflé

Merry Berry Frozen Soufflé

PREP: 15 MIN; FREEZE: 8 HR; STAND: 30 MIN
6 SERVINGS

4 egg whites

1/4 teaspoon salt

1/3 cup water

3/4 cup sugar

1 can (16 ounces) whole berry cranberry sauce

2 cups frozen (thawed) whipped topping

Candied Cranberries (right)

Fresh mint leaves, if desired

Beat egg whites and salt in large bowl with electric mixer on high speed until soft peaks form. Heat water and sugar to boiling in 1-quart saucepan over medium-high heat, stirring frequently, until sugar is dissolved. Cook over medium heat to 245° on candy thermometer or until small amount of mixture dropped into very cold water forms a firm ball.

Slowly beat sugar mixture into egg whites on low speed. Beat on medium speed about 8 minutes or until mixture cools to room temperature.

Fold cranberry sauce and whipped topping into egg white mixture. Spoon into 6 individual soufflé dishes, about 1 1/4 cups each; smooth tops. Cover with plastic wrap and freeze at least 8 hours, but no longer than 24 hours.

Let stand at room temperature 30 minutes before serving. Garnish with Candied Cranberries and mint leaves.

1 Serving: Calories 270 (Calories from Fat 35); Fat 4g (Saturated 3g); Cholesterol 15mg; Sodium 180mg; Carbohydrate 57g (Dietary Fiber 1g); Protein 3g
% Daily Value: Vitamin A 4%; Vitamin C 2%; Calcium 2%; Iron 0%
Diet Exchanges: 4 Fruit, 1/2 Fat

Candied Cranberries

1/2 cup water

3/4 cup sugar

1/2 cup cranberries

Cover cookie sheet with waxed paper. Heat water and 1/2 cup of the sugar to boiling in 1-quart saucepan over medium-high heat, stirring frequently, until sugar is dissolved. Cook over medium-high heat to 234° on candy thermometer or until small amount of mixture dropped into very cold water forms a soft ball that flattens when removed from water. Remove from heat; stir in cranberries. Let stand about 2 minutes or until cranberries are softened. Remove cranberries with slotted spoon to cookie sheet. Place remaining 1/4 cup sugar on plate; roll cranberries in sugar to coat. (Cranberries can be prepared up to 6 hours before using; keep refrigerated.)

Holiday Hints

Don't worry if you don't have individual soufflé dishes. Just use a freezerproof 2 1/2-quart glass serving bowl or soufflé dish. Serve a scoop of soufflé on dessert plates dusted with baking cocoa, and offer chocolate syrup on the side.

Merry Muffins (page 172) and Lemon-
Glazed Coffee Wreath (page 177)

CHAPTER 5

Holiday Breads

The warmth of a baking oven on a cold winter's day and the sweet smells of spice wafting from the kitchen bring back memories of Christmas past.

Pumpkin-Marmalade Bread

PREP: 15 MIN; BAKE: 1 HR 10 MIN; COOL: 1 HR
1 LOAF (24 SLICES)

2 1/4 cups all-purpose flour

3/4 cup packed brown sugar

3/4 cup granulated sugar

4 1/2 teaspoons pumpkin pie spice

2 1/4 teaspoons baking powder

3/4 teaspoon ground cinnamon

1/4 teaspoon salt

4 eggs

1 1/4 cups canned pumpkin

1/2 cup butter or margarine, melted

1/3 cup orange marmalade

3 tablespoons orange-flavored liqueur or orange
   juice

Marmalade Glaze (right)

Heat oven to 350°. Grease bottom only of loaf pan,
8 1/2×4 1/2×2 1/2 inches or 9×5×3 inches. Mix
flour, brown sugar, granulated sugar, pumpkin pie spice,
baking powder, cinnamon and salt in medium bowl.

Beat eggs, pumpkin, butter, marmalade and liqueur in
large bowl with electric mixer on medium speed until
blended. Gradually beat in flour mixture on low speed.
Spread in pan.

Bake 1 hour 5 minutes to 1 hour 10 minutes or until
toothpick inserted in center comes out clean. Cool 10
minutes. Loosen sides of loaf from pan; remove from
pan to wire rack. Spread warm loaf with Marmalade
Glaze; cool completely. Store tightly wrapped in refrigerator up to 1 week.

1 Slice: Calories 155 (Calories from Fat 45); Fat 5g (Saturated 3g);
Cholesterol 45mg; Sodium 110mg; Carbohydrate 27g (Dietary Fiber
1g); Protein 2g
% Daily Value: Vitamin A 32%; Vitamin C 0%; Calcium 4%; Iron 6%
Diet Exchanges: 1 Starch, 1 Fruit, 1/2 Fat

Marmalade Glaze

2 tablespoons orange marmalade

1 tablespoon orange-flavored liqueur or orange
   juice

Mix ingredients.

New Twist

Turn this bread into a divine dessert. Thickly slice the
leftover bread, then cut into "fingers" or cubes for dipping into chocolate, fruit or other dessert sauces. Or frost
fingers or cubes with thinned leftover frosting and roll in
chopped nuts or coconut for a sweet snack.

Poppy Seed Bread

PREP: 15 MIN; BAKE: 1 HR 20 MIN; COOL: 1 HR
1 LOAF (24 SLICES)

2 1/2 cups all-purpose flour

1 cup sugar

1/4 cup poppy seed

1 1/4 cups milk

1/3 cup vegetable oil

3 1/2 teaspoons baking powder

1 teaspoon salt

1 teaspoon vanilla

1 egg

Heat oven to 350°. Grease bottom only of loaf pan, 9×5×3 inches.

Mix all ingredients; beat 30 seconds with spoon. Pour into pan.

Bake 1 hour 10 minutes to 1 hour 20 minutes, or until toothpick inserted in center comes out clean. Cool 10 minutes. Loosen sides of loaves from pan; remove from pan to wire rack. Cool completely.

1 Slice: Calories 120 (Calories from Fat 35); Fat 4g (Saturated 1g); Cholesterol 10mg; Sodium 180mg; Carbohydrate 19g (Dietary Fiber 0g); Protein 2g
% Daily Value: Vitamin A 0%; Vitamin C 0%; Calcium 8%; Iron 4%
Diet Exchanges: 1 Starch, 1 Fat

Pumpkin-Marmalade Bread (page 168) and Poppy Seed Bread

Gifts for Giving

Whether shared at mealtime or given as a gift, this bread is a real winner. Make your quick-bread gifts memorable by wrapping first in plastic wrap and next in a holiday dish towel. For a more special gift, place wrapped bread in a basket along with cookie cutter butter pats (page 196) and a fancy butter knife.

Spirited Eggnog Bread
with Rum Glaze

PREP: 20 MIN; BAKE: 1 HR 5 MIN; COOL: 1 HR
1 LOAF (24 SLICES)

2 1/4 cups all-purpose flour

3/4 cup sugar

1 cup eggnog or half-and-half

3 tablespoons vegetable oil

2 tablespoons rum or 1 1/2 tablespoons water plus
   1 teaspoon rum extract

3 1/2 teaspoons baking powder

1/2 teaspoon salt

1/4 teaspoon ground nutmeg

1 egg

1/2 cup chopped pistachio nuts or slivered
   almonds, if desired

Rum Glaze (right)

Heat oven to 350°. Grease bottom only of loaf pan,
8 1/2×4 1/2×2 1/2 inches or 9×5×3 inches. Mix all
ingredients except nuts and Rum Glaze in large bowl;
beat 30 seconds with spoon. Stir in nuts. Pour into pan.

Bake 55 to 65 minutes or until toothpick inserted in center comes out clean. Cool 10 minutes. Loosen sides of
loaf from pan; remove from pan to wire rack. Cool completely. Drizzle with Rum Glaze. Sprinkle with additional
ground nutmeg and chopped pistachio nuts.

1 Slice: Calories 100 (Calories from Fat 20); Fat 2g (Saturated 1g);
Cholesterol 15mg; Sodium 130mg; Carbohydrate 19g (Dietary Fiber
0g); Protein 2g
% Daily Value: Vitamin A 0%; Vitamin C 0%; Calcium 4%; Iron 4%
Diet Exchanges: 1 Starch, 1/2 Fat

Rum Glaze

1/2 cup powdered sugar

2 teaspoons eggnog or half-and-half

1 teaspoon rum or 1/2 teaspoon rum extract

Mix all ingredients until smooth and thin enough to
drizzle.

Gifts for Giving

Wrap the unglazed bread in plastic wrap, and place in a
holiday basket. Place the glaze in a decorative container
and the pistachios for the garnish in a separate holiday
container or decorative see-through bag. Include a premium container of ground nutmeg or for the avid cook,
buy whole nutmeg and enclose a small nutmeg grater.

Spirited Eggnog Bread with Rum Glaze

Merry Muffins

PREP: 15 MIN; BAKE: 25 MIN
12 MUFFINS

3/4 cup milk

1/2 cup vegetable oil

1 tablespoon grated orange peel, if desired

1 egg

2 cups all-purpose or whole wheat flour

1/2 cup sugar

3 teaspoons baking powder

1/2 teaspoon salt

1 cup fresh or frozen cranberries, cut in half, or dried cranberries

1/3 cup chopped pistachio nuts or pecans, if desired

Heat oven to 400°. Grease bottoms only of 12 medium muffin cups, 2 1/2 × 1 1/4 inches, or place paper baking cup in each muffin cup. Mix milk, oil, orange peel and egg in large bowl. Stir in flour, sugar, baking powder and salt all at once just until flour is moistened (batter will be lumpy). Fold in cranberries and nuts.

Divide batter evenly among muffin cups. Bake 20 to 25 minutes or until golden brown. Immediately remove from pan to wire rack. Serve warm if desired.

1 Muffin: Calories 205 (Calories from Fat 80); Fat 9g (Saturated 2g); Cholesterol 20mg; Sodium 240mg; Carbohydrate 28g (Dietary Fiber 1g); Protein 4g
% Daily Value: Vitamin A 2%; Vitamin C 0%; Calcium 10%; Iron 8%
Diet Exchanges: 1 Starch, 1 Fruit, 1 1/2 Fat

APRICOT-GINGER MUFFINS: Add 1/2 cup chopped dried apricots and 2 tablespoons chopped crystallized ginger. Drizzle these muffins with a powdered sugar glaze, and sprinkle with additional chopped crystallized ginger.

APPLE-CINNAMON MUFFINS: Stir in 1 medium apple, peeled and chopped, with the milk, and stir in 1/2 teaspoon ground cinnamon with the salt. Sprinkle brown sugar over batter in cups before baking if desired.

DATE-NUT MUFFINS: Stir in 1/2 cup chopped dates and 1/3 cup chopped nuts with the milk.

Holiday Hints

For very merry muffins:

• Dip tops of muffins into warm melted butter, then dip into coarse decorating sugar, granulated sugar, red or green sugar or holiday decors.

• Brush freshly baked muffins with honey, jelly, apple butter or maple syrup.

Gingerbread Muffins

PREP: 15 MIN; BAKE: 20 MIN

12 MUFFINS

1/4 cup packed brown sugar

1/2 cup molasses

1/3 cup milk

1/3 cup vegetable oil

1 egg

2 cups all-purpose flour

1 teaspoon baking powder

1 teaspoon ground ginger

1/2 teaspoon salt

1/2 teaspoon baking soda

1/2 teaspoon ground cinnamon

1/4 teaspoon ground allspice

Heat oven to 400°. Grease bottoms only of 12 medium muffin cups, 2 1/2 × 1 1/4 inches, or place paper baking cup in each muffin cup. Beat brown sugar, molasses, milk, oil and egg in large bowl, using spoon. Stir in remaining ingredients just until flour is moistened.

Divide batter evenly among muffin cups. Bake 18 to 20 minutes or until toothpick inserted in center comes out clean. Immediately remove from pan to wire rack. Serve warm if desired.

1 Muffin: Calories 190 (Calories from Fat 65); Fat 7g (Saturated 1g); Cholesterol 20mg; Sodium 210mg; Carbohydrate 30g (Dietary Fiber 1g); Protein 3g
% Daily Value: Vitamin A 0%; Vitamin C 0%; Calcium 6%; Iron 10%
Diet Exchanges: 1 Starch, 1 Fruit, 1 Fat

New Twist

For a festive holiday finish:

- Dip muffin tops into melted butter and then into a mixture of ground cinnamon and sugar.

- Drizzle tops with melted white baking chips.

- Slice muffins in half, and fill with vanilla pudding or ice cream. Top with caramel or lemon sauce, and sprinkle with ground cinnamon or nutmeg.

Apricot Jeweled Scones

PREP: 15 MIN; BAKE: 18 MIN
8 SCONES

1 3/4 cups all-purpose flour

1/4 cup sugar

2 teaspoons baking powder

1/4 teaspoon salt

1/3 cup butter or margarine

1/3 cup finely chopped dried apricots

1/3 cup white baking chips

1 egg

About 1/3 cup half-and-half

Heat oven to 400°. Mix flour, sugar, baking powder and salt in large bowl. Cut in butter, using pastry blender or crisscrossing 2 knives, until mixture looks like fine crumbs. Stir in apricots and baking chips. Stir in egg and just enough half-and-half so dough leaves side of bowl and forms a ball.

Turn dough onto lightly floured surface. Knead lightly 10 times. Pat or roll into 8-inch circle on ungreased cookie sheet. Cut into 8 wedges, but do not separate. Sprinkle with sugar if desired.

Bake 16 to 18 minutes or until golden brown. Carefully separate wedges; remove from cookie sheets to wire rack. Serve warm, if desired.

1 Scone: Calories 285 (Calories from Fat 115); Fat 13g (Saturated 8g); Cholesterol 55mg; Sodium 270mg; Carbohydrate 38g (Dietary Fiber 1g); Protein 5g
% Daily Value: Vitamin A 12%; Vitamin C 0%; Calcium 10%; Iron 10%
Diet Exchanges: 1 Starch, 1 1/2 Fruit, 2 1/2 Fat

Holiday Hints

Add a little holiday sparkle to your scones:

- Vary the "jewels" in your scones by using dried cranberries, dried cherries, raisins or fruitcake mix instead of the apricots.
- Add 1 tablespoon grated lemon or orange peel.

- Add 1/4 cup chopped pecans, pistachio nuts, almonds, walnuts or sunflower nuts.
- Stir in 1/4 cup chopped crystallized ginger.
- Brush tops of scones with melted butter and sprinkle with sliced almonds or your favorite chopped nuts before baking.

- Sprinkle scones before baking with coarse decorating sugar.
- Drizzle melted semisweet chocolate chips or white baking chips over baked scones.
- Top baked scones with jam or spreadable fruit.

New Twist

Slather your scones with a delightful topper, such as **Honey-Chestnut Spread**. To make this yummy spread, place 1/2 cup creamy honey spread and 1 can (10 ounces) whole chestnuts in water (not water chestnuts), drained, in a blender or food processor. Cover and blend on medium speed, stopping blender often to scrape sides, until smooth. Cover and store in refrigerator up to one week.

Apricot Jeweled Scones

Cherry Swirl Coffee Cake

PREP: 20 MIN; BAKE: 45 MIN
18 SERVINGS

1 1/2 cups sugar

1/2 cup butter or margarine, softened

1/2 cup shortening

1 1/2 teaspoons baking powder

1 teaspoon vanilla

1 teaspoon almond extract

4 eggs

3 cups all-purpose flour

1 can (21 ounces) cherry pie filling

Powdered Sugar Glaze (right)

Heat oven to 350°. Generously grease jelly roll pan, 15 1/2 × 10 1/2 × 1 inch. Beat sugar, butter, shortening, baking powder, vanilla, almond extract and eggs in large bowl with electric mixer on low speed, scraping bowl constantly. Beat on high speed 3 minutes, scraping bowl occasionally. Stir in flour.

Spread two-thirds of the batter in pan. Spread pie filling over batter. Drop remaining batter by tablespoonfuls onto pie filling.

Holiday Hints

Any can of fruit pie filling will work in this recipe; we particularly like the festive colors of cherry, raspberry and strawberry pie fillings. For a finishing touch, garnish with sliced almonds, fresh mint and frozen cranberries tossed in sugar.

Bake about 45 minutes or until toothpick inserted in center comes out clean. Drizzle Powdered Sugar Glaze over warm coffee cake. Serve warm or let stand until cool.

1 Serving: Calories 300 (Calories from Fat 110); Fat 12g (Saturated 5g); Cholesterol 60mg; Sodium 90mg; Carbohydrate 45g (Dietary Fiber 1g); Protein 4g
% Daily Value: Vitamin A 6%; Vitamin C 0%; Calcium 4%; Iron 6%
Diet Exchanges: 1 Starch, 2 Fruit, 2 Fat

Powdered Sugar Glaze

1 cup powdered sugar

1 to 2 tablespoons milk or water

Mix ingredients until smooth and thin enough to drizzle.

Lemon-Glazed Coffee Wreath

PREP: 25 MIN; BAKE: 50 MIN; COOL: 1 HR

12 SERVINGS

1/2 cup butter or margarine, softened

2 cups all-purpose flour

2 tablespoons cold water

1/2 cup butter or margarine

1 cup water

1/2 cup golden raisins, chopped dried apricots or chopped fruitcake mix

1 teaspoon vanilla or rum extract

3 eggs

Lemon Glaze (right)

Heat oven to 350°. Cut 1/2 cup butter into 1 cup of the flour, using pastry blender or crisscrossing 2 knives, until particles are size of small peas. Sprinkle 2 tablespoons cold water over flour mixture; mix with fork.

Gather dough into a ball. Shape into about 12-inch rope. Form rope into circle on ungreased cookie sheet. Press to form wreath shape, 11 1/2 inches in diameter with 4-inch-wide side and 3 1/2-inch hole in center.

Heat 1/2 cup butter, 1 cup water and the raisins to boiling over medium heat. Add remaining 1 cup flour and the vanilla. Stir constantly over low heat about 1 minute or until mixture forms a ball. Remove from heat. Add eggs; beat with spoon until smooth and glossy. Spread evenly over dough wreath to within 1/4 inch of edges.

Bake 45 to 50 minutes or until topping is crisp and brown (topping will shrink and fall, forming a custard-like top). Cool completely on cookie sheet. Remove from cookie sheet to wire rack. Drizzle with Lemon Glaze.

1 Serving: Calories 325 (Calories from Fat 170); Fat 19g (Saturated 11g); Cholesterol 100mg; Sodium 130mg; Carbohydrate 36g (Dietary Fiber 1g); Protein 4g
% Daily Value: Vitamin A 14%; Vitamin C 0%; Calcium 2%; Iron 6%
Diet Exchanges: 1 Starch, 1 1/2 Fruit, 3 1/2 Fat

Lemon Glaze

1 1/2 cups powdered sugar

2 tablespoons butter or margarine, softened

1/2 teaspoon vanilla

1 to 2 tablespoons lemon juice

Mix all ingredients until smooth and thin enough to drizzle.

New Twist

Everything tastes better with some chocolate! After patting dough into wreath shape, sprinkle with 1/2 cup semisweet chocolate and 1/4 cup chopped nuts to within 1/2 inch of edges. Add topping as directed. After baking, cool and sprinkle with powdered sugar.

Holiday Hints

Add a little holiday sparkle by decorating this coffee cake with sugared dried fruits. Toss dried fruits, such as coarsely cut apricot halves, cherries, raisins, cranberries and thin strips of fresh lemon peel, with granulated sugar until evenly coated. Fill center of wreath with fresh fruit.

Candy Cane Coffee Cake

PREP: 30 MIN; RISE: 1 HR; BAKE: 25 MIN
3 COFFEE CAKES (12 SERVINGS EACH)

2 packages regular or quick active dry yeast

1/2 cup warm water (105° to 115°)

1 1/4 cups buttermilk

2 eggs

5 1/2 to 6 cups bread flour or all-purpose flour

1/2 cup butter or margarine, softened

1/2 cup sugar

2 teaspoons baking powder

2 teaspoons salt

1 1/2 cups chopped dried apricots

1 1/2 cups chopped drained maraschino cherries

Powdered Sugar Glaze (page 176)

1 1/2 cups red cinnamon candies, if desired

Dissolve yeast in warm water in large bowl. Add buttermilk, eggs, 2 1/2 cups of the flour, the butter, sugar, baking powder and salt. Beat with electric mixer on low speed 30 seconds, scraping bowl constantly. Beat on medium speed 2 minutes, scraping bowl frequently. Stir in enough remaining flour to make dough easy to handle. (Dough should remain soft and sticky.)

Grease 3 cookie sheets. Turn dough onto lightly floured surface. Knead about 5 minutes or until smooth and elastic. Divide dough into 3 equal parts. Roll one part into rectangle, 15×9 inches. Place rectangle on cookie sheet.

Mix apricots and chopped cherries. Spread one-third of the apricot mixture in a strip about 2 1/2 inches wide lengthwise down center of rectangle. Make cuts in dough at 1/2-inch intervals on both 15-inch sides almost to filling. Fold strips over filling, overlapping and crossing in center. Carefully stretch dough until 22 inches long; curve one end to form top of cane. Repeat with remaining 2 parts of dough. Cover and let rise in warm place about 1 hour or until double. (Dough is ready if indentation remains when touched.)

Heat oven to 375°. Bake 20 to 25 minutes or until golden brown. Drizzle Powdered Sugar Glaze over warm coffee cakes. Decorate with cinnamon candies.

1 Serving: Calories 180 (Calories from Fat 65); Fat 7g (Saturated 1g); Cholesterol 20mg; Sodium 240mg; Carbohydrate 27g (Dietary Fiber 1g); Protein 3g
% Daily Value: Vitamin A 2%; Vitamin C 0%; Calcium 10%; Iron 6%
Diet Exchanges: 1 Starch, 1 Fruit, 1 Fat

Gifts for Giving

These festive fruit-filled coffee cakes would be perfect for placing—wrapped and ribboned—beneath someone's Christmas tree. For a festive touch, wrap in holiday cellophane found in party stores.

Candy Cane Coffee Cake

Saint Lucia Crown

PREP: 40 MIN; RISE: 2 1/4 HR; BAKE: 25 MIN; COOL: 1 HR
1 LARGE LOAF (32 SLICES)

1/16 to 1/8 teaspoon crushed saffron or 2 to 3
   drops yellow food color

1/2 cup warm milk (105° to 115°)

2 packages regular or quick active dry yeast

1/2 cup warm water (105° to 115°)

1/2 cup sugar

1 teaspoon salt

2 eggs, beaten

1/4 cup butter or margarine, softened

4 1/2 to 5 cups bread flour or all-purpose flour

1/2 cup chopped citron or lemon peel

1/4 cup chopped blanched almonds

1 tablespoon grated lemon peel

Powdered Sugar Glaze (page 176)

Green and red candied cherries, if desired

Stir saffron into warm milk. Dissolve yeast in warm water in large bowl. Stir in saffron-milk mixture, sugar, salt, eggs, butter and 2 1/2 cups of the flour. Beat with spoon until smooth. Stir in citron, almonds, lemon peel and enough remaining flour to make dough easy to handle.

Turn dough onto lightly floured surface. Knead about 10 minutes or until smooth and elastic. Place in greased bowl; turn greased side up. Cover and let rise in warm place about 1 1/2 hours or until double. (Dough is ready if indentation remains when touched.)

Grease 2 cookie sheets. Punch down dough. Cut off one-third of dough for top braid and reserve. Divide remaining dough into 3 equal parts; roll each part into rope, 25 inches long. Place ropes close together on cookie sheet. Braid ropes loosely; shape into circle and pinch ends to seal.

Divide reserved dough into 3 equal parts; roll each part into rope, 16 inches long. Place ropes close together on second cookie sheet. Braid ropes loosely; shape into circle and pinch ends to seal. Cover both braids and let rise in warm place about 45 minutes or until double.

Heat oven to 375°. Bake 20 to 25 minutes or until golden brown. Remove from cookie sheets to wire rack. Cool completely. Drizzle Powdered Sugar Glaze over both braids. Make holes for 5 candles in small braid. Place small braid on large braid. Garnish with cherries. Insert candles.

1 Slice: Calories 125 (Calories from Fat 25); Fat 3g (Saturated 1g); Cholesterol 15mg; Sodium 100mg; Carbohydrate 23g (Dietary Fiber 1g); Protein 3g
% Daily Value: Vitamin A 2%; Vitamin C 0%; Calcium 0%; Iron 6%
Diet Exchanges: 1 1/2 Starch

SAINT LUCIA BUNS: After punching down dough, cut dough into pieces about 2 1/2 inches in diameter. Roll each piece into 12-inch rope; form into tightly coiled S shape. Place a raisin in center of each coil. Place on greased cookie sheet. Brush tops lightly with softened butter or margarine. Cover and let rise in warm place about 45 minutes or until double. Bake about 15 minutes or until golden brown. About 1 1/2 dozen buns.

Holiday Hints

Saint Lucia Day is the Swedish holiday celebrated December 13. Saint Lucia, a beautiful maiden, wore a crown of candles to help light the way when she carried food to Christian martyrs hiding in caves from persecution. Since then, Saint Lucia Day is celebrated by having the oldest daughter be the first to rise and bring buns to all who are sleeping in the household.

Saint Lucia Crown

Raspberry and Cream Cheese Coffee Rounds

PREP: 25 MIN; RISE: 55 MIN; BAKE: 35 MIN; COOL: 20 MIN
2 COFFEE CAKES (6 SERVINGS EACH)

3 1/2 to 4 cups bread flour or all-purpose flour

1/3 cup sugar

1 teaspoon salt

1 package regular or quick active dry yeast

1/3 cup shortening

1/2 cup water

1/2 cup milk

1 egg

Cream Cheese Filling (right)

1 can (21 ounces) raspberry pie filling

1 egg white

1/2 cup sliced almonds

1/4 cup sugar

Grease 2 round pans, 9×1 1/2 inches. Mix 2 cups of the flour, 1/3 cup sugar, the salt and yeast in large bowl.

Heat shortening, water and milk over medium heat to 125° to 130° (shortening will not melt); stir into flour mixture. Add egg; beat with electric mixer on medium speed about 2 minutes or until smooth. Stir in enough of the remaining flour to make dough easy to handle.

Turn dough onto lightly floured surface. Knead 3 to 5 minutes or until smooth. Cover and let rest 10 minutes. Prepare Cream Cheese Filling.

Divide dough in half. Roll each half into 15-inch circle. Fold each circle into fourths; place each in pan. Unfold; press dough against bottom and side of each pan, allowing edge to hang over side. Spread half of the Cream Cheese Filling over dough in each pan; top each with half of the pie filling.

Make cuts around edge of dough at 1-inch intervals to within 1/2 inch of filling. Twist strips of dough once or twice and fold over filling. Beat egg white until foamy; brush over dough. Sprinkle each coffee cake with 1/4 cup of the almonds and 2 tablespoons sugar. (Coffee cakes can be covered and refrigerated up to 24 hours; rising time may be slightly longer.) Cover and let rise in warm place 45 minutes.

Heat oven to 375°. Bake 30 to 35 minutes or until golden brown. Cool 20 minutes. Cover and refrigerate any remaining coffee cake.

1 Serving: Calories 410 (Calories from Fat 145); Fat 16g (Saturated 6g); Cholesterol 55mg; Sodium 280mg; Carbohydrate 60g (Dietary Fiber 2g); Protein 8g
% Daily Value: Vitamin A 8%; Vitamin C 0%; Calcium 4%; Iron 14%
Diet Exchanges: 3 Starch, 1 Fruit, 2 1/2 Fat

Cream Cheese Filling

1 package (8 ounces) cream cheese, softened

1/4 cup sugar

3 tablespoons all-purpose flour

1 egg yolk

Mix all ingredients until smooth.

Holiday Hints

Fresh pineapple mint leaves make an especially festive garnish for this colorful coffe cake. Use kitchen scissors to cut the mint into holly leaf shapes.

Raspberry and Cream Cheese Coffee Rounds

Julekake

PREP: 25 MIN; RISE: 2 1/4 HR; BAKE: 40 MIN
1 LOAF (16 SLICES)

Because Julekake is one of our most requested recipes, we knew you'd love a version you could make in your bread machine.

1 package regular or quick active dry yeast

1/4 cup very warm water (120° to 130°)

3/4 cup very warm milk (120° to 130°)

1/2 cup sugar

2 tablespoons shortening

1/2 teaspoon salt

1/2 teaspoon ground cardamom

1 egg

1/2 cup raisins

1/3 cup fruitcake mix (mixed candied fruit)

3 1/4 to 3 3/4 cups bread flour or all-purpose flour

1 egg yolk

2 tablespoons water

Dissolve yeast in warm water in large bowl. Stir in warm milk, sugar, shortening, salt, cardamom, egg, raisins, fruit cake mix and 1 1/2 cups of the flour. Beat with spoon until smooth. Stir in enough remaining flour to make dough easy to handle.

Turn dough onto lightly floured surface. Knead about 5 minutes or until smooth and elastic. Place in greased bowl; turn greased side up. Cover and let rise in warm place about 1 1/2 hours or until double. (Dough is ready if indentation remains when touched.)

Grease round pan, 9 × 1 1/2 inches. Punch down dough. Shape into round loaf. Place in pan. Cover and let rise in warm place about 45 minutes or until double.

Heat oven to 350°. Beat egg yolk and 2 tablespoons water; brush over dough. Bake 30 to 40 minutes or until golden brown.

1 Slice: Calories 195 (Calories from Fat 45); Fat 5g (Saturated 3g); Cholesterol 30mg; Sodium 240mg; Carbohydrate 35g (Dietary Fiber 1g); Protein 4g
% Daily Value: Vitamin A 4%; Vitamin C 0%; Calcium 2%; Iron 10%
Diet Exchanges: 1 Starch, 1 Fruit, 1 Fat

Julekake Bread Machine Variation

1 egg plus enough water to equal 1 cup plus 2 tablespoons

1/2 teaspoon ground cardamom

1 teaspoon salt

1 tablespoon plus 1 teaspoon sugar

1/4 cup butter, softened*

3 cups bread flour

1 teaspoon bread machine yeast

1/3 cup raisins

1/3 cup fruitcake mix (mixed candied fruit)

Make this recipe with bread machines that use 3 cups flour.

Measure carefully, placing all ingredients except raisins and fruitcake mix in bread machine pan in the order recommended by the manufacturer. Add raisins and fruit cake mix at the raisin/nut signal or 5 to 10 minutes before last kneading cycle ends.

Select Basic/White cycle. Use Medium or Light crust color.

Do not use delay cycles. Remove baked bread from pan, and cool on wire rack.

*We do not recommend margarine for this recipe.

Julekake

Whole Wheat-Cranberry Bread

PREP: 15 MIN; BREAD MACHINE CYCLE: ABOUT 3 1/2 HR; COOL: 1 HR

1-Pound Recipe (8 slices)		1 1/2-Pound Recipe (12 slices)
		1 cup plus
3/4 cup	Water	2 tablespoons
2 tablespoons	Honey	1/4 cup
	Butter or margarine,	
1 tablespoon	softened	2 tablespoons
1 1/4 cups	Bread flour	2 cups
3/4 cup	Whole wheat flour	1 1/4 cups
1 teaspoon	Salt	1 1/2 teaspoons
1/4 teaspoon	Ground mace	3/4 teaspoon
1 1/4 teaspoons	Bread machine yeast	2 teaspoons
	Dried cranberries	
1/3 cup	or golden raisins	1/2 cup

Make 1 1/2-Pound Recipe with bread machines that use 3 cups flour, or make 1-Pound Recipe with bread machines that use 2 cups flour.

Measure carefully, placing all ingredients except cranberries in bread machine pan in the order recommended by the manufacturer. Add cranberries at the raisin/nut signal or 5 to 10 minutes before last kneading cycle ends.

Select Whole Wheat or Basic/White cycle. Use Medium or Light crust color.

Do not use delay cycles. Remove baked bread from pan, and cool on wire rack.

1 Slice: Calories 185 (Calories from Fat 25); Fat 3g (Saturated 1g); Cholesterol 5mg; Sodium 310mg; Carbohydrate 38g (Dietary Fiber 4g); Protein 5g
% Daily Value: Vitamin A 2%; Vitamin C 4%; Calcium 0%; Iron 10%
Diet Exchanges: 1 1/2 Starch, 1 Fruit

New Twist

You'll love making these flavorful butters. Prepare them to serve or to give with a loaf of bread. Be sure to store them in the refrigerator until ready to serve.

- **Cranberry-Orange Butter:** Mix 1/2 cup butter or margarine, softened, and 2 tablespoons cranberry-orange relish or sauce until blended.

- **Strawberry Butter:** Blend 1/2 cup butter or margarine, 1/2 cup sliced strawberries and 2 teaspoons grated orange peel in blender or food processor until smooth.

- **Pecan Butter:** Mix 1 cup butter or margarine, softened, 1/4 cup packed brown sugar and 1/2 cup chopped pecans until smooth.

- **Maple-Peanut Butter Spread:** Mix 1/2 cup butter or margarine, softened, 1/2 cup peanut butter and 1/4 cup maple-flavored syrup until smooth.

Whole Wheat-Cranberry Bread and Pecan Butter

Dinner Rolls

PREP: 30 MIN; RISE: 1 1/2 HR; BAKE: 15 MIN
15 ROLLS

Each year we receive countless requests for homemade dinner rolls. Perhaps it's the irresistible aroma of freshly baked bread or the endless pairing possibilities of these light-as-a-feather rolls. Whatever the reason, Christmas and bread baking are a match made in heaven during the holiday season.

3 1/2 to 3 3/4 cups bread flour or all-purpose flour

1/4 cup sugar

1/4 cup butter or margarine, softened

1 teaspoon salt

1 package regular or quick active dry yeast

1/2 cup very warm water (120° to 130°)

1/2 cup very warm milk (120° to 130°)

1 egg

Butter or margarine, melted, if desired

Mix 2 cups of the flour, the sugar, softened butter, salt and yeast in medium bowl. Add warm water, warm milk and egg. Beat with electric mixer on low speed 1 minute, scraping bowl frequently. Beat on medium speed 1 minute, scraping bowl frequently. Stir in enough remaining flour to make dough easy to handle.

Turn dough onto lightly floured surface. Knead about 5 minutes or until smooth and elastic. Place in greased bowl; turn greased side up. Cover and let rise in warm place about 1 hour or until double. (Dough is ready if indentation remains when touched.)

Grease rectangular pan, 13×9×2 inches. Punch down dough. Divide into 15 equal pieces. Shape each piece into a ball; place into pan. Cover and let rise in warm place about 30 minutes or until double.

Heat oven to 375°. Bake 12 to 15 minutes or until golden brown. Brush with melted butter. Serve warm or cool on wire rack.

1 Roll: Calories 135 (Calories from Fat 20); Fat 02g (Saturated 1g); Cholesterol 20mg; Sodium 170mg; Carbohydrate 26g (Dietary Fiber 1g); Protein 4g
% Daily Value: Vitamin A 2%; Vitamin C 0%; Calcium 0%; Iron 8%
Diet Exchanges: 1 1/2 Starch

Timesaving Tips

You can make this melt-in-your-mouth dinner roll recipe using the convenience of a bread machine. Follow this simple conversion:

- Decrease bread flour to 3 1/4 cups.

- Decrease softened butter to 2 tablespoons.

- Omit the milk, and increase water to 1 cup.

- Substitute 3 teaspoons bread machine yeast for the package of active dry yeast.

- Place all ingredients except melted butter in bread machine pan in the

order recommended by the manufacturer. Select Dough/Manual cycle. Do not use delay cycle. Follow above recipe for shaping, rising and baking.

Holiday Hints

Before baking, brush rolls with mixture of 1 egg white beaten with

1 tablespoon water; top with sprig of fresh Italian parsley and brush again

with egg white mixture.

Garlic Bread Wreath

PREP: 20 MIN; RISE: 3 HR; BAKE: 30 MIN
8 SERVINGS

1/4 cup shredded Parmesan cheese

1 loaf (1 pound) frozen white bread dough (from
3-pound package), thawed

1 tablespoon olive or vegetable oil

1 small clove garlic, finely chopped

Grease cookie sheet. Sprinkle 2 tablespoons of the cheese
over flat surface. Roll bread dough in cheese into 24-inch
rope. Place rope on cookie sheet and form into circle;
pinch ends to seal.

Make cuts in dough at about 1 1/2-inch intervals from
the outer edge of the circle, cutting two-thirds of the way
through, using kitchen scissors. Lift and turn every other
section of dough toward center of the circle. Cover and
let rise in warm place 2 to 3 hours or until double.
(Dough is ready if indentation remains when touched.)

Heat oven to 350°. Mix oil and garlic; brush over dough.
Sprinkle with remaining 2 tablespoons cheese. Bake 25
to 30 minutes or until golden brown.

1 Serving: Calories 170 (Calories from Fat 35); Fat 4g (Saturated
1g); Cholesterol 2mg; Sodium 350mg; Carbohydrate 28g (Dietary
Fiber 1g); Protein 6g
% Daily Value: Vitamin A 0%; Vitamin C 0%; Calcium 10%; Iron
10%
Diet Exchanges: 2 Starch

Holiday Hints

Fill the center of the wreath with a dish of:

- **Sun-Dried Tomato Butter:** Beat 1/4 cup butter, softened, with 2 tablespoons chopped, drained, oil-packed
  sun-dried tomatoes. Garnish with fresh dill weed.

- **Basil Butter:** Beat 1/4 cup butter, softened, with 2
  tablespoons chopped fresh basil leaves or 2 teaspoons
  dried basil leaves. Garnish with fresh basil.

- Olive oil, garnished with fresh rosemary sprigs.

Savory Onion Twist

PREP: 15 MIN; CHILL: 8 HR; RISE: 25 MIN; BAKE: 25 MIN
1 LOAF (16 SLICES)

Easy Refrigerator Dough (right)

1 cup shredded Swiss or mozzarella cheese
(4 ounces)

1/4 cup finely chopped red or green bell pepper

2 tablespoons finely chopped onion

2 tablespoons mayonnaise or salad dressing

1 tablespoon chopped fresh or 1 teaspoon dried
cilantro

1/2 teaspoon ground cumin

Prepare Easy Refrigerator Dough. Divide dough in half;
cover and refrigerate half of dough for another use.

Grease large cookie sheet. Roll remaining half of dough
on lightly floured surface into rectangle, 15 × 10 inches.
Mix 1/2 cup of the cheese and the remaining ingredients. Spread cheese mixture over dough to within 1/2
inch of edges. Roll up dough, beginning at 15-inch side;
pinch edge of dough into roll to seal.

Cut roll lengthwise in half. Place halves, filling sides up
and side by side, on cookie sheet; twist together gently
and loosely. Pinch edges to fasten. Cover and let rise in
warm place about 25 minutes or until double. (Dough is
ready if indentation remains when touched.)

Heat oven to 375°. Bake 20 to 25 minutes or until gold-
en brown. Immediately sprinkle with 1/2 cup remaining
cheese. Serve warm.

1 Slice: Calories 185 (Calories from Fat 70); Fat 8g (Saturated 3g);
Cholesterol 20mg; Sodium 160mg; Carbohydrate 24g (Dietary Fiber
1g); Protein 5g
% Daily Value: Vitamin A 2%; Vitamin C 4%; Calcium 6%; Iron 6%
Diet Exchanges: 1 1/2 Starch, 1 1/2 Fat

Easy Refrigerator Dough

1 package regular or quick active dry yeast

1 1/2 cups very warm water (120° to 130°)

1 cup unseasoned lukewarm mashed potatoes

2/3 cup sugar

2/3 cup shortening

1 1/2 teaspoons salt

2 eggs

6 to 7 cups bread flour or all-purpose flour

Dissolve yeast in warm water in large bowl. Stir in potatoes, sugar, shortening, salt, eggs and 3 cups of the flour.
Beat with spoon until smooth. Stir in enough remaining
flour to make dough easy to handle. Turn dough onto
lightly floured surface. Knead about 5 minutes or until
smooth and elastic. Place in greased bowl; turn greased
side up. Cover bowl tightly; refrigerate at least 8 hours
but no longer than 5 days. Punch down dough before
using.

Holiday Hints

We think you'll love this twist so much you'll want to
make another one right away! If you prefer, shape the
second half of dough into 24 rolls, and place on greased
cookie sheet. Cover and let rise in warm place about 1
hour or until double. Bake at 400° for about 15 minutes
or until golden brown.

Savory Onion Twist

Festive Focaccia

PREP: 25 MIN; RISE: 1 HR 50 MIN; BAKE: 15 MIN
2 FOCACCIAS (12 SLICES EACH)

2 1/2 to 3 cups bread flour or all-purpose flour

2 teaspoons sugar

1/4 teaspoon salt

1 package regular or quick active dry yeast

1/4 cup olive or vegetable oil

1 cup very warm water (120° to 130°)

2 tablespoons olive or vegetable oil

2 medium red bell peppers, cut into 1/4-inch strips

2 small onions, sliced

1 to 2 tablespoons olive or vegetable oil

2 tablespoons chopped fresh herb leaves (such as basil, oregano or rosemary)

2 tablespoons shredded Parmesan cheese

Mix 1 cup of the flour, the sugar, salt and yeast in large bowl. Add 1/4 cup oil and the warm water. Beat with electric mixer on medium speed 3 minutes, scraping bowl occasionally. Stir in enough remaining flour until dough is soft and leaves side of bowl.

Turn dough onto lightly floured surface. Knead 5 to 10 minutes or until dough is smooth and elastic. Place in greased bowl; turn greased side up. Cover and let rise in warm place 1 to 1 1/2 hours or until double. (Dough is ready if indentation remains when touched.)

Heat oven to 425°. Grease 2 cookie sheets. Punch down dough. Divide in half. Shape each half into flattened 12-inch round on cookie sheet. Cover and let rise in warm place 20 minutes.

Meanwhile, heat 2 tablespoons oil in 10-inch skillet over medium heat. Cook bell peppers and onions in oil, stirring occasionally, until tender.

Prick centers of focaccias and 1 inch in from edges thoroughly with fork. Brush with 1 to 2 tablespoons oil. Spread bell pepper mixture over focaccias. Sprinkle each with 1 tablespoon herb leaves and cheese. Bake 12 to 15 minutes or until golden brown. Serve warm.

1 Slice: Calories 80 (Calories from Fat 25); Fat 3g (Saturated 0g); Cholesterol 0mg; Sodium 35mg; Carbohydrate 12g (Dietary Fiber 1g); Protein 2g
% Daily Value: Vitamin A 6%; Vitamin C 16%; Calcium 0%; Iron 4%
Diet Exchanges: 1 Starch

Timesaving Tips

If you're in a pinch, why not use frozen bread dough for this recipe? Just thaw the dough and follow directions above.

Festive Focaccia

Cheesy Roasted Red Pepper Bread

PREP: 20 MIN; BAKE: 20 MIN
12 SLICES

1 loaf (1 pound) French bread

1 cup shredded mozzarella cheese (4 ounces)

1/2 cup mayonnaise or salad dressing

1/4 cup finely chopped roasted red bell peppers
(from 7-ounce jar), well drained

1 tablespoon chopped fresh cilantro, if desired

1/2 teaspoon ground cumin

1 small onion, finely chopped (1/4 cup)

Heat oven to 400°. Cut bread loaf horizontally into 3 layers. Mix remaining ingredients.

Spread half of the cheese mixture over bottom layer. Top with second layer; spread with remaining cheese mixture. Top with third layer; press firmly.

Wrap loaf securely in heavy-duty aluminum foil. Bake 15 to 20 minutes or until hot. Serve warm.

1 Slice: Calories 190 (Calories from Fat 90); Fat 10g (Saturated 2g); Cholesterol 10mg; Sodium 320mg; Carbohydrate 20g (Dietary Fiber 1g); Protein 6g
% Daily Value: Vitamin A 2%; Vitamin C 4%; Calcium 10%; Iron 6%
Diet Exchanges: 1 Starch, 1 Vegetable, 2 Fat

Holiday Hints

This recipe is as easy as it is delicious!

• You can substitute finely chopped fresh red bell pepper for the roasted red bell peppers in this recipe.

• Preparing your holiday dinner on the grill? You can heat this bread on the grill over medium heat for 15 to 20 minutes.

Cheesy Roasted Red Pepper Bread

Pesto Biscuits

PREP: 15 MIN; BAKE: 12 MIN
10 BISCUITS

2 cups all-purpose flour

3 teaspoons baking powder

1/2 teaspoon salt

1/3 cup shortening

1/4 cup pesto

About 1/2 cup milk

Finely shredded Parmesan cheese, if desired

Red or green hot pepper (jalapeño) jelly, if desired

Heat oven to 450°. Mix flour, baking powder and salt in large bowl. Cut in shortening and pesto, using pastry blender or crisscrossing 2 knives, until mixture looks like fine crumbs. Stir in just enough milk so dough leaves side of bowl and forms a ball.

Turn dough onto lightly floured surface. Knead lightly 10 times. Roll or pat 1/2 inch thick. Cut with floured 2 1/2-inch cookie or biscuit cutter. Place about 1 inch apart on ungreased cookie sheet. Sprinkle with cheese.

Bake 10 to 12 minutes or until golden brown. Immediately remove from cookie sheet. Serve warm with pepper jelly.

1 Biscuit: Calories 235 (Calories from Fat 100); Fat 11g (Saturated 3g); Cholesterol 0mg; Sodium 320mg; Carbohydrate 30g (Dietary Fiber 1g); Protein 5g
% Daily Value: Vitamin A 0%; Vitamin C 0%; Calcium 12%; Iron 10%
Diet Exchanges: 2 Starch, 2 Fat

Holiday Hints

It's easy to get even your butter into the act of being festive. Slice chilled butter 1/4 inch thick and cut slices with mini-cookie cutters. Use cutters with open tops so you can push the butter through. Simple shapes work best (such as stars, hearts, etc.). Place butter on waxed paper; refrigerate until ready to serve. Butter scraps can be softened and reshaped or used in baking.

To make large butter pats, place a 3-inch cookie cutter on a plate; fill with softened butter or margarine, spreading even with top of cutter. To unmold, run a knife dipped in hot water along the inside of cookie cutter, and remove the cutter.

Refrigerate butter shapes until ready to serve, or wrap in colorful plastic wrap, tie with bow and refrigerate until ready to give as a gift with homemade breads.

Pesto Biscuits

Savory Mini-Scones

PREP: 20 MIN; BAKE: 17 MIN
24 SCONES

2 1/2 cups all-purpose flour

1/2 cup shredded Cheddar cheese (2 ounces)

3 medium green onions, chopped (3 tablespoons)

3 tablespoons chopped fresh cilantro or parsley

2 teaspoons baking powder

3/4 teaspoon baking soda

1/2 teaspoon salt

1/4 teaspoon ground red pepper (cayenne)

1/4 cup butter or margarine

1/2 cup apple juice

1/3 cup plain fat-free yogurt

1 egg

2 tablespoons plain fat-free yogurt

Heat oven to 400°. Spray 2 cookie sheets with cooking spray. Mix flour, cheese, onions, cilantro, baking powder, baking soda, salt and red pepper in large bowl. Cut in butter, using pastry blender or crisscrossing 2 knives, until mixture looks like fine crumbs. Mix apple juice, 1/3 cup yogurt and the egg; stir into flour mixture until dough leaves side of bowl.

Turn dough onto lightly floured surface. Knead about 1 minute or until smooth. Divide dough in half. Roll each half into 9-inch circle that is 1/4 inch thick. Place each circle on cookie sheet. Cut each circle into 12 wedges with floured knife, but do not separate. Brush 1 tablespoon yogurt over each circle.

Bake 15 to 17 minutes or until golden brown. Carefully separate wedges; remove from cookie sheets to wire rack. Serve warm.

1 Scone: Calories 85 (Calories from Fat 25); Fat 3g (Saturated 2g); Cholesterol 10mg; Sodium 160mg; Carbohydrate 11g (Dietary Fiber 0g); Protein 3g
% Daily Value: Vitamin A 2%; Vitamin C 0%; Calcium 4%; Iron 4%
Diet Exchanges: 1 Starch

Holiday Hints

Surrounded with smoked or poached fish, smoked turkey, chicken or pastrami, these scones are a perfect addition to any party platter.

Gifts for Giving

Tuck savory scones and a jar of Apple-Pepper Jelly (page 294) into a decorative basket or box. You've just created the perfect gift for the person who appreciates a not-so-sweet treat!

Easy Puff Twists

PREP: 25 MIN; BAKE: 8 MIN PER SHEET
ABOUT 48 TWISTS

2/3 cup grated Parmesan cheese

1 tablespoon paprika

1 package (17 1/4 ounces) frozen puff pastry,
thawed

1 egg, slightly beaten

Heat oven to 425°. Cover 2 cookie sheets with cooking parchment paper or heavy brown paper. Mix cheese and paprika. Roll 1 sheet of pastry into rectangle, 12 × 10 inches, on lightly floured surface with floured cloth-covered rolling pin.

Brush egg over pastry. Sprinkle with 3 tablespoons of the cheese mixture; press gently into pastry. Turn pastry over. Brush egg over other side of pastry. Sprinkle with 3 tablespoons of the cheese mixture; press gently into pastry. Fold pastry lengthwise in half.

Cut pastry crosswise into 1/2-inch strips. Unfold strips; roll each end in opposite directions to twist. Place twists on cookie sheet. Bake 7 to 8 minutes or until puffed and golden brown. Remove from cookie sheet to wire rack. Repeat with remaining sheet of pastry, egg and cheese mixture. Serve warm, if desired.

1 Twist: Calories 60 (Calories from Fat 35); Fat 4g (Saturated 2g); Cholesterol 15mg; Sodium 45mg; Carbohydrate 5g (Dietary Fiber 0g); Protein 1g
% Daily Value: Vitamin A 0%; Vitamin C 0%; Calcium 2%; Iron 2%
Diet Exchanges: 1/2 Starch, 1/2 Fat

New Twist

These easy breadsticks are welcome additions to any bread basket—the crisp-tender morsels will melt in your mouth!

- For a peppery twist, mix 2 teaspoons cracked black pepper or lemon pepper seasoning with the Parmesan cheese mixture.

- For an appetizer-size bread, cut twists in half before baking.

Popovers

PREP: 15 MIN; BAKE: 45 MIN
6 TO 8 POPOVERS

2 eggs

1 cup all-purpose flour

1 cup milk

1/2 teaspoon salt

Honey-Walnut Cream Cheese (right)

Heat oven to 450°. Generously grease 6-cup popover pan, six 6-ounce custard cups or 8 medium muffin cups, 2 1/2 × 1 1/4 inches.

Beat eggs slightly in medium bowl. Stir in flour, milk and salt with fork or wire whisk just until smooth (do not overbeat). Fill popover pan or custard cups half full, muffin cups three-fourths full. Bake 25 minutes.

Reduce oven temperature to 350°. Bake 15 to 20 minutes longer or until deep golden brown. Immediately remove from pan. Serve warm with Honey-Walnut Cream Cheese.

1 Popover: Calories 180 (Calories from Fat 70); Fat 8g (Saturated 4g); Cholesterol 90mg; Sodium 280mg; Carbohydrate 21g (Dietary Fiber 1g); Protein 7g
% Daily Value: Vitamin A 8%; Vitamin C 0%; Calcium 6%; Iron 8%
Diet Exchanges: 1 1/2 Starch, 1 1/2 Fat

LEMON-POPPY SEED POPOVERS: Add 1 tablespoon poppy seed and 1 teaspoon grated lemon peel to batter.

CINNAMON-NUT POPOVERS: Add 1/2 teaspoon ground cinnamon and 1/4 cup finely chopped nuts to batter.

Honey-Walnut Cream Cheese

1 package (3 ounces) cream cheese, softened

1 tablespoon finely chopped walnuts, toasted (page 31), if desired

2 teaspoons honey

Beat all ingredients with spoon until blended.

Timesaving Tips

Do you love popovers but don't feel you have enough time to make them? You may like to make a batch when you do have time and freeze them! Pierce each freshly baked popover with the point of a knife to let the steam out. Cool them on a wire rack, wrap tightly and freeze.

Popovers with Honey-Walnut Cream Cheese

Ginger Cookie Cut-Outs (page 220, variation of Gingersnaps), Truffles (page 243) and Peppermint Bark (page 234)

CHAPTER 6

Sweet Shop Favorites

Nothing compares to a busy kitchen at Christmastime: fresh fudge begging to be tasted, while sugar cookie cut-outs await sprinkles of brightly-colored sugars.

Melt-in-Your-Mouth Sugar Cookies

PREP: 25 MIN; CHILL: 2 HR; BAKE: 8 MIN PER SHEET; COOL: 30 MIN
ABOUT 5 DOZEN COOKIES

1 1/2 cups powdered sugar

1 cup butter or margarine, softened

1 teaspoon vanilla

1/2 teaspoon almond extract

1 egg

2 1/2 cups all-purpose flour

1 teaspoon baking soda

1 teaspoon cream of tartar

Creamy Decorator's Frosting, Decorator's Glaze or
    Royal Icing (right)

Beat powdered sugar, butter, vanilla, almond extract and
egg in large bowl with electric mixer on medium speed,
or mix with spoon. Stir in flour, baking soda and cream
of tartar. Cover and refrigerate at least 2 hours.

Heat oven to 375°. Lightly grease cookie sheet. Divide
dough in half. Roll each half 1/4 inch thick on lightly
floured surface. Cut into desired shapes with 2 1/2-inch
cookie cutters. Place about 2 inches apart on cookie
sheet.

Bake 7 to 8 minutes or until edges are light brown.
Remove from cookie sheet to wire rack; cool completely.
Frost with Creamy Decorator's Frosting; decorate as
desired (see Holiday Hints, page 206).

1 Cookie: Calories 65 (Calories from Fat 25); Fat 3g (Saturated 2g);
Cholesterol 10mg; Sodium 35mg; Carbohydrate 8g (Dietary Fiber
0g); Protein 1g
% Daily Value: Vitamin A 2%; Vitamin C 0%; Calcium 0%; Iron 0%
Diet Exchanges: 1/2 Starch, 1/2 Fat

Creamy Decorator's Frosting

1 cup powdered sugar

1/2 teaspoon vanilla

1 tablespoon water or 1 to 2 tablespoons milk

Few drops of food color, if desired

Mix all ingredients in small bowl with spoon until
smooth and spreadable.

Decorator's Glaze

2 cups powdered sugar

2 tablespoons water

2 tablespoons light corn syrup

1/2 teaspoon almond extract

Beat all ingredients in small bowl with electric mixer on
low speed until smooth.

Royal Icing

1 package (16 ounces) powdered sugar (4 1/2 cups)

1/3 cup warm water (105° to 115°)

3 tablespoons meringue powder

1 teaspoon vanilla or almond extract

1/2 teaspoon cream of tartar

Food colors, if desired

Beat all ingredients in large bowl with electric mixer on
low speed until mixed. Beat on high speed 7 to 10 minutes or until very stiff. Divide and tint with food colors.

Melt-in-Your-Mouth Sugar Cookies

Holiday Hints

- Creamy Decorator's Frosting (page 204) is so versatile, it makes cookie decorating a snap. To make a thinner frosting or glaze, add more milk. If you want a colored frosting, stir in liquid food color, 1 drop at a time, until frosting is desired color. If you desire an intense, vivid frosting, use paste food color (too much liquid color will break down the frosting, causing it to separate and curdle).

- Decorator's Glaze (page 204) adds a smooth and glossy sheen to your holiday cookies. Thin the glaze with a little water and drizzle or pour over cookies for a fast and shiny finish. Feel free to use vanilla instead of the almond extract, but almond extract will make for a whiter glaze.

- Royal Icing (page 204) is a stiff decorator icing and makes very crisp lines. When decorating cookies, first pipe a thin border of Royal Icing around the outside edge and let dry. Then fill in the cookies with thinned Royal Icing or frosting, using a small metal spatula or medium-size paintbrush. The icing will not drip over the edges, and you'll have cookies that look professionally decorated.

New Twist

If you want to express your artistic abilities, try painting, marbling or flocking cookies. Paint cookies with Egg Yolk Paint (below) before baking, or paint cookies with Food Color Paint or Milk Paint (right) before or after baking, using fine-tip paintbrushes.

Egg Yolk Paint: Stir together 1 egg yolk and 1/4 teaspoon water. Divide mixture among several small custard cups. Tint with food color to desired brightness (Egg Yolk Paint creates opaque, bright colors). Paint on cookie dough before baking. If paint thickens while standing, add a few drops of water. For food-safety reasons, use Egg Yolk Paint only on cookie dough that will be baked; do not paint on cookies that have already been baked.

Food Color Paint: Stir together small amounts of water and food color. Paint on cookie dough before baking, or use to paint designs on frosted cookies that are set.

Milk Paint: Stir together small amounts of evaporated milk and food color. Paint on cookie dough before baking or on frosted cookies that are set.

Marbling: Using a fine-tip brush, paint a different color of Milk Paint or Food Color Paint on *freshly* iced, glazed or frosted cookies. Or drizzle or pipe on frosting, or squeeze on decorating gels sold in tubes at supermarkets. (Do not allow glaze, frosting or icing to dry or harden before marbling, or this technique won't work.) Use a brush or toothpick to swirl the colors or create marbleized patterns. Let paint or gel dry completely before storing cookies.

Flocking: Pipe or drizzle a design on completely dried and hardened glazed or frosted cookie. Sprinkle colored sugar over design while design is still fresh (do not allow design to dry or harden before flocking, or this technique won't work). Shake off any excess sugar. Or instead of adding a design, you can flock the entire surface of a freshly glazed or frosted cookie.

Sensational Shortbread Cookies

PREP: 20 MIN; BAKE: 12 MIN PER SHEET; COOL: 30 MIN
ABOUT 2 DOZEN COOKIES

3/4 cup butter or margarine, softened

1/4 cup sugar

2 cups all-purpose flour

1/2 teaspoon almond extract, if desired

Heat oven to 350°. Beat butter and sugar in large bowl with electric mixer on medium speed, or mix with spoon. Stir in flour and almond extract. (If dough is crumbly, mix in additional 1 to 2 tablespoons butter or margarine, softened.)

Roll dough 1/2 inch thick on lightly floured surface. Cut into about 1-inch shapes with knife or cookie cutters. Place about 1 inch apart on ungreased cookie sheet.

Bake 10 to 12 minutes or until set. Remove from cookie sheet to wire rack; cool completely.

1 Cookie: Calories 100 (Calories from Fat 55); Fat 6g (Saturated 4g); Cholesterol 15mg; Sodium 40mg; Carbohydrate 6g (Dietary Fiber 0g); Protein 1g
% Daily Value: Vitamin A 4%; Vitamin C 0%; Calcium 0%; Iron 2%
Diet Exchanges: 1/2 Starch, 1 Fat

New Twist

Ready for knockout new bright ideas for shortbread? Try Shortbread Buttons, Ornaments or Trees, and your cookies will get oohs and aahs!

- **Shortbread Buttons:** Tint cookie dough with food color (use paste food color for the brightest colors). Roll dough 1/4 inch thick; cut with 1 1/2-inch round cookie cutter. Make button holes with toothpick or end of straw. Bake as directed. About 3 dozen cookies.

- **Shortbread Ornaments:** Prepare dough as directed. Divide into 3 equal parts. Tint each part dough with food colors to make bright red, green and purple. Roll dough between sheets of waxed paper to 1/4-inch thickness; cut with 3-inch round biscuit cutter. Cut dough rounds with knife or pastry wheel

to form 1/4-inch strips. Combine different colors of dough strips to form striped round ornaments. Pinch small pea-size amount of dough; place on ornament to form top. Punch hole near top with end of plastic straw to hang ornament. Bake as directed. Decorate with decorating gels if desired. About 2 dozen cookies.

- **Shortbread Trees:** Prepare dough as directed. Divide into 6 equal parts. Mix 2 parts dough, 2 tablespoons chopped pistachio nuts and enough green food color to tint dough a light green. Mix another 2 parts dough and enough green food color to tint dough a medium green. Mix remaining 2 parts dough and enough green food color to tint dough a deep green.

Pat light green dough into 9 × 2-inch rectangle, 3/4 inch thick, on plastic wrap. Pat medium green dough into 9 × 1 3/4-inch rectangle, 1/2 inch thick; place on top of light green dough. Pat deep green dough into 9 × 3/4-inch roll, 1/2 inch thick place on top of medium green dough. Shape dough into triangle so that it looks like a tree shape (layers need not be perfect). Wrap dough in plastic wrap and refrigerate about 2 hours or until firm. Cut dough into 1/4-inch slices. Place about 1 inch apart on ungreased cookie sheet. Bake 10 to 12 minutes or until set. Cool on cookie sheet 1 minute before removing to wire rack. About 2 dozen cookies.

Shortbread Buttons, Shortbread Ornaments and Shortbread Trees (variations of Sensational Shortbread Cookies)

TINTING TIPS AND COLORING CUES

If you like pastel colors for cookie dough, tint using traditional food colors. If you want to make brightly colored doughs, you'll get the best results with paste food colors. Paste food colors are available in craft and specialty kitchen stores. To color the doughs for Shortbread Ornaments, Shortbread Trees and Shortbread Buttons, we used paste food colors, kneading the color into the dough in a 1-quart resealable bag. This is an activity kids love!

New Twist

Shortbread is so simple and yet so scrumptious! With a little imagination, you can turn these melt-in-your-mouth cookies into decorated delights.

- Dip edges of shortbread cookies into melted chocolate and then into chopped pistachio nuts.

- Drizzle tops of shortbread cookies with melted semisweet chocolate chips or white baking chips.

- Roll or pat the dough into two 4-inch circles, 1/2 inch thick. Scallop the edges using your fingers or a small spoon. Decorate with whole nuts and melted white baking chips or sprinkle lightly with cocoa in desired design.

- For itty-bitty shortbread bites, cut the rolled dough with canapé or 3/4-inch cookie cutters or cut into 1/2-inch squares. These mini-cookies will need to bake only about 10 minutes, and they are perfect for those who want a little nibble of each cookie on the holiday platter. Top shortbread bites with Creamy Decorator's Frosting (page 204) and dried cranberries or chocolate-covered coffee beans.

- For shortbread cookies with a textured top, use a meat mallet to lightly pound the rolled dough.

Holiday Spritz

PREP: 25 MIN; BAKE: 8 MIN PER SHEET; COOL: 30 MIN
ABOUT 5 DOZEN COOKIES

1 cup butter or margarine, softened

1/2 cup sugar

1 egg

2 1/2 cups all-purpose flour

1/4 teaspoon salt

1/4 teaspoon almond extract or vanilla

Few drops of food color, if desired

Heat oven to 400°. Beat butter, sugar and egg in large bowl with electric mixer on medium speed, or mix with spoon. Stir in remaining ingredients.

Place dough in cookie press. Form desired shapes on ungreased cookie sheet.

Bake 5 to 8 minutes or until set but not brown. Immediately remove from cookie sheet to wire rack; cool completely.

1 Cookie: Calories 50 (Calories from Fat 25); Fat 3g (Saturated 2g); Cholesterol 10mg; Sodium 30mg; Carbohydrate 5g (Dietary Fiber 0g); Protein 1g
% Daily Value: Vitamin A 2%; Vitamin C 0%; Calcium 0%; Iron 0%
Diet Exchanges: 1/2 Starch

CHOCOLATE SPRITZ: Stir 2 ounces unsweetened baking chocolate, melted and cooled, into butter-sugar mixture. Omit food color.

RUM BUTTER SPRITZ: Substitute rum extract for the almond extract. Tint dough with food colors. After baking, spread cooled cookies with **Butter Rum Glaze**: Melt 1/4 cup butter or margarine in 1-quart saucepan; remove from heat. Stir in 1 cup powdered sugar and 1 teaspoon rum extract. Stir in 1 to 2 tablespoons hot water until glaze is spreadable. Tint glaze with food color to match cookies.

SPICY SPRITZ: Stir in 1 teaspoon ground cinnamon, 1/2 teaspoon ground nutmeg and 1/4 teaspoon ground allspice with the flour.

Holiday Hints

Before baking spruce up your Spritz with:

• Currants, raisins, small candies, chopped nuts, slices of candied fruits or candied fruit peels arranged in festive patterns.

After baking decorate with:

• Edible glitter, colored sugar, nonpareils, red cinnamon candies or finely chopped nuts. A drop of corn syrup will hold the decorations in place nicely.

Holiday Spritz (Chocolate, Rum Butter and Spicy—variations)

Snowballs

PREP: 25 MIN; BAKE: 9 MIN PER SHEET; COOL: 30 MIN
ABOUT 4 DOZEN COOKIES

1 cup butter or margarine, softened

1/2 cup powdered sugar

1 teaspoon vanilla

2 1/4 cups all-purpose flour

1/4 teaspoon salt

3/4 cup finely chopped nuts

Powdered sugar

Heat oven to 400°. Beat butter, 1/2 cup powdered sugar and the vanilla in large bowl with electric mixer on medium speed, or mix with spoon. Stir in flour and salt. Stir in nuts.

Shape dough into 1-inch balls. Place about 2 inches apart on ungreased cookie sheet.

Bake 8 to 9 minutes or until set but not brown. Immediately remove from cookie sheet; roll in powdered sugar. Cool completely on wire rack. Roll in powdered sugar again.

1 Cookie: Calories 75 (Calories from Fat 45); Fat 5g (Saturated 2g); Cholesterol 10mg; Sodium 40mg; Carbohydrate 7g (Dietary Fiber 0g); Protein 1g
% Daily Value: Vitamin A 2%; Vitamin C 0%; Calcium 0%; Iron 2%
Diet Exchanges: 1/2 Starch, 1 Fat

New Twist

This is the cookie of many names! Whether you call them Snowballs, Russian Tea Cakes, Swedish Tea Cakes, Mexican Wedding Cakes or Butterballs, these rich and buttery cookies have become a holiday favorite. Try these flavorful variations.

Lemon Snowballs: Substitute lemon extract for the vanilla. For an extra lemon punch, add 1 teaspoon grated lemon peel. Crush 1/2 cup lemon drops in food processor or blender. Stir in 1/4 cup of the crushed lemon drops with the flour; reserve remaining candy. Bake as directed. Immediately roll baked cookies in powdered sugar; wait 10 minutes, then roll in reserved crushed lemon drops. Reroll, if desired.

Peppermint Snowballs: Crush 3/4 cup hard peppermint candies in food processor or blender. Stir in 1/4 cup of the crushed candies with the flour; reserve remaining candy. Bake as directed. Immediately roll baked cookies in powdered sugar; wait 10 minutes, then roll in reserved crushed candy. Reroll, if desired.

Snowballs (Lemon and Peppermint—variations)

Almond Bonbons

PREP: 25 MIN; BAKE: 12 MIN PER SHEET; COOL: 30 MIN
ABOUT 3 DOZEN COOKIES

1 1/2 cups all-purpose flour

1/2 cup butter or margarine, softened

1/3 cup powdered sugar

2 tablespoons milk

1/2 teaspoon vanilla

1/2 package (7- or 8-ounce size) almond paste

Almond Glaze (right)

Coarse sugar crystals (decorating sugar), if desired

Heat oven to 375°. Beat flour, butter, powdered sugar, milk and vanilla in large bowl with electric mixer on medium speed, or mix with spoon. Cut almond paste into 1/2-inch slices; cut each slice into fourths.

Shape 1-inch ball of dough around each piece of almond paste. Gently roll to form ball. Place about 1 inch apart on ungreased cookie sheet.

Bake 10 to 12 minutes or until set and bottom is golden brown. Remove from cookie sheet to wire rack; cool completely. Dip tops of cookies into Almond Glaze; sprinkle with sugar crystals.

1 Cookie: Calories 70 (Calories from Fat 25); Fat 3g (Saturated 2g); Cholesterol 5mg; Sodium 20mg; Carbohydrate 10g (Dietary Fiber 0g); Protein 1g
% Daily Value: Vitamin A 2%; Vitamin C 0%; Calcium 0%; Iron 2%
Diet Exchanges: 1/2 Starch, 1/2 Fat

Almond Glaze

1 cup powdered sugar

1/2 teaspoon almond extract

4 to 5 teaspoons milk

Mix all ingredients until smooth.

New Twist

For a flavorful twist, instead of almond paste wrap the dough around:

• Candied cherries for Cherry Bonbons.

• Dried apricots for Apricot Bonbons.

• Dates for Date Bonbons.

• Malted milk balls for Malted Bonbons.

• Hazelnuts or macadamia nuts for Hazelnut Bonbons.

Holiday Hints

Add a winter wonderland touch by tinting the glaze with a few drops of food colors in pastel shades. When set, drizzle with additional white glaze. For gifts, pack small cookies in mini paper baking cups or fluted bonbon cups.

Almond Bonbons

Minty Middle Treasures

PREP: 25 MIN; BAKE: 10 MIN PER SHEET; COOL: 30 MIN
ABOUT 2 DOZEN COOKIES

1/2 cup granulated sugar

1/4 cup packed brown sugar

1/4 cup shortening

1/4 cup butter or margarine, softened

1/2 teaspoon vanilla

1 egg

1 2/3 cups all-purpose flour

1/2 teaspoon baking soda

1/4 teaspoon salt

About 2 dozen foil-wrapped rectangular chocolate
   mints, unwrapped

Almond Frosting (right)

Candy sprinkles

Heat oven to 400°. Beat sugars, shortening, butter, vanilla and egg in large bowl with electric mixer on medium
speed, or mix with spoon. Stir in flour, baking soda, salt.

Shape about 1 tablespoon dough around each mint.
Place about 2 inches apart on ungreased cookie sheet.

Bake 9 to 10 minutes or until light brown. Remove from
cookie sheet to wire rack; cool completely. Dip tops of
cookies into Almond Frosting. Sprinkle with candy decorations.

1 Cookie: Calories 145 (Calories from Fat 55); Fat 6g (Saturated
3g); Cholesterol 15mg; Sodium 70mg; Carbohydrate 21g (Dietary
Fiber 0g); Protein 2g
% Daily Value: Vitamin A 2%; Vitamin C 0%; Calcium 2%; Iron 2%
Diet Exchanges: 1 1/2 Starch, 1 Fat

Almond Frosting

1 cup powdered sugar

1 tablespoon plus 1 to 2 teaspoons milk

1/4 teaspoon almond extract or vanilla

Few drops of food color, if desired

Mix all ingredients until smooth and thick enough to
coat.

Party Pointers

Call it a Sweets Swap or a Cookie
Exchange; you'll get the same great
results—and lighten your baking
load, too. Why not start this tradition of sharing with your friends this
year? Here's how:

• Send out invitations a month in
advance. Think about limiting your
group to fewer than twelve to make
managing the event easier. You may
want to mail labels for the sweets
along with the invitations.

• Ask guests to bring their sweets on
paper or plastic plates or in nonre-
turnable containers and covered
with clear plastic wrap so the contents are easily seen. Each person
needs to bring enough treats to
share and sample.

• Everyone will want the recipes, so
have guests bring a copy; e-mail
the recipes or print them out on
the computer.

• As host, you will need to provide
the space for guests and their
goodies. Be sure you have lots of
piping-hot coffee and tea to go
with the cookie samples.

Minty Middle Treasures

Holiday Melting Moments

PREP: 25 MIN; CHILL: 1 HOUR; BAKE: 12 MIN PER SHEET; COOL: 30 MIN
ABOUT 3 1/2 DOZEN COOKIES

1 cup butter, softened (do not use margarine)

1 egg yolk

1 cup plus 2 tablespoons all-purpose flour

1/2 cup cornstarch

1/2 cup powdered sugar

2 tablespoons baking cocoa

1/8 teaspoon salt

Vanilla Frosting (right)

2 candy canes, about 6 inches long, finely crushed

Beat butter and egg yolk in large bowl with electric mixer on medium speed, or mix with spoon. Stir in flour, cornstarch, powdered sugar, cocoa and salt. Cover and refrigerate about 1 hour or until firm.

Heat oven to 375°. Shape dough into 1-inch balls. Place about 2 inches apart on ungreased cookie sheet.

Bake 10 to 12 minutes or until set but not brown. Remove from cookie sheet to wire rack; cool completely. Frost with Vanilla Frosting. Sprinkle with crushed candy canes.

1 Cookie: Calories 90 (Calories from Fat 45); Fat 5g (Saturated 3g); Cholesterol 20mg; Sodium 40mg; Carbohydrate 10g (Dietary Fiber 0g); Protein 1g
% Daily Value: Vitamin A 4%; Vitamin C 0%; Calcium 0%; Iron 0%
Diet Exchanges: 1/2 Starch, 1 Fat

Vanilla Frosting

1 cup powdered sugar

2 tablespoons butter or margarine, softened

2 to 3 teaspoons milk

1 teaspoon vanilla

Mix all ingredients until smooth and spreadable.

Holiday Hints

Pssst . . . looking for a few cookie baking secrets?

- Have at least three or four cookie sheets on hand, so as you bake one sheet you can get another one ready to go. Use cookie sheets that are at least 2 inches narrower and shorter than the inside dimensions of your oven, so the heat will circulate around them.

- We recommend baking only one cookie sheet at a time, using the middle oven rack. If you wish to bake two sheets at the same time, place one on the oven rack in the upper third of the oven and one on the oven rack in the lower third. Remember to switch their positions halfway through baking time.

- Check cookies at the minimum bake time. Even one minute can make a difference with cookies, especially those high in sugar and fat. The longer cookies bake, the more brown, crisp or hard they become.

- Always put cookie dough on completely cooled cookie sheets. Cookies spread too much if put on a hot, or even a warm, cookie sheet. You can cool cookie sheets quickly by popping them in the refrigerator or freezer or by running cold water over them (dry completely and grease again if needed).

Holiday Melting Moments

Gingersnaps

PREP: 25 MIN; CHILL: 1 HR; BAKE: 12 MIN PER SHEET; COOL: 30 MIN
ABOUT 4 DOZEN COOKIES

1 cup packed brown sugar

3/4 cup shortening

1/4 cup molasses

1 egg

2 1/4 cups all-purpose flour

2 teaspoons baking soda

1 teaspoon ground cinnamon

1 teaspoon ground ginger

1/2 teaspoon ground cloves

1/4 teaspoon salt

Granulated sugar

Beat brown sugar, shortening, molasses and egg in large bowl with electric mixer on medium speed, or mix with spoon. Stir in remaining ingredients except granulated sugar. Cover and refrigerate at least 1 hour. Heat oven to 375°. Lightly grease cookie sheet.

Shape dough by rounded teaspoonfuls into balls; dip tops into granulated sugar. Place balls, sugared sides up, about 3 inches apart on cookie sheet.

Bake 9 to 12 minutes or just until set. Remove from cookie sheet to wire rack; cool completely.

1 Cookie: Calories 80 (Calories from Fat 25); Fat 3g (Saturated 1g); Cholesterol 5mg; Sodium 70mg; Carbohydrate 12g (Dietary Fiber 0g); Protein 1g
% Daily Value: Vitamin A 0%; Vitamin C 0%; Calcium 0%; Iron 2%
Diet Exchanges: 1 Starch

New Twist

If you love ginger, you'll love this cookie with triple the zing: Simply add 1/4 cup chopped crystallized ginger and 1 tablespoon grated gingerroot to the dough before shaping into balls.

LACED GINGERSNAPS: Cover cookie sheet with waxed paper. Heat 1/2 cup semisweet chocolate chips or white baking chips and 1 teaspoon shortening until melted. Drizzle over cookies.

GINGER COOKIE CUT-OUTS: Roll the chilled dough for Gingersnaps, one-fourth at a time, on lightly floured cloth-covered surface. Cut into desired shapes with floured cookie cutters. Bake as directed. Frost and decorate cooled cookies if desired.

SNOWCAPPED GINGERSNAPS: Cover cookie sheet with waxed paper. Place 3 packages (6 ounces each) white baking bars, broken up, and 1 tablespoon shortening in microwavable bowl. Microwave uncovered on Medium-High (70%) 1 1/2 to 2 minutes, stirring every 15 seconds, until smooth. Dip half of each cooled cookie into melted mixture; sprinkle with chopped crystallized ginger if desired. Place on waxed paper; let stand until coating is firm.

BLACK-AND-WHITE GINGERSNAPS: Prepare Snowcapped Gingersnaps, as directed—except do not sprinkle with crystallized ginger. After white coating is set, dip half of each cookie into melted chocolate-flavored candy coating (almond bark) so that chocolate covers half of white coating. Place on waxed paper; let stand until chocolate is set.

Timesaving Tips

If you don't have time to shape the dough into balls, divide dough into 4 equal parts. Shape each part into a roll, 1 inch in diameter and about 12 inches long. Place rolls on greased cookie sheet; flatten slightly to about 5/8-inch thickness. Sprinkle with sugar. Bake 10 to 12 minutes or just until set. While warm, slice diagonally into about 1-inch strips. Drizzle with melted white baking chips if desired.

Gingersnaps (Snowcapped, Black-and-White and Laced—variations)

Slice-It-Easy Cookies

PREP: 25 MIN; CHILL: 4 HR; BAKE: 10 MIN PER SHEET; COOL: 30 MIN
ABOUT 7 DOZEN COOKIES

1 cup butter or margarine, softened

1 cup sugar

1 1/2 teaspoons vanilla

2 eggs

3 cups all-purpose flour

1 teaspoon salt

1/2 teaspoon baking soda

Beat butter, sugar, vanilla and eggs in large bowl with electric mixer on medium speed, or mix with spoon. Stir in remaining ingredients. Divide into 3 equal parts. Shape each part into roll, about 1 1/2 inches in diameter. Wrap and refrigerate at least 4 hours.

Heat oven to 400°. Cut rolls into 1/8-inch slices. Place about 1 inch apart on ungreased cookie sheet.

Bake 8 to 10 minutes or just until golden brown around edges. Immediately remove from cookie sheet to wire rack; cool completely.

1 Cookie: Calories 45 (Calories from Fat 20); Fat 2g (Saturated 1g); Cholesterol 10mg; Sodium 50mg; Carbohydrate 6g (Dietary Fiber 0g); Protein 1g
% Daily Value: Vitamin A 2%; Vitamin C 0%; Calcium 0%; Iron 0%
Diet Exchanges: 1/2 Starch

CHRISTMAS TREES: Shape each roll into a triangle; coat sides with green sugar. Refrigerate and cut into slices as directed. Cut tree trunks from several slices; attach trunks to unbaked trees on cookie sheet, overlapping slightly. Sprinkle with candy decorations. Bake as directed. About 6 dozen cookies.

HOLIDAY COOKIE TARTS: Cut out centers of half of the unbaked cookie slices with 3/4-inch holiday cutters, or design your own patterns. Place slice with cutout on top of slice without cutout; press edges to seal. Spoon 1/2 teaspoon red jelly or jam into cutout. Bake as directed. Lightly sprinkle powdered sugar over cookies. About 3 1/2 dozen sandwich cookies.

PEPPERMINT PINWHEELS: Using 1/2 Slice-It-Easy Cookie dough, divide dough in half again. Stir 1/2 teaspoon peppermint extract and 1/4 teaspoon red or green food color into 1 half. Cover both halves and refrigerate 1 hour. Roll plain dough into rectangle, about 9×8 inches, on lightly floured surface. Repeat with colored dough; place on plain dough. Roll doughs together until about 1/4 inch thick. Roll up tightly, beginning at 9-inch side. Refrigerate at least 4 hours; cut into slices and bake as directed. About 3 dozen cookies. (Photo on page 225.)

RIBBON BAR COOKIES: Decrease vanilla to 1 teaspoon; add 1 teaspoon peppermint extract. Divide dough in half. Stir 1/2 teaspoon red or green food color into 1 half. Cover both halves and refrigerate 1 hour. Shape each half into 2 strips, each about 9×2 1/2 inches, on very lightly floured surface. Layer strips, alternating colors; press together. Refrigerate, cut into slices and bake as directed. About 5 1/2 dozen cookies. (Photo on page 225.)

SUGAR-COATED SLICES: Coat rolls with red or green sugar, small multicolored candies or chopped nuts. Refrigerate, cut into slices and bake as directed.

No-Bake Apricot Gems

PREP: 20 MIN
ABOUT 7 1/2 DOZEN COOKIES

1 package (6 ounces) dried apricots

1 cup hazelnuts

2 1/2 cups graham cracker crumbs

1 can (14 ounces) sweetened condensed milk

Place apricots and hazelnuts in food processor. Cover and process, using quick on-and-off motions, until finely chopped. Place mixture in large bowl. Stir in cracker crumbs and milk.

Shape mixture into 1-inch balls. Cover tightly and store in refrigerator up to 2 weeks or freeze up to 2 months.

1 Cookie: Calories 45 (Calories from Fat 20); Fat 2g (Saturated 0g); Cholesterol 5mg; Sodium 20mg; Carbohydrate 6g (Dietary Fiber 0g); Protein 1g
% Daily Value: Vitamin A 2%; Vitamin C 0%; Calcium 2%; Iron 0%
Diet Exchanges: 1/2 Starch

NO-BAKE APPLE GEMS: Substitute dried apples for the apricots and walnuts for the hazelnuts.

NO-BAKE CHERRY GEMS: Substitute dried cherries for the apricots and slivered almonds for the hazelnuts.

NO-BAKE CRANBERRY GEMS: Substitute dried cranberries for the apricots and pistachio nuts for the hazelnuts.

Chocolate Crinkles

PREP: 20 MIN; CHILL: 3 HR; BAKE: 12 MIN PER SHEET; COOL: 30 MIN
ABOUT 6 DOZEN COOKIES

2 cups granulated sugar

1/2 cup vegetable oil

2 teaspoons vanilla

4 ounces unsweetened baking chocolate, melted
    and cooled

4 eggs

2 cups all-purpose flour

2 teaspoons baking powder

1/2 teaspoon salt

1 cup powdered sugar

Mix granulated sugar, oil, vanilla and chocolate in large
bowl. Stir in eggs, one at a time. Stir in flour, baking
powder and salt. Cover and refrigerate at least 3 hours.

Heat oven to 350°. Grease cookie sheet. Drop dough by
teaspoonfuls into powdered sugar; roll in sugar to coat.
Shape dough into balls. Place about 2 inches apart on
cookie sheet.

Bake 10 to 12 minutes or until almost no indentation
remains when touched. Remove from cookie sheet to
wire rack; cool completely.

1 Cookie: Calories 70 (Calories from Fat 3); Fat 25g (Saturated 1g);
Cholesterol 10mg; Sodium 35mg; Carbohydrate 10g (Dietary Fiber
0g); Protein 1g
% Daily Value: Vitamin A 0%; Vitamin C 0%; Calcium 0%; Iron 2%
Diet Exchanges: 1/2 Starch, 1/2 Fat

Gifts for Giving

Give a little dough this holiday.
Homemade cookie dough that's
ready to bake makes an especially
thoughtful gift for someone who
appreciates homemade taste. Place
the dough in a decorative tin that
also can be used to store the cookies.
Be sure to tuck in a little note of
baking instructions.

Sending a homemade treat to out-of-
town friends and family? Here are
some tips for mailing your cookies:

• Wrap cookies in pairs, back to back,
  and place them flat or on end in a
  can, box or other sturdy container.
  Or place cookies in single layers
  with waxed paper in between.

• Fill each container as full as practi-
  cal, padding the top with crushed
  waxed paper to prevent shaking
  and breakage.

• Pack containers in a foil-lined cor-
  rugated or fiberboard packing box.
  Fill with crumpled newspapers,
  shredded paper or foam packing
  peanuts.

Chocolate Crinkles, Peppermint Pinwheels and Ribbon Bar Cookies (page 222, variations of Slice-It-Easy Cookies)

Rum-Cashew Biscotti

PREP: 25 MIN; BAKE: 45 MIN PER SHEET; COOL: 45 MIN
ABOUT 3 DOZEN BISCOTTI

2/3 cup sugar

1/2 cup vegetable oil

2 teaspoons rum extract

2 eggs

2 1/2 cups all-purpose flour

1 cup unsalted cashew pieces

1 teaspoon baking powder

1/4 teaspoon baking soda

1/4 teaspoon salt

Rum Glaze (page 170), if desired

Heat oven to 350°. Beat sugar, oil, rum extract and eggs in large bowl with spoon. Stir in remaining ingredients except Rum Glaze.

Turn dough onto lightly floured surface. Knead until smooth. Shape half of dough at a time into rectangle, 10×3 inches, on ungreased cookie sheet.

Bake 25 to 30 minutes or until toothpick inserted in center comes out clean. Cool on cookie sheet 15 minutes. Cut rectangle crosswise into 1/2-inch slices. Place slices, cut sides down, on cookie sheet.

Bake about 15 minutes, turning once, until crisp and light brown. Immediately remove from cookie sheet to wire rack; cool completely. Drizzle with Rum Glaze.

1 Biscotti: Calories 80 (Calories from Fat 25); Fat 3g (Saturated 1g); Cholesterol 10mg; Sodium 40mg; Carbohydrate 13g (Dietary Fiber 1g); Protein 1g
% Daily Value: Vitamin A 0%; Vitamin C 2%; Calcium 0%; Iron 2%
Diet Exchanges: 1 Starch

MERRY CHERRY BISCOTTI: Use vanilla for the rum extract. Omit cashews. Add 3/4 cup dried cherries or 3/4 cup chopped candied cherries and 1/2 cup chopped slivered almonds.

PISTACHIO BISCOTTI: Use vanilla for the rum extract. Omit cashews. Add 1/2 cup coarsely chopped pistachio nuts.

Gifts for Giving

Biscotti are the trendy Italian cookies that are baked twice—first as a loaf, then a second time sliced—until they are thoroughly dry and crisp. Great served with coffee or just right for munching, they make great gifts wrapped in cellophane and tied with festive ribbon. Pretty glass containers are ideal for giving biscotti. Tie curly ribbons on the containers, and add a handmade gift tag. Or package biscotti in cellophane, and tuck in a glass coffee mug. Because this is a hardy cookie, it's also a great one for mailing.

New Twist

Make your biscotti look festive. Heat 3 ounces semisweet baking chocolate or white baking bar and 1/2 teaspoon shortening until melted and smooth. Drizzle chocolate over biscotti, or dip half of each biscotti into melted chocolate. Immediately sprinkle with your choice of crushed hard peppermint candy, chopped pistachio or other nuts, coarse decorating sugar, chopped candied ginger or holiday candy decorations. Place on waxed paper until chocolate is set.

Rum-Cashew Biscotti (Merry Cherry and Pistachio—variations)

Heirloom Holiday Fruit Drops

PREP: 20 MIN; CHILL: 1 HR; BAKE: 10 MIN PER SHEET; COOL: 30 MIN
ABOUT 4 DOZEN COOKIES

Would you believe this cookie dates back to 1945? Since the advent of holiday baking, this timeless and treasured recipe has been a constant request from cooks of all ages.

1 cup packed brown sugar

1/2 cup shortening

1/4 cup buttermilk or water

1 egg

1 3/4 cups all-purpose flour

1/2 teaspoon baking soda

1/2 teaspoon salt

1 cup candied cherries, cut in half

1 cup chopped dates

3/4 cup chopped nuts

Pecan halves, if desired

Beat brown sugar, shortening, buttermilk and egg in large bowl with electric mixer on medium speed until blended, or mix with spoon. Gradually stir in flour, baking soda and salt. Stir in cherries, dates and chopped nuts. Cover and refrigerate 1 hour.

Heat oven to 400°. Grease cookie sheet. Drop dough by rounded teaspoonfuls about 2 inches apart onto cookie sheet. Place a pecan half on each cookie.

Bake 8 to 10 minutes or until almost no indentation remains when touched lightly with finger. Immediately remove from cookie sheet to wire rack; cool completely.

1 Cookie: Calories 85 (Calories from Fat 35); Fat 4g (Saturated 1g); Cholesterol 5mg; Sodium 45mg; Carbohydrate 12g (Dietary Fiber 1g); Protein 1g
% Daily Value: Vitamin A 0%; Vitamin C 0%; Calcium 0%; Iron 2%
Diet Exchanges: 1 Starch

Holiday Hints

Invite a few friends or neighbors in, and do your holiday baking in just one or two days. To ensure the event is well organized, here are a few suggestions:

• Choose a combination of oven, microwave and no-bake recipes to ensure sufficient cooking space.

• Early in the week, select recipes, buy groceries and organize equipment. You also can ask each person to bring the ingredients for one or two recipes or the prepared cookie dough.

• Set up work stations. You may include a mixing area, rolling out and baking station and decorating area.

• Ask guests to bring containers. Pack your goodies for storing or gift giving, and label them.

At the end of your event, you'll have your baking done, and the best part is everyone helps with the cleanup!

Heirloom Holiday Fruit Drops, No-Bake Apricot Gems (page 223) and No-Bake Cranberry Gems (variation, page 223)

Sweet Shop Favorites

Almond-Toffee Triangles

PREP: 20 MIN; BAKE: 40 MIN; COOL: 30 MIN
4 DOZEN BARS

2/3 cup butter or margarine, softened

1/2 cup packed brown sugar

1/2 cup corn syrup

1 teaspoon vanilla

1 egg

2 cups all-purpose flour

1/2 teaspoon salt

1/3 cup packed brown sugar

1/3 cup corn syrup

1/4 cup butter or margarine

1/4 cup whipping (heavy) cream

1 teaspoon vanilla

1 cup sliced almonds

Heat oven to 350°. Grease jelly roll pan, 15 1/2 × 10 1/2 × 1 inch, or line with aluminum foil.

Mix 2/3 cup butter, 1/2 cup brown sugar, 1/2 cup corn syrup, 1 teaspoon vanilla and the egg in large bowl. Stir in flour and salt. Spread in pan. Bake 18 to 20 minutes or until light golden brown.

Meanwhile, cook 1/3 cup brown sugar and 1/3 cup corn syrup in 1 1/2-quart saucepan over low heat, stirring constantly, until sugar is dissolved. Stir in 1/4 cup butter and the whipping cream. Heat to boiling; remove from heat. Stir in vanilla.

Sprinkle almonds over baked layer. Pour cooked mixture over almonds; spread evenly. Bake 15 to 20 minutes or until light brown and set; cool completely. Cut into 6 rows by 4 rows; cut squares diagonally in half.

1 Bar: Calories 100 (Calories from Fat 45); Fat 5g (Saturated 3g); Cholesterol 15mg; Sodium 60mg; Carbohydrate 13g (Dietary Fiber 0g); Protein 1g
% Daily Value: Vitamin A 2%; Vitamin C 0%; Calcium 0%; Iron 2%
Diet Exchanges: 1 Starch, 1/2 Fat

New Twist

We think the triangle shape adds a fun addition to a holiday cookie tray, but you can also cut these cookies into squares or bars. These bars are so easy you'll want to try these two new flavor twists.

• **Coffee-Hazelnut Bars:** Substitute chopped hazelnuts for the almonds. Add 1 tablespoon instant coffee (dry) to the brown sugar-corn syrup mixture.

• **Maple-Praline Bars:** Substitute chopped pecans for the almonds and maple-flavored syrup for the corn syrup.

Almond-Toffee Triangles (Coffee-Hazelnut Bars and Maple-Praline Bars—variation)

Tom-and-Jerry Brownies

PREP: 25 MIN; BAKE: 35 MIN

2 DOZEN BROWNIES

1 package (1 pound 6 1/2 ounces) brownie mix (with pouch of chocolate syrup)

1/3 cup water

1/3 cup vegetable oil

2 eggs

1 package (8 ounces) cream cheese, softened

1/3 cup granulated sugar

1 tablespoon brandy or 2 teaspoons brandy extract

1 teaspoon ground nutmeg

1 egg

Powdered sugar, if desired

Heat oven to 375°. Grease bottom only of rectangular pan, 13×9×2 inches. Prepare brownie mix as directed on package, using water, oil and 2 eggs. Pour half of batter into pan.

Stir remaining ingredients except powdered sugar in small bowl until smooth. Drop cheese mixture by spoonfuls onto brownie batter. Pour remaining brownie batter over cheese mixture. Swirl cheese mixture through brownie batter with knife for marbled design.

Bake 30 to 35 minutes or until toothpick inserted 2 inches from side of pan comes out clean or almost clean; cool. Sprinkle with powdered sugar. Cut into 6 rows by 4 rows. Store covered in refrigerator.

1 Brownie: Calories 180 (Calories from Fat 70); Fat 8g (Saturated 3g); Cholesterol 35mg; Sodium 125mg; Carbohydrate 24g (Dietary Fiber 0g); Protein 3g
% Daily Value: Vitamin A 4%; Vitamin C 0%; Calcium 2%; Iron 4%
Diet Exchanges: 1 1/2 Starch, 1 Fat

CHOCOLATE-COVERED CHERRY BROWNIES: Omit brandy and nutmeg. Add 1 teaspoon almond extract and 1 cup chopped candied cherries to cream cheese mixture. Do not swirl cheese mixture.

CINNAMON-SPICED BROWNIES: Omit brandy and nutmeg. Add 1 tablespoon baking cocoa and 2 teaspoons ground cinnamon to cream cheese mixture.

CREAMY CAPPUCCINO BROWNIES: Decrease granulated sugar to 3 tablespoons; omit brandy and nutmeg. Dissolve 1 teaspoon instant espresso coffee (dry) in 2 tablespoons warm water; stir into cream cheese mixture.

Holiday Hints

The secret to cutting perfect bars is to line the pan with aluminum foil. To shape foil, turn the pan upside down, and form a piece of aluminum foil over it, leaving the foil about 1 inch longer on two opposite sides (for lifting). Carefully remove foil, turn pan over and fit foil into pan. Grease foil as directed in recipe.

When the bars have baked and cooled, lift the aluminum foil and bars out of the pan onto a cutting surface. Peel foil back and cut bars. When cutting brownies, use a plastic knife for nice, even cuts.

Tom-and-Jerry Brownies (Chocolate-Covered Cherry Brownies—variation)

Creamy Chocolate Marble Fudge

PREP: 20 MIN; COOK: 20 MIN; CHILL: 3 HR
8 DOZEN CANDIES

6 cups sugar

1 can (12 ounces) evaporated milk

1 cup butter or margarine

1 package (8 ounces) cream cheese, softened

2 jars (7 ounces each) marshmallow creme or 1
package (10 1/2 ounces) miniature marshmallows

1 tablespoon vanilla

1 package (12 ounces) white baking chips (2 cups)

1 cup milk chocolate chips

1 package (6 ounces) semisweet chocolate chips
(1 cup)

2 tablespoons baking cocoa

1/2 cup chopped nuts, if desired

Butter rectangular pan, 13×9×2 inches, or line with aluminum foil, leaving 1 inch of foil overhanging at 2 opposite sides of pan. Heat sugar, milk, butter and cream cheese to boiling in 6-quart Dutch oven over medium-high heat and cook 6 to 8 minutes, stirring constantly.

Reduce heat to medium. Cook about 10 minutes, stirring occasionally, to 225° on candy thermometer; remove from heat.

Quickly stir in marshmallow creme and vanilla. Pour 4 cups hot marshmallow mixture over white baking chips in large bowl; stir to mix. Stir milk chocolate chips, semisweet chocolate chips, cocoa and nuts into remaining marshmallow mixture.

Pour one-third of the white mixture into pan, spreading evenly. Quickly pour one-third of the chocolate mixture over top, spreading evenly. Repeat twice. Swirl knife greased with butter through mixtures for marbled design. Cool until set.

Refrigerate uncovered about 3 hours or until set. Cut into 12 rows by 8 rows with knife greased with butter. Store covered in refrigerator.

1 Candy: Calories 130 (Calories from Fat 45); Fat 5g (Saturated 3g); Cholesterol 10mg; Sodium 30mg; Carbohydrate 20g (Dietary Fiber 0g); Protein 1g
% Daily Value: Vitamin A 2%; Vitamin C 0%; Calcium 2%; Iron 0%
Diet Exchanges: 1 Starch, 1 Fat

Gifts for Giving

Let us share another recipe for gift giving—**Layered Brownies**. To make the gift, layer the following ingredients in a 2-quart glass jar and seal the jar:

• 1/3 cup baking cocoa

• 2/3 cup sugar

• 1/2 cup semisweet chocolate chips

• 1/2 cup white baking chips

• 2/3 cup packed brown sugar

• 1 cup plus 2 tablespoons all-purpose flour

• 1/2 teaspoon salt

• 1/2 cup coarsely chopped nuts, if desired

Attach a small wooden spoon to the jar with a festive ribbon along with these directions for baking:

Directions for Baking: Mix contents of jar with 2/3 cup vegetable oil, 3 eggs and 1 teaspoon vanilla in large bowl with spoon. Pour into greased 9-inch square pan, and bake at 350° for about 30 minutes.

Truffles

PREP: 25 MIN; CHILL: 25 MIN; FREEZE: 30 MIN
ABOUT 15 CANDIES

6 ounces semisweet baking chocolate, chopped

2 tablespoons butter or margarine

1/4 cup whipping (heavy) cream

1 cup semisweet or milk chocolate chips or white baking chips

1 tablespoon shortening

Finely chopped nuts, if desired

Coarse sugar crystals (decorating sugar), if desired

1/4 cup powdered sugar and 1/2 teaspoon milk, if desired

Melt baking chocolate in heavy 2-quart saucepan over low heat, stirring constantly; remove from heat. Stir in butter. Stir in whipping cream. Refrigerate 10 to 15 minutes, stirring frequently, just until thick enough to hold a ball shape.

Cover cookie sheet with aluminum foil. Drop refrigerated mixture by teaspoonfuls onto cookie sheet. Shape into balls. (If mixture is too sticky, refrigerate until firm enough to shape.) Freeze 30 minutes.

Heat chocolate chips and shortening over low heat, stirring constantly, until chocolate is melted and mixture is smooth; remove from heat.

Dip 1 truffle at a time into melted chocolate, using fork, until coated. Place on foil-covered cookie sheet. Immediately sprinkle some of the truffles with nuts or sugar crystals. Or mix powdered sugar and milk; drizzle over some of the truffles. Refrigerate truffles about 10 minutes or until chocolate is set. Serve at room temperature. Store in airtight container at room temperature.

1 Candy: Calories 145 (Calories from Fat 90); Fat 10g (Saturated 6g); Cholesterol 10mg; Sodium 15mg; Carbohydrate 14g (Dietary Fiber 1g); Protein 1g
% Daily Value: Vitamin A 2%; Vitamin C 0%; Calcium 0%; Iron 4%
Diet Exchanges: 1 Starch, 1 1/2 Fat

Holiday Hints

• Personalize truffles with flavored liqueurs. Stir 2 tablespoons brandy or almond, apricot, cherry or coffee liqueur into whipping cream.

• We've all been there—afraid to pick up that piece of candy because we're not sure what's in it. To avoid that situation, just identify candy flavors, using melted chocolate, with initials on top of candies.

Gifts for Giving

• To make an attractive serving tray or to present as gifts, pack truffles in mini paper baking cups.

• Wrap truffles in festive gold or silver cellophane and tie with metallic ribbons to make unforgettable gifts.

Deluxe Christmas Fudge

PREP: 20 MIN; CHILL: 2 HR

6 DOZEN CANDIES

1 1/2 packages (12-ounce size) semisweet chocolate chips (3 cups)

2 cups miniature marshmallows or 16 large marshmallows, cut in half

1 can (14 ounces) sweetened condensed milk

1 teaspoon vanilla

1 cup pistachio nuts

1/2 cup chopped candied cherries

1/4 cup white baking chips, melted, if desired

Line square pan, 9×9×2 inches, with aluminum foil, leaving 1 inch of foil overhanging at 2 opposite sides of pan. Grease foil with butter.

Place chocolate chips, marshmallows and milk in 8-cup microwavable measuring cup. Microwave uncovered on High 3 to 5 minutes, stirring every minute, until marshmallows and chips are melted and can be stirred smooth.

Stir in vanilla, nuts and cherries. Immediately pour into pan. Drizzle with melted white baking chips. Refrigerate about 2 hours or until firm. Remove fudge from pan, using foil edges to lift. Cut into 9 rows by 8 rows or cut into diamond shapes

1 Candy: Calories 75 (Calories from Fat 35); Fat 3g (Saturated 2g); Cholesterol 5mg; Sodium 15mg; Carbohydrate 11g (Dietary Fiber 1g); Protein 1g
% Daily Value: Vitamin A 0%; Vitamin C 0%; Calcium 2%; Iron 2%
Diet Exchanges: 1 Fruit, 1 Fat

HAZELNUT FUDGE: Omit cherries; substitute hazelnuts for the pistachios and add 2 tablespoons hazelnut liqueur.

Gifts for Giving

Looking for a fun way to package fudge for holiday gifts? Cut out shapes, using deep, open cookie cutters. Personalize fudge by writing a name or holiday greeting with white decorator frosting from a tube. You can either remove the cookie cutter from the fudge or keep the cutter surrounding the fudge; wrap in holiday cellophane bags, and tie with curly ribbons.

Deluxe Christmas Fudge and Creamy Chocolate Marble Fudge (page 234)

Chocolate-Covered Peanut Butter Candies

PREP: 25 MIN; CHILL: 2 HR
64 CANDIES

1/2 cup creamy peanut butter

1/4 cup butter or margarine, softened

1/4 cup chopped peanuts

1/2 teaspoon vanilla

2 cups powdered sugar

1 package (12 ounces) semisweet chocolate chips
  (2 cups)

1 tablespoon plus 1 teaspoon shortening

Peanut Butter Icing (right)

Line square pan, 8×8×2 or 9×9×2 inches, with aluminum foil, leaving 1 inch of foil overhanging at 2 opposite sides of pan. Grease foil with butter.

Mix peanut butter, butter, peanuts and vanilla in medium bowl. Stir in powdered sugar, 1/2 cup at a time, until stiff dough forms. (Work in powdered sugar with hands if necessary.) If dough is crumbly, work in additional 1 tablespoon peanut butter. Pat mixture in pan. Cover and refrigerate about 1 hour or until firm. Remove from pan, using foil edges to lift. Cut into 8 rows by 8 rows.

Cover cookie sheet with waxed paper. Melt chocolate chips and shortening in 1-quart saucepan over low heat,

stirring constantly. Dip peanut butter squares, one at a time, into chocolate mixture (see Holiday Hints, below). Place on cookie sheet. Refrigerate uncovered about 30 minutes or until firm.

Drizzle Peanut Butter Icing over tops of chocolate-covered squares. Refrigerate uncovered about 30 minutes or until firm. Store candies loosely covered in refrigerator.

1 Candy: Calories 70 (Calories from Fat 35); Fat 4g (Saturated 2g); Cholesterol 0mg; Sodium 200mg; Carbohydrate 9g (Dietary Fiber 1g); Protein 1g
% Daily Value: Vitamin A 0%; Vitamin C 0%; Calcium 0%; Iron 0%
Diet Exchanges: 1/2 Starch, 1/2 Fat

Peanut Butter Icing

1/2 cup powdered sugar

2 tablespoons creamy peanut butter

About 1 tablespoon milk

Mix powdered sugar and peanut butter. Beat in milk with wire whisk until smooth. Stir in additional milk, if necessary, 1 teaspoon at a time, until thin enough to drizzle.

Holiday Hints

To make dipping the candies easy, here are some handy tips:

- Using a dry fork, dip one candy at a time completely into the melted chocolate. Lift up and draw the fork across the side of the pan or bowl to remove excess chocolate.

- Using another fork, push the candy off the dipping fork onto a cookie sheet covered with waxed paper. Refrigerate candies 5 to 10 minutes or just until coating has hardened.

Chocolate-Covered Peanut Butter Candies

Cappuccino-Pecan Nuggets

PREP: 45 MIN; CHILL: 1 HR 10 MIN

3 DOZEN CANDIES

1/4 cup packed brown sugar

1 tablespoon instant espresso coffee (dry)

2/3 cup sweetened condensed milk

12 ounces vanilla-flavored candy coating (almond bark), chopped

12 vanilla or chocolate caramels

1/4 cup semisweet chocolate chips

1 tablespoon whipping (heavy) cream

72 large pecan halves (about 1 1/2 cups)

10 to 12 ounces milk chocolate, semisweet or bittersweet baking chocolate, chopped

3 tablespoons shortening

Finely chopped pecans, instant espresso coffee (dry) or baking cocoa, if desired

Line square pan, 8×8×2 or 9×9×2 inches, with aluminum foil, leaving 1 inch of foil overhanging at 2 opposite sides of pan; spray with cooking spray.

Mix brown sugar and 1 tablespoon coffee in 8-cup microwavable measuring cup. Stir in milk. Microwave uncovered on High 2 to 3 minutes, stirring every minute, until boiling. Stir in candy coating until melted. Pour into pan. Refrigerate uncovered about 30 minutes or until firm. Remove mixture from pan, using foil edges to lift. Cut into 6 rows by 6 rows.

Place caramels, chocolate chips and whipping cream in 2-cup microwavable measuring cup. Microwave uncovered on Medium (50%) 1 1/2 to 2 1/2 minutes, stirring every minute, until mixture is almost melted. Stir until smooth. Refrigerate uncovered about 15 minutes, stirring once or twice, until mixture holds its shape and is cool enough to handle.

Cover cookie sheet with waxed paper. For each nugget, roll 1/2 teaspoon caramel-chocolate mixture into ball.

Press 2 pecan halves on ball in sandwich shape, flattening ball slightly between bottom sides of pecan halves. Flatten slightly and shape 1 square coffee mixture evenly around pecan cluster; roll between hands to form ball. Place on cookie sheet. Refrigerate about 15 minutes or until firm.

Cover cookie sheet with aluminum foil. Place chocolate and shortening in microwavable 4-cup measuring cup or bowl. Microwave uncovered on Medium (50%) 3 to 4 minutes, stirring every minute, until chocolate is almost melted. Stir until smooth.

Dip 1 nugget at a time into chocolate, using fork, until coated. Place on foil-lined cookie sheet. Immediately sprinkle some of the nuggets with finely chopped pecans, coffee or cocoa. Drizzle some of the nuggets with remaining melted chocolate if desired. Refrigerate about 10 minutes or just until set. Serve at room temperature. Store in airtight container at room temperature.

1 Candy: Calories 175 (Calories from Fat 100); Fat 11g (Saturated 4g); Cholesterol 5mg; Sodium 20mg; Carbohydrate 18g (Dietary Fiber 1g); Protein 2g
% Daily Value: Vitamin A 0%; Vitamin C 0%; Calcium 4%; Iron 2%
Diet Exchanges: 1 Starch, 2 Fat

Holiday Hints

Create dramatic chocolate drizzles in a couple of ways:

- Dip fork or small tableware-type spoon into melted chocolate, allowing the first large drop of chocolate to drip back into the bowl. Then, using back-and-forth motions, drizzle chocolate over cookies, bars or candy.

- Spoon melted chocolate into a decorating bag with a writing tip, and squeeze out the chocolate. Or spoon melted chocolate into a small, resealable plastic bag, snip off a very tiny piece of one corner of the bag and gently squeeze out the melted chocolate.

Cappuccino-Pecan Nuggets

Peppermint Bark

PREP: 15 MIN; STAND: 1 HR
ABOUT 16 CANDIES

1 package (16 ounces) vanilla-flavored candy coating (almond bark), broken into pieces

24 hard peppermint candies

Cover cookie sheet with waxed paper, aluminum foil or cooking parchment paper. Place candy coating in 8-cup microwavable measure or 2-quart microwavable casserole. Microwave uncovered on High 2 to 3 minutes, stirring every 30 seconds, until almost melted. Stir until smooth.

Place peppermint candies in heavy plastic bag; crush with rolling pin or bottom of small heavy saucepan. Pour crushed candies into wire strainer. Shake strainer over melted coating until all of the tiniest candy pieces fall into the coating; reserve the larger candy pieces. Stir coating to mix evenly.

Spread coating evenly on cookie sheet. Sprinkle evenly with remaining candy pieces. Let stand about 1 hour or until cool and hardened. Break into pieces.

1 Candy: Calories 40 (Calories from Fat 20); Fat 2g (Saturated 2g); Cholesterol 0mg; Sodium 5mg; Carbohydrate 6g (Dietary Fiber 0g); Protein 0g
% Daily Value: Vitamin A 0%; Vitamin C 0%; Calcium 2%; Iron 0%
Diet Exchanges: 1/2 Starch

Holiday Hints

Several brands of candy coating are available, and each may melt a bit differently. The white color varies, and when melted, some are thinner than others. Make a note of the brand you prefer to work with, and watch carefully while melting.

New Twist

Let your imagination run wild! Leave out the crushed peppermint candy, and try some of the following combinations:

• Chocolate-covered coffee beans and chopped hazelnuts

• Dried cranberries and chopped almonds

• Crushed red and green ring-shaped hard candy

• Chopped candied pineapple and macadamia nuts

• Red and green plain or mint candy-coated chocolate candies

Toffee

PREP: 15 MIN; STAND: 1 HR
ABOUT 3 DOZEN CANDIES

1 cup sugar

1 cup butter or margarine

1/4 cup water

1/2 cup semisweet chocolate chips

1/2 cup finely chopped pecans

Heat sugar, butter and water to boiling in 2-quart saucepan, stirring constantly; reduce heat to medium. Cook, stirring constantly, to 300° on candy thermometer or until small amount of mixture dropped into cup of very cold water separates into hard, brittle threads. (Watch carefully so mixture does not burn.)

Immediately pour toffee onto ungreased large cookie sheet. If necessary, quickly spread mixture to 1/4-inch thickness. Sprinkle with chocolate chips; let stand about 1 minute or until chips are completely softened. Spread softened chocolate evenly over toffee. Sprinkle with nuts. Let stand at room temperature about 1 hour, or refrigerate if desired, until firm. Break into bite-size pieces.

1 Candy: Calories 91 (Calories from Fat 65); Fat 7g (Saturated 4g); Cholesterol 14mg; Sodium 35mg; Carbohydrate 7g (Dietary Fiber 0g); Protein 0g
% Daily Value: Vitamin A 4%; Vitamin C 0%; Calcium 0%; Iron 0%
Diet Exchanges: 1/2 Fruit, 1 1/2 Fat

Gifts for Giving

Packaging gifts for the holidays can be as fun as making them. If you're looking for some fresh ideas, try these:

• Fill a holiday stocking with a batch of favorite candies that you have individually wrapped in holiday cellophane.

• Fill unused Chinese takeout containers with colored tissue paper and colorful confetti. Pack with individually wrapped candies.

• Wrap coffee tins with holiday paper or aluminum foil. Fill with candies, separating layers with waxed paper.

• Shop garage sales and flea markets for antique candy molds or mixing bowls. Place candy in container, wrap in cellophane and tie with a bow.

Chocolate-Wine Balls

PREP: 20 MIN
ABOUT 3 1/2 DOZEN CANDIES

1/4 cup honey

1 package (6 ounces) semisweet chocolate chips
(1 cup)

2 1/2 cups finely crushed vanilla wafer cookies
(about 55 cookies)

2 cups ground walnuts

1/3 cup port, sweet red wine or apple juice

About 1/2 cup coarse sugar crystals (decorating
sugar)

Heat honey and chocolate chips in 3-quart saucepan over
low heat, stirring constantly, until chocolate is melted;
remove from heat. Stir in crushed cookies, walnuts and
port. Shape into 1-inch balls; roll in sugar crystals.

Store in tightly covered container. Let stand several days
to blend flavors. Flavor improves with age up to 4 weeks.

1 Candy: Calories 75 (Calories from Fat 35); Fat 4g (Saturated 1g);
Cholesterol 0mg; Sodium 15mg; Carbohydrate 10g (Dietary Fiber
1g); Protein 1g
% Daily Value: Vitamin A 0%; Vitamin C 0%; Calcium 0%; Iron 2%
Diet Exchanges: 1/2 Starch, 1 Fat

WHITE WINE BALLS: Omit chocolate chips and do
not heat honey. Substitute dry white wine for the port.
Mix all ingredients except sugar. Shape into 1-inch balls;
roll in sugar. Continue as directed.

RUM BALLS OR BOURBON BALLS: Just substitute
rum or bourbon for the port. Prepare as directed.

Gifts for Giving

To give as a gift, wrap candies individually in colorful
plastic wrap or cellophane, and tie with metallic ribbons.
Fill a wine glass with candies, and be sure to include the
candy recipe with your gift.

Chocolate-Wine Balls (White Wine Balls—variation)

Maple-Nut Brittle

PREP: 15 MIN; COOK: 13 MIN; COOL: 1 HR
ABOUT 3 DOZEN CANDIES

1 cup packed brown sugar

1/2 cup maple-flavored syrup

1 can (about 12 ounces) lightly salted mixed nuts
(2 cups)

1 tablespoon butter or margarine

1 teaspoon baking soda

Heat oven to 200°. Generously butter large cookie sheet; keep warm in oven.

Mix brown sugar and maple syrup in 8-cup microwavable measure. Microwave uncovered on High 5 minutes. Stir in nuts.

Microwave uncovered on High 5 to 7 minutes or until syrup is bubbling and nuts are toasted—syrup will be very hot. Stir in butter.

Microwave uncovered 1 minute. Quickly and thoroughly stir in baking soda until mixture is light and foamy. Pour onto cookie sheet; quickly spread candy.

Cool 30 to 60 minutes or until hardened. Break into pieces. Store candy in airtight container at room temperature up to 2 weeks.

1 Candy: Calories 90 (Calories from Fat 45); Fat 5g (Saturated 1g); Cholesterol 0mg; Sodium 55mg; Carbohydrate 11g (Dietary Fiber 1g); Protein 2g
% Daily Value: Vitamin A 0%; Vitamin C 0%; Calcium 2%; Iron 2%
Diet Exchanges: 1 Fruit, 1 Fat

Holiday Hints

If you're not fond of mixed nuts, feel free to use an equal amount of your favorite nut. Out of maple syrup? Use corn syrup instead.

New Twist

For a festive touch, drizzle melted semisweet chocolate or white baking chips in a zigzag pattern over nut brittle.

Maple-Nut Brittle and Toffee (page 243)

Praline Truffle Cups

PREP: 30 MIN; CHILL: 1 HOUR 5 MIN

2 DOZEN CANDIES

6 ounces vanilla-flavored candy coating (almond bark), cut up

24 mini paper candy cups

6 ounces semisweet baking chocolate, cut up

2 tablespoons butter or margarine, cut into pieces

1/4 cup finely ground pecans

1/3 cup whipping (heavy) cream

1 tablespoon praline liqueur or maple-flavored syrup

Melt candy coating in double boiler over hot water. Spread 1 teaspoon coating evenly in bottoms and up sides of paper candy cups. Let stand until hardened.

Melt chocolate in heavy 2-quart saucepan over low heat, stirring constantly; remove from heat. Stir in remaining ingredients. Refrigerate about 35 minutes, stirring frequently, until mixture is thickened and mounds when dropped from a spoon.

Spoon mixture into decorating bag with star tip. Pipe mixture into candy-coated cups. Refrigerate about 30 minutes or until chocolate mixture is firm. Peel paper from cups before serving if desired. Store tightly covered in refrigerator.

1 Candy: Calories 105 (Calories from Fat 65); Fat 7g (Saturated 4g); Cholesterol 5mg; Sodium 15mg; Carbohydrate 9g (Dietary Fiber 0g); Protein 1g
% Daily Value: Vitamin A 2%; Vitamin C 0%; Calcium 2%; Iron 2%
Diet Exchanges: 1/2 Starch, 1 1/2 Fat

CHERRY TRUFFLE CUPS: Omit pecans. Substitute 2 tablespoons cherry liqueur for the praline liqueur. Place candied cherry half in each cup before filling with chocolate mixture. Garnish with candied cherries.

CRÈME DE MENTHE TRUFFLE CUPS: Substitute 1/4 cup finely ground almonds for the pecans and 2 tablespoons crème de menthe for the praline liqueur. Garnish with ground nuts.

RASPBERRY TRUFFLE CUPS: Omit pecans. Substitute 2 tablespoons raspberry liqueur for the praline liqueur. Place fresh raspberry in each cup before filling with chocolate mixture. Garnish with fresh raspberries.

Praline Truffle Cups (Cherry, Crème de Menthe and Raspberry—variations)

Divinity

PREP: 20 MIN; COOK: 35 MIN; STAND: 4 HR
ABOUT 4 DOZEN CANDIES

Sweet dreams of divinity dance in the minds of many around the holidays. One bite of these melt-in-your-mouth morsels is sure to send your taste buds twirling.

2 2/3 cups sugar

2/3 cup light corn syrup

1/2 cup water

2 egg whites

1 teaspoon vanilla

2/3 cup coarsely chopped nuts

Cook sugar, corn syrup and water (use 1 tablespoon less water on humid days) in 2-quart saucepan over low heat, stirring constantly, until sugar is dissolved. Cook without stirring to 260° on candy thermometer or until small amount of mixture dropped into very cold water forms a hard ball that holds its shape but is pliable.

Beat egg whites in medium bowl with electric mixer on high speed until stiff peaks form. (For best results, use electric stand mixer, not a portable handheld mixer because total beating time is about 6 minutes and mixture is thick.) Continue beating while pouring hot syrup in a thin stream into egg whites, beating constantly on medium speed. Add vanilla. Beat until mixture holds its shape and becomes slightly dull. (If mixture becomes too stiff for mixer, continue beating with wooden spoon.) Fold in nuts. Quickly drop mixture from buttered spoon onto waxed paper. Let stand at room temperature at least 4 hours, but no longer than 12 hours, until candies feel firm and dry to the touch. Store in airtight container at room temperature.

1 Candy: Calories 70 (Calories from Fat 10); Fat 1g (Saturated 0g); Cholesterol 0mg; Sodium 10mg; Carbohydrate 15g (Dietary Fiber 0g); Protein 0g
% Daily Value: Vitamin A 0%; Vitamin C 0%; Calcium 0%; Iron 0%
Diet Exchanges: 1 Fruit

New Twist

Divinity is a divine candy. To add your final touch, indulge in one of these variations:

• **Cherry-Almond:** Add 1/2 cup chopped candied cherries; use almond extract instead of the vanilla.

• **Peppermint:** Add 1/2 cup crushed hard peppermint candies and, if desired, 2 or 3 drops of red food color.

• **Chocolate-Mint:** Add 1/2 cup semisweet chocolate chips, 2 drops green food color and 1/4 teaspoon mint extract.

Holiday Hints

Making Divinity can be a little tricky, but it helps if you start with the spoonful test. Drop a spoonful of the divinity mixture onto waxed paper. If it stays in a mound, it has been beaten long enough. If the mixture flattens out, beat another 30 seconds and check again.

If the mixture is too stiff to spoon, beat in a few drops of hot water until a softer consistency is reached.

Divinity (Chocolate-Mint, Cherry-Almond and Peppermint—variations)

Oven Caramel Corn (Caramel-Apple, Red and White Christmas and Hawaiian—variations)

Oven Caramel Corn

PREP: 25 MIN; BAKE: 1 HR
ABOUT 15 CUPS CARAMEL CORN

15 cups popped popcorn (about 2/3 cup
   unpopped)

1 cup packed brown sugar

1/2 cup butter or margarine

1/4 cup light corn syrup

1/2 teaspoon salt

1/2 teaspoon baking soda

Heat oven to 200°. Divide popcorn between 2 ungreased rectangular pans, 13×9×2 inches. Heat brown sugar, butter, corn syrup and salt in 3-quart saucepan over medium heat, stirring occasionally, until bubbly around edges. Cook 5 minutes, stirring occasionally; remove from heat. Stir in baking soda.

Pour mixture over popcorn; stir until well coated. Bake 1 hour, stirring every 15 minutes.

1 Cup: Calories 180 (Calories from Fat 80); Fat 9g (Saturated 4g); Cholesterol 15mg; Sodium 270mg; Carbohydrate 25g (Dietary Fiber 1g); Protein 1g
% Daily Value: Vitamin A 4%; Vitamin C 0%; Calcium 2%; Iron 2%
Diet Exchanges: 1 1/2 Starch, 1 1/2 Fat

New Twist

Surprise your family and those on your gift list with some new flavor twists. Use 12 cups popped popcorn; toss with ingredients (below) after stirring in brown sugar mixture. Bake as directed.

- **Caramel-Apple Oven Caramel Corn:** Divide 2 cups dried apple slices, coarsely chopped, and 1 1/2 cups caramels, cut into fourths, between each pan of popcorn.

- **Hawaiian Oven Caramel Corn:** Divide 1 1/2 cups dried tropical fruit mix and 1 cup coarsely chopped macadamia nuts between each pan of popcorn.

- **Red and White Christmas Oven Caramel Corn:** Divide 2 cups dried cranberries and 1 1/2 cups white baking chips between each pan of popcorn

Winter Wonderland Castle (page 280)
and Winterland Critters (page 278)

CHAPTER 7

Festive Family Fun

Christmas is the time to create family memories: sticky fingers and chocolate-smeared faces, lopsided gingerbread palaces and smiles that make your heart melt.

No-Roll Sugar Cookies

PREP: 30 MIN; BAKE: 10 MIN PER SHEET; COOL: 30 MIN
ABOUT 8 DOZEN COOKIES

Kids and cookies go hand in hand at the holidays. Except for the occasional spilled sugar scattered on the floor, making these yummy cookies with Santa's little helpers is perfect for an afternoon of family fun.

Rainbow Dust (right) or purchased colored sugars

2 cups sugar

1 1/2 cups butter or margarine, softened

1 cup flaked coconut

1 teaspoon vanilla

3 cups all-purpose flour

1 teaspoon baking soda

1/2 teaspoon salt

Prepare Rainbow Dust. Heat oven to 350°.

Beat 2 cups sugar, the butter, coconut and vanilla in large bowl with electric mixer on medium speed, or mix with spoon. Stir in flour, baking soda and salt.

Shape dough by rounded teaspoonfuls into balls. Place about 3 inches apart on ungreased cookie sheet. Press bottom of glass into dough to grease, then dip into Rainbow Dust; press on shaped dough to flatten slightly.

Bake 8 to 10 minutes or until edges are golden brown. Remove from cookie sheet to wire rack; cool completely.

1 Cookie: Calories 65 (Calories from Fat 25); Fat 3g (Saturated 2g); Cholesterol 10mg; Sodium 45mg; Carbohydrate 9g (Dietary Fiber 0g); Protein 0g
% Daily Value: Vitamin A 2%; Vitamin C 0%; Calcium 0%; Iron 0%
Diet Exchanges: 1/2 Starch, 1/2 Fat

Rainbow Dust (Colored Sugar)

1/2 cup sugar

Food colors (see chart)

Place sugar in resealable plastic bag. Choose a color from the chart, and add food colors to sugar in bag. Seal bag. Squeeze sugar in bag until it becomes colored. Store sugar in sealed bag or bottle with tight-fitting lid.

COLOR	NUMBER OF DROPS OF LIQUID FOOD COLOR
Orange	2 drops yellow and 2 drops red
Peach	4 drops yellow and 1 drop red
Yellow	4 drops yellow
Pale yellow	2 drops yellow
Green	8 drops green
Lime green	3 drops yellow and 1 drop green
Blue	5 drops blue
Turquoise blue	3 drops blue and 1 drop green
Baby blue	2 drops blue
Purple	3 drops red and 2 drops blue
Red	10 drops red
Rose	5 drops red and 1 drop blue
Pink	1 drop red

New Twist

Want a big hit? Make **Giant No-Roll Sugar Cookies**! Shape 1/4 cupfuls of dough into 2-inch balls. Place about 3 inches apart on ungreased cookie sheet. Bake about 12 minutes or until edges are golden brown. Cool 3 minutes before removing from cookie sheet to wire rack. Makes about 17 giant cookies.

No-Roll Sugar Cookies

Hidden Treasure Cookies

PREP: 25 MIN; BAKE: 12 MIN PER SHEET; COOL: 30 MIN
ABOUT 4 DOZEN COOKIES

1/2 cup powdered sugar

1 cup butter or margarine, softened

1 teaspoon vanilla

2 1/4 cups all-purpose flour

1/2 cup finely chopped nuts

1/4 teaspoon salt

12 caramels, each cut into 4 pieces

Powdered sugar

Heat oven to 400°. Mix 1/2 cup powdered sugar, the butter and vanilla in large bowl. Stir in flour, nuts and salt until dough holds together.

Mold portions of dough around pieces of caramels to form 1-inch balls. Place about 1 inch apart on ungreased cookie sheet.

Bake 10 to 12 minutes or until set but not brown. Roll in powdered sugar while warm. Cool completely on wire rack. Roll in powdered sugar again.

1 Cookie: Calories 85 (Calories from Fat 45); Fat 5g (Saturated 3g); Cholesterol 10mg; Sodium 40mg; Carbohydrate 9g (Dietary Fiber 0g); Protein 1g
% Daily Value: Vitamin A 2%; Vitamin C 0%; Calcium 0%; Iron 2%
Diet Exchanges: 1/2 Starch, 1 Fat

New Twist

Vary the treasures in your cookies! Instead of caramels, try these precious ideas:

- Candied cherries
- Malted milk balls
- Chocolate-covered raisins
- Gummy fruit candies

Lemon Stampers

PREP: 25 MIN; CHILL: 2 HR; BAKE: 9 MIN PER SHEET; COOL: 30 MIN
ABOUT 5 DOZEN COOKIES

1 cup butter or margarine, softened

1 package (3 ounces) cream cheese, softened

1/2 cup sugar

1 tablespoon grated lemon peel

2 cups all-purpose flour

Carrot Cookie Press (right) or purchased cookie
     press

Sugar

Beat butter and cream cheese in large bowl with electric
mixer on medium speed, or mix with spoon. Stir in
1/2 cup sugar and the lemon peel. Gradually stir in flour.
Cover and refrigerate about 2 hours or until firm. While
dough is chilling, prepare Carrot Cookie Press.

Heat oven to 375°. Shape dough into 1-inch balls. Place
about 2 inches apart on ungreased cookie sheet. Flatten
to about 1/4-inch thickness with cookie press dipped
into sugar.

Bake 7 to 9 minutes or until set but not brown. Remove
from cookie sheet to wire rack; cool completely.

1 Cookie: Calories 45 (Calories from Fat 25); Fat 3g (Saturated 2g);
Cholesterol 10mg; Sodium 20mg; Carbohydrate 5g (Dietary Fiber
0g); Protein 0g
% Daily Value: Vitamin A 2%; Vitamin C 0%; Calcium 0%; Iron 0%
Diet Exchanges: 1/2 Starch

Carrot Cookie Press

Cut carrot, about 1 1/2 inches in diameter, into 2-inch
lengths. Cut decorative design about 1/8 inch deep in
cut end of carrot, using small sharp knife, tip of
vegetable peeler or other small sharp kitchen tool.

Holiday Hints

• Here's a tip to remember when shaping dough into
  balls: Use a level tablespoon of dough to create a perfect 1-inch ball.

• For a bright, festive touch, use Rainbow Dust (page
  256) to decorate these cookies.

• If you don't want to make the Carrot Cookie Press,
  stamp your cookies with a potato masher, the bottom
  of a glass or the bumpy side of a meat mallet.

Festive Family Fun

Fudgy No-Bakes

PREP: 20 MIN; CHILL: 1 HR
36 SQUARES

1 3/4 cups graham cracker crumbs (about 20 squares)

1 cup flaked coconut

1/4 cup baking cocoa

2 tablespoons granulated sugar

1/2 cup butter or margarine, melted

2 tablespoons water

2 cups powdered sugar

1/4 cup butter or margarine, softened

1 tablespoon milk

1 teaspoon vanilla

Candy decorations, if desired

Mix cracker crumbs, coconut, cocoa and granulated sugar in medium bowl. Stir in 1/2 cup butter and the water. Press in ungreased square pan, 9×9×2 inches. Refrigerate while preparing topping.

Mix remaining ingredients except candy decorations. (If necessary, stir in additional 1 to 2 teaspoons milk until spreadable.) Spread over layer in pan. Refrigerate 1 hour. Cut into 6 rows by 6 rows. Decorate with candy decorations. Store loosely covered in refrigerator.

1 Square: Calories 95 (Calories from Fat 45); Fat 5g (Saturated 3g); Cholesterol 10mg; Sodium 55mg; Carbohydrate 12g (Dietary Fiber 0g); Protein 0g
% Daily Value: Vitamin A 2%; Vitamin C 0%; Calcium 0%; Iron 0%
Diet Exchanges: 1 Starch, 1/2 Fat

Timesaving Tips

You can save time (and mess) by purchasing already crushed graham crackers at your supermarket.

Gifts for Giving

Get the whole family involved in making this recipe the "family gift" for neighbors and friends. Use decorator frostings to make wreaths and red cinnamon candies for holly berries. Personalize Fudgy No-Bakes by using decorator frosting to write names or holiday greetings. Use disposable aluminum pans to make gift giving a breeeze.

Fudgy No-Bakes

Peanut Butter Squares

PREP: 20 MIN; CHILL: 30 MIN

36 BARS

1 1/2 cups powdered sugar

1 cup graham cracker crumbs (about 12 squares)

1/2 cup butter or margarine

1/2 cup peanut butter

1 cup semisweet chocolate chips or white baking
chips

Candy decorations, if desired

Mix powdered sugar and cracker crumbs in medium
bowl. Heat butter and peanut butter in 1-quart saucepan
over low heat, stirring occasionally, until melted. Stir
into crumb mixture. Press in ungreased square pan,
8 × 8 × 2 inches.

Heat chocolate chips in 1-quart saucepan over low heat,
stirring frequently, until melted. Spread over crumb mixture. Immediately sprinkle with candy decorations.
Refrigerate about 30 minutes or until firm. Cut into
6 rows by 6 rows. (To cut diamond shapes, first cut
straight parallel lines 1 to 1 1/2 inches apart down the
length of the pan. Second, cut diagonal lines 1 to 1 1/2
inches apart across the straight cuts.) Store loosely covered in refrigerator.

1 Bar: Calories 95 (Calories from Fat 55); Fat 6g (Saturated 3g);
Cholesterol 5mg; Sodium 45mg; Carbohydrate 10g (Dietary Fiber
1g); Protein 1g
% Daily Value: Vitamin A 2%; Vitamin C 0%; Calcium 0%; Iron 0%
Diet Exchanges: 1/2 Starch, 1 Fat

PEANUT BUTTER BONBONS: Instead of pressing
crumb mixture into pan, shape it into 1-inch balls. Heat
chocolate chips or white baking chips with 1 tablespoon
shortening. Dip the balls into melted chocolate, using
tongs, to coat and place them on a sheet of waxed paper.
Decorate with candies if desired and then refrigerate the
bonbons until firm.

Peanut Butter Squares and Peanut Butter Bonbons (variation)

Christmas Mice Shortbread

PREP: 30 MIN; COOL: 1 HR

15 COOKIES

15 maraschino cherries with stems, drained

2/3 cup white baking chips or chocolate chips

1/2 teaspoon vegetable oil

1 package (5.3 ounces) shortbread triangles

30 sliced almonds

15 white baking chips or chocolate chips

Shredded coconut

15 red cinnamon candies

Cover work area with piece of waxed paper about 18 inches long. Dry cherries with paper towels.

Place 2/3 cup chips and the oil in 6-ounce custard cup. Microwave uncovered on High 1 minute to 1 minute 10 seconds or until chips are softened; stir until smooth.

Hold 1 cherry by stem (mouse tail), and dip into melted chips, covering completely. Immediately place on shortbread triangle, with tail at 45-degree angle. Place 2 of the sliced almonds against front of cherry to form mouse ears. Repeat with remaining cherries, shortbread and almonds.

Using the remaining melted chips as glue and a toothpick to spread the melted chips, attach the flat side of a whole chip (flat side back) to the base of the almonds to form the mouse head. Using melted chips as glue, attach a few shreds of coconut for the whiskers and a cinnamon candy for the nose.

Let cool without moving 50 to 60 minutes or until melted chip mixture is firm and completely set. Store in cool place up to 1 week.

1 Cookie: Calories 110 (Calories from Fat 55); Fat 6g (Saturated 2g); Cholesterol 2mg; Sodium 50mg; Carbohydrate 14g (Dietary Fiber 1g); Protein 1g
% Daily Value: Vitamin A 0%; Vitamin C 0%; Calcium 0%; Iron 4%
Diet Exchanges: 1 Fruit, 1 Fat

Holiday Hints

We think the shortbread cookies resemble a wedge of cheese, but you can use other purchased or homemade flat-surfaced cookies for the base of your mice decorations.

A merry mouse can add the final touch to your holiday food platters. Kids will have fun placing mice on a saucer next to Grandma and Grandpa's cups of coffee or on a plate of cookies for Santa.

Teddy Bear Snack Toss

PREP: 10 MIN
ABOUT 6 CUPS SNACK

2 cups teddy bear-shaped graham snacks

2 cups Honey Nut Cheerios® cereal

1 cup honey-roasted peanuts or 2 cups chocolate-covered peanuts

1/2 cup raisins

Toss all ingredients in large bowl. Store tightly covered at room temperature up to 2 weeks.

1/2 Cup: Calories 160 (Calories from Fat 70); Fat 8g (Saturated 1g); Cholesterol 0mg; Sodium 190mg; Carbohydrate 20g (Dietary Fiber 2g); Protein 4g
% Daily Value: Vitamin A 4%; Vitamin C 2%; Calcium 2%; Iron 8%
Diet Exchanges: 1 1/2 Starch, 1 Fat

Teddy Bear Snack Toss and Reindeer Snack (page 265)

Holiday Hints

Dry snacks, such as nuts, popcorn, mints and other hard candies, are perfect mates for unusual containers. A Santa cookie jar, a box wrapped with holiday gift wrap or a mason jar tied with raffia or ribbon make interesting containers for giving and serving finger foods. Look for unusual items around your house to serve your holiday nibbles in.

If necessary, line containers with plastic wrap to keep the food clean and to keep the food from staining the container. Or, you can use a holiday napkin to hide the plastic wrap before filling the container with snacks.

Reindeer Snack

PREP: 10 MIN; MICROWAVE: 9 MIN; COOL: 20 MIN
ABOUT 9 CUPS SNACK

1/3 cup butter or margarine

1/2 teaspoon chili powder

1/4 teaspoon garlic powder

3 cups popped popcorn

3 cups Bugles® nacho cheese flavor snacks

2 cups pretzel sticks

1 can (4 ounces) shoestring potatoes

Place butter, chili powder and garlic powder in 3-quart microwavable casserole or bowl. Microwave uncovered on High about 1 minute or until butter is melted; stir.

Stir in remaining ingredients. Toss until well coated. Microwave uncovered 6 to 8 minutes, stirring every 2 minutes; cool completely. Store loosely covered at room temperature up to 2 weeks.

1/2 Cup: Calories 110 (Calories from Fat 70); Fat 8g (Saturated 4g); Cholesterol 10mg; Sodium 180mg; Carbohydrate 10g (Dietary Fiber 1g); Protein 1g
% Daily Value: Vitamin A 2%; Vitamin C 4%; Calcium 0%; Iron 2%
Diet Exchanges: 1/2 Starch, 1 1/2 Fat

Holiday Hints

You can make this snack in the oven, too! Heat the oven to 300°. Mix popcorn, snacks, pretzels and shoestring potatoes in a large bowl. Melt butter, and mix with chili powder and garlic powder. Drizzle over popcorn mixture while tossing until evenly coated. Spread in ungreased jelly roll pan, 15 1/2 × 10 1/2 × 1 inch. Bake uncovered 15 minutes, stirring twice; cool.

Gifts for Giving

This is a perfect snack to make with the kids and leave for Santa's reindeer. Have fun creating ideas for packaging it. Perhaps Santa would like it in a doggie bag for the road trip!

Double-Frosted Chocolate Sandwich Cookies

PREP: 30 MIN; MICROWAVE: 10 MIN; STAND: 10 MIN
3 1/2 DOZEN COOKIES

1 package (10 ounces) white baking chips

4 teaspoons shortening

1 package (16 ounces) creme-filled chocolate sandwich cookies

1 package (10 ounces) mint-chocolate chips

Candy decorations, colored glitter sugars or coarse sugar crystals (decorating sugar)

Cover cookie sheet with waxed paper. Place white baking chips and 2 teaspoons of the shortening in microwavable bowl. Microwave uncovered on Medium (50%) 4 to 5 minutes or until mixture can be stirred smooth. Dip 21 of the cookies, one at a time, into white chip mixture; place on waxed paper on cookie sheet. Refrigerate 5 to 10 minutes or until coating is set.

Place mint-chocolate chips and remaining 2 teaspoons shortening in microwavable bowl. Microwave uncovered on Medium (50%) 4 to 5 minutes or until mixture can be stirred smooth. Dip remaining cookies, one at a time, into chocolate mixture; place on waxed paper on cookie sheet. Refrigerate 5 to 10 minutes or until coating is set.

Drizzle remaining chocolate melted mixture (reheat slightly if mixture has hardened) over tops of white-coated cookies. Sprinkle with candy decorations. Let stand until set. Drizzle remaining white melted mixture (reheat slightly if mixture has hardened) over tops of chocolate-coated cookies. Sprinkle with candy decorations. Let stand about 10 minutes or until set.

1 Cookie: Calories 130 (Calories from Fat 65); Fat 7g (Saturated 3g); Cholesterol 5mg; Sodium 85mg; Carbohydrate 16g (Dietary Fiber 1g); Protein 2g
% Daily Value: Vitamin A 0%; Vitamin C 0%; Calcium 2%; Iron 2%
Diet Exchanges: 1 Starch, 1 Fat

Party Pointers

Here's a fun inside activity for kids to do on a cold wintry day plus a few tips for you to make cookie dipping easy to clean up. Let the fun begin!

- Cover work surface with butcher's paper or a vinyl tablecloth.

- Apron all children. If aprons aren't available, tie large dish towels around them.

- Keep moistened cloths ready for sticky fingers and spills.

For the fun stuff, gather:

- Three or more styles of purchased sandwich cookies.

- At least two bowls of melted chocolates.

- Assorted candies, raisins, licorice, decorator icings and Rainbow Dust (page 256).

Double-Frosted Chocolate Sandwich Cookies

Chocolate Spoons

PREP: 30 MIN
18 TO 24 SPOONS

1 cup semisweet chocolate chips, white baking chips or mint-chocolate chips

18 to 24 gold- or silver-colored plastic spoons

Candy decorations, crushed hard peppermint candies, miniature candy-coated chocolate chips or coarse sugar crystals (decorating sugar), if desired

Melt chocolate in heavy 1-quart saucepan over lowest possible heat, stirring constantly. Dip spoons into melted chocolate, coating only the bowl of each spoon. Sprinkle with candy decorations. Place spoons on waxed paper until chocolate is set.

Wrap spoons in plastic wrap or cellophane.

Holiday Hints

For the young at heart, serve spoons with cups of piping hot cocoa. The chocolate will melt as the beverage is stirred.

Gifts for Giving

Get the whole family involved with this fun recipe.

- Delegate dipping, sprinkling and wrapping to different individuals or teams. Another person or group can be in charge of gift tags.

- Double dipping is encouraged for spoons. Dip first into white chocolate, then after white chocolate has set, dip into dark chocolate, leaving a hint of the white chocolate. Or drizzle melted chocolate in a zig-zag design over spoons.

- For a larger gift, place several wrapped chocolate spoons in holiday mugs. Include pouches of cocoa mix or special coffees.

Keep a basket of wrapped and tied with ribbon chocolate spoons by your entryway. As guests leave, surprise them with a momento of their visit.

Chocolate Spoons and Peppermint Wands (page 270)

Peppermint Wands

PREP: 25 MIN; STAND: 12 MIN
16 CANDY CANES

1/2 cup semisweet chocolate chips or white baking chips

2 teaspoons shortening

16 peppermint sticks or candy canes, about 6 inches long

Crushed hard peppermint candies, miniature chocolate chips, candy decorations, colored glitter sugars or coarse sugar crystals (decorating sugar), if desired

Line jelly roll pan, 15 1/2 × 10 1/2 × 1 inch, with waxed paper. Heat chocolate chips and shortening in 1-quart saucepan over low heat, stirring occasionally, until melted.

Tip saucepan so chocolate runs to one side. Dip 1 candy cane at a time into chocolate, coating about three-fourths of each cane with chocolate. Place on waxed paper in pan. Let stand about 2 minutes or until chocolate is partially dry.

Roll chocolate-dipped ends in crushed peppermint candies. Place on waxed paper in pan. Let stand about 10 minutes or until chocolate is dry. Store loosely covered at room temperature up to 2 weeks.

1 Candy Cane: Calories 140 (Calories from Fat 20); Fat 2g (Saturated 1g); Cholesterol 0mg; Sodium 10mg; Carbohydrate 31g (Dietary Fiber 0g); Protein 0g
% Daily Value: Vitamin A 0%; Vitamin C 0%; Calcium 0%; Iron 0%
Diet Exchanges: 2 Fruit

Holiday Hints

Using the microwave eliminates hot stove top preparation. Place chocolate chips and shortening in 2-cup microwavable measuring cup. Microwave uncovered on Medium (50%) about 3 minutes or until chips are softened; stir until smooth. Continue as directed.

Chocolate-Marshmallow Dip

PREP: 5 MIN
1 1/2 CUPS DIP

1 jar (7 ounces) marshmallow creme

1 container (4 ounces) snack-size chocolate fudge
pudding

Assorted holiday cookies, if desired

Assorted fruits, if desired

Small pretzel twists, if desired

Stir marshmallow creme until smooth. Just before serving, layer marshmallow creme and pudding in small
bowl. Swirl through layers, using tip of knife. Serve dip
with cookies, fruits and pretzels.

1/4 Cup: Calories 135 (calories from fat 10); Fat 1g (saturated 1g);
Cholesterol 0mg; Sodium 40mg; Carbohydrate 31g (Dietary Fiber
0g); Protein 1g
%Daily Value: Vitamin A 0%; Vitamin C 0%; Calcium 2%, Iron 0%
Diet exchanges: 2 Fruit

Holiday Hints

Kids love this dynamite dipper. For fun serving ideas:

- Layer this dip in a soda fountain-style sundae glass to
  show off the layers and swirls. For a festive finish, top
  with candy decorations, miniature candy-coated chocolate candies or chopped peanuts.

- Skewer banana chunks, strawberries, kiwifruit pieces,
  grapes and pineapple chunks on 4-inch drinking straws
  for funky fruit dippers.

If you're concerned about double dippers, use individual
clear serving dishes, and let the dipping begin.

North Pole Strawberry Smoothie

PREP: 5 MIN
2 SERVINGS

1 package (10 ounces) frozen strawberries in syrup, partially thawed and undrained

1/4 cup water

2 cups vanilla frozen yogurt

2 tablespoons vanilla reduced-fat yogurt

1 strawberry-flavored or peppermint candy cane, about 6 inches long, finely crushed

Green decorating gel

Place strawberries and water in blender. Cover and blend on medium-high speed until slushy. Blend on medium speed until smooth. Transfer to 2-cup measure.

Wash and dry blender. Place frozen yogurt and reduced-fat yogurt in blender. Cover and blend on medium speed until smooth.

Place crushed candy cane on small plate. Pipe decorating gel around rim of two 12-ounce glasses. Dip rims into crushed candy.

Carefully pour yogurt mixture and strawberries at the same time into glasses, creating a half-and-half design. Serve with large drinking straws if desired.

1 Serving: Calories 425 (Calories from Fat 20); Fat 2g (Saturated 1g); Cholesterol 10mg; Sodium 130mg; Carbohydrate 95g (Dietary Fiber 3g); Protein 10g
% Daily Value: Vitamin A 2%; Vitamin C 100%; Calcium 32%; Iron 6%
Diet Exchanges: 3 Starch, 3 Fruit

Party Pointers

Host a Santa's Breakfast for the neighborhood kids! Here are a few helpful organizing tips:

• Send out invitations immediately after Thanksgiving.

• Limit the party to six guests, plus a couple parents you think could be helpful.

• Enlist a Santa (the earlier the better) to join the kids for breakfast.

• Have a small wrapped gift at each place setting or in Santa's sack to be distributed.

HOLIDAY MENU

Santa's Breakfast Menu

• North Pole Strawberry Smoothie

• Scrambled eggs and hashbrowns

• Merry Muffins (page 172), dipped into colored sugars

North Pole Strawberry Smoothie

Christmas Vacation Peanut Butter Fondue

PREP: 10 MIN; COOK: 5 MIN
1 1/2 CUPS FONDUE

2/3 cup packed brown sugar

1/4 cup half-and-half

1 tablespoon honey

3/4 cup creamy peanut butter

Pieces of assorted cakes, candies and fruit, if desired (see Holiday Hints, below)

Heat brown sugar, half-and-half and honey to boiling in 2-quart saucepan over medium heat, stirring occasionally.

Stir in peanut butter until smooth. Pour into fondue pot or individual serving bowls. Dip assorted cakes, candies and fruit into fondue.

1/4 Cup: Calories 320 (Calories from Fat 160); Fat 18g (Saturated 4g); Cholesterol 5mg; Sodium 160mg; Carbohydrate 33g (Dietary Fiber 2g); Protein 8g
% Daily Value: Vitamin A 0%; Vitamin C 0%; Calcium 4%; Iron 6%
Diet Exchanges: 2 Starch, 3 1/2 Fat

Party Pointers

Have the Christmas Vacation Peanut Butter Fondue ready, and invite the neighbor kids to a children's holiday party. Activities could include building a Winter Wonderland Castle (page 280) or cookie decorating.

Holiday Hints

To make fondue even more fun:

- Use chocolate-covered candy dessert sticks for dipping.
- Use sugar-cone sundae cups for individual-size fondue.
- Place chocolate sprinkles in a separate bowl into which to dip fondue-coated foods.

Try these tempting dippers:

- Purchased pound cake cut into cubes or seasonal shapes
- Animal crackers or graham cracker squares
- Marshmallows

- Strawberries, grapes, pineapple chunks, banana slices, apple slices and pear slices
- Small pretzel twists—plain or fudge-covered

Christmas Vacation Peanut Butter Fondue

Festive Family Fun

Gingerbread Drum

PREP: 45 MIN; BAKE: 12 MIN; COOL: 30 MIN; STAND: 30 MIN

1 DRUM

1 package (14 1/2 ounces) gingerbread cake and cookie mix

1/4 cup hot water

2 tablespoons all-purpose flour

2 tablespoons butter or margarine, melted

Royal Icing (page 204)

7 graham cracker squares, 2 1/2 inches

Any color of gummy candy strips

Small candies, if desired

1 piece shoestring licorice, about 12 inches long, if desired

2 peppermint sticks, about 6 inches long

2 large marshmallows

Heat oven to 375°. Prepare gingerbread mix as directed on package for gingersnaps, using hot water, flour and butter. Divide dough in half. Roll each half 1/4 inch thick on lightly floured cloth-covered surface.

Cut two 6-inch circles from dough by inverting 6-inch-diameter bowl onto dough and cutting around bowl with knife. Make 2 holes in one circle 3 inches apart and 1/2 inch from edge, using end of drinking straw (holes will be used to insert licorice drum handle). Place circles on ungreased cookie sheet. Bake 9 to 12 minutes or until firm and edges begin to brown. Cool 3 minutes; remove from cookie sheet to wire rack. Cool completely.

Prepare Royal Icing. Place gingerbread circle without holes on work surface to use as bottom of drum. Attach graham crackers to drum bottom at right angle, using icing as glue, to form side of drum. Let stand about 30 minutes or until icing is completely set.

Attach gingerbread circle with holes to graham crackers, using icing, to form top of drum; or if desired, do not attach top of drum and use top as a lid instead. Cut desired lengths of gummy candy strips. Attach in V-shape pattern around side of drum, using icing. Attach small candies to top and bottom edges and side of drum, using icing. Loop licorice through holes on top of drum to make handle. Make drumsticks by inserting end of each peppermint stick into a marshmallow.

Holiday Hints

Using graham crackers for the side of the drum is easy for little hands, but if you prefer, make side of drum from the prepared gingerbread dough. One package of the gingerbread mix will make either two complete drums with sides or two rounds for one drum plus cookies to tuck inside.

The dough for the Gingerbread Village (page 306) can also be used to make this drum. Prepare and bake as directed, using the drum measurements.

Gifts for Giving

Fill the gingerbread drum with treats, and leave it out for Santa and his reindeer. You may like to fill it with Teddy Bear Snack Toss (page 264), small gingerbread cookies or wrapped candies.

A child will love making a drum for Grandma and Grandpa filled with their favorite cookies or candies. Or instead of cookies or candies, a handwritten "I love you and made this just for you" note may be a perfect filler.

Gingerbread Drum

Winterland Critters

PREP: 30 MIN; STAND: 20 MIN
ABOUT 30 COOKIES

For All Critters

1 package (20 ounces) vanilla-flavored candy coating (almond bark)

1 package (16 ounces) Vienna-style creme-filled sandwich cookies

Cover cookie sheet with waxed paper. Place 6 squares of candy coating in 4-cup microwavable measuring cup. Microwave uncovered on High 1 minute; stir. Microwave 1 to 2 minutes longer, stirring well every 30 seconds, until smooth. Candy coating will be used to coat cookies and to attach candies to cookies. Add squares of coating as needed, and microwave 10 to 15 seconds at a time, stirring until smooth.

Follow directions for decorating about 10 each of Penguins, Reindeer and Santas.

1 Cookie: Calories 175 (Calories from Fat 80); Fat 9g (Saturated 5g); Cholesterol 5mg; Sodium 65mg; Carbohydrate 2g (Dietary Fiber 0g); Protein 2g
%Daily Value: Vitamin A 0%; Vitamin C 0%; Calcium 4%; Iron 2%
Diet Exchanges: 1 1/2 Starch, 1 Fat

Holiday Hints

Kids will have a ball making a winter wonderland scene! To finish your wintry scene, consider these additions:

• Skating Pond: Place a small mirror on the board, and surround it with marshmallow snow.

• Snow Skis: Create skis by using sticks of chewing gum; create poles with black string licorice.

• Sleds: For a Santa's sled, use candy canes for runners and graham crackers for the sleigh to hold Santa.

Penguins

Black string licorice, cut into 3-inch lengths for body and about 1/2-inch pieces for eyes

Candy corn, cut crosswise in half (discard large ends)

White fudge or yogurt-covered small pretzel twists

Any color of chewy fruit snack rolls (from 5-ounce package) or red string licorice, cut into 7-inch strips

Assorted large and small gumdrops

Dip one cookie at a time into candy coating to cover completely. Place on waxed paper on cookie sheet. Immediately place 3-inch lengths of licorice on cookie to form outline of penguin; insert 1/2-inch pieces of licorice into coating for eyes. Insert pointed ends of candy corn pieces into coating for beaks. Let stand about 20 minutes until coating is completely set.

Attach pretzel to end of cookie, using candy coating, for feet. Let stand until coating is set.

Cut 6 × 1/2-inch strip of fruit snack roll for scarf; tie scarf around neck of penguin. For earmuffs, flatten 2 small gumdrops for ends of earmuffs; cut 2 × 1/4-inch strip of fruit snack roll for headband of earmuffs. For hat, cut triangle shape from fruit snack roll. Attach to penguin, using candy coating. Let stand until coating is set.

Reindeer

Small pretzel twists

Assorted candy decorations

Candy-coated chocolate candies

Whole almonds

Any color of chewy fruit snack rolls (from 5-ounce package)

Dip each end of cookie into candy coating, leaving middle of cookie uncoated. Place on waxed paper on cookie sheet. Attach pretzel to end of cookie, using candy coating, for hooves. Let stand about 20 minutes or until coating is set.

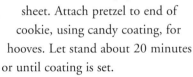

Break off end of rounded tips of pretzel to resemble antlers. Dip cookie top into melted coating; immediately attach antlers.

Attach candies for eyes using melted coating. Attach almond for nose, using melted coating. Cut $3 \times 1/8$-inch strip of fruit snack roll for collar; attach collar around reindeer neck, using coating. Attach candies to collar if desired. Let stand until coating is set.

Santas

Red sugar

White fudge or yogurt-covered small pretzel twists (from 7 1/2-ounce package)

Santa face candy decorations

Any color of chewy fruit snack rolls (from 5-ounce package)

Large red and green gumdrops

Green miniature candy-coated chocolate candies

Dip one cookie at a time into candy coating to cover completely; immediately sprinkle with red sugar. Place on waxed paper on cookie sheet. Attach pretzel to end of cookie, using coating, for feet. Let stand about 20 minutes or until coating is set.

Dip cookie top into melted coating; sprinkle with red sugar. Attach Santa face to front of cookie, using extra coating if needed.

Cut $3 \times 1/8$-inch strip of fruit snack roll for belt; attach belt around Santa, using coating. Cut large red gumdrop into fourths; attach 2 of the pieces to each cookie, using coating, for arms. Attach candies to end of arms for mittens. Attach other candies for decorations if desired.

Attach large green gumdrop to Santa's back, using coating, for Santa's toy bag. Let stand until coating is set.

Holiday Hints

Purchased cookies are ideal for little hands to decorate and for big people's patience. Here are a few tips:

- Cookies that are firm, such as sandwich-style cookies, work best.

- Melt white baking chips, milk chocolate chips and semisweet chocolate chips in microwavable dishes in the microwave.

- Let kids do their thing. They may want red trees or green Santa faces, but we guarantee they will have fun!

- Have small dishes of the decorations kids like most.

Winter Wonderland Castle

PREP: 2 HR
1 CASTLE

16 pretzel rods, about 9 inches long

1 package (20 ounces) vanilla-flavored candy coating (almond bark)

9 sugar-style ice-cream cones with pointed ends

Red colored sugars

Red and green candy decorations

Foamcore board or heavy cardboard, 16×14 inches

Aluminum foil

7 graham cracker squares, 2 1/2 inches

About 9 small gumdrops, if desired

Red string licorice, cut into 5-inch strips

Chewy fruit snack rolls (from 5-ounce package)

6 candy canes, 3 inches long

1 roll (0.9 ounce) ring-shaped hard candy

1 bag (10 ounces) large marshmallows

1 bag (10 1/2 ounces) miniature marshmallows

Blue, purple and white coarse sugar crystals (decorating sugar), if desired

Tube of decorating icing, if desired

Make corner posts of castle by securing 4 pretzel rods with twist tie or rubber band at the middle. Make sure that one end of group of pretzel rods is even so they stand upright easily. Repeat 3 times to make 4 corner posts; set aside.

Place 6 squares of candy coating in 4-cup microwavable measuring cup. Microwave uncovered on High 1 minute; stir. Microwave 1 to 2 minutes longer, stirring well every 30 seconds, until smooth. Candy coating will be used to attach pieces of castle. Add squares coating as needed, and microwave 10 to 15 seconds at a time, stirring until smooth.

Dip 2 inches of bottoms (level end) of 1 corner post of pretzels into coating. Place upright on waxed paper, letting coating pool slightly to form a base. Let stand about 30 minutes or until coating is completely set. Repeat with remaining corner posts.

Spread melted coating over ice-cream cones. Roll 4 cones in red sugar for castle towers; roll remaining cones in candy decorations for trees. Place upright on waxed paper. Let stand about 20 minutes or until coating is completely set.

Cover foamcore board with aluminum foil. Dip tops of each corner post into coating; top with red cones. Let stand about 30 minutes or until coating is completely set; remove twist ties or rubber band from pretzels.

Attach 1 graham cracker square between each set of corner posts, using coating, to form square castle. Attach half of a graham cracker square above 3 of the whole cracker squares, leaving 1/2 inch space between crackers. Attach gumdrops along top of cracker halves, using coating. Attach licorice along sides of corner posts.

Attach 1 graham cracker square at right angle to cracker square at fourth side, using coating, to form drawbridge. Cut strip from fruit roll; attach to drawbridge for walkway. Attach candy canes for braces for drawbridge.

Attach ring-shaped candies at top of each cone tower; attach candy cane to ring-shaped candy at each tower. Cut pennant-style flags from fruit roll, about 2×1/2 inch; attach to candy canes.

Spread melted coating randomly over foil surrounding castle. Sprinkle with large and miniature marshmallows to create snow. Sprinkle sugar crystals around castle to create moat. Arrange green tree cones to create winter scene. Create a sign for the castle with 6×1-inch strip of fruit roll; add letters to sign with decorating icing. Add Winterland Critters (page 278) to complete the castle scene.

P B and "Jay" Bird Feeder Treat

PREP: 15 MIN

1 BIRD FEEDER

4 unsalted rice cakes, about 3 inches in diameter

About 1/4 cup peanut butter

Birdseed

About 3 tablespoons jelly or peanut butter

1 length of twine, 2 feet long

Cranberry Heart (right) or orange slice

Ribbon, 6 to 12 inches long, if desired

Poke a hole in the middle of each rice cake, using a skewer. Spread peanut butter over 2 rice cakes. Top with other 2 rice cakes to make 2 sandwiches.

Spread birdseed on cookie sheet. Spread honey on edges of each sandwich; roll in birdseed until edges are completely covered.

Tie a double knot about 6 inches from one end of twine. Thread sandwich, through center hole, on other end of twine. Tie another double knot in twine about 6 inches from sandwich. Thread on second sandwich.

Tie a loop in top end of twine to allow bird feeder to hang. Tie Cranberry Heart to bottom end of twine. Tie ribbon around twine into bow.

Cranberry Heart

Thread dried cranberries (from 6-ounce package) on 1-foot length of floral wire, leaving 1 inch of bare wire on each end. Twist ends together to form a circle; form into a heart shape.

Holiday Hints

Trim a tree in your yard with edible decorations to help the birds celebrate the season.

- Spread peanut butter on pinecones, roll in birdseed and nestle in branches.
- Slice oranges, and hang from branches with brightly colored waterproof ribbon.
- Thread popcorn and cranberries onto string to hang from branches.

Santa's Chimney (page 316)

CHAPTER 8

Holiday Giifts and Decorations

During the holidays, mantels and vases

overflow with evergreens and holly,

while treasured gifts wrapped in shiny bows

rest unopened beneath the tree.

Maple-Cranberry Syrup

PREP: 5 MIN; COOK: 5 MIN
1 1/2 CUPS SYRUP

1 cup maple-flavored syrup

1/2 cup whole berry cranberry sauce

1/4 cup chopped walnuts, if desired

Heat maple syrup and cranberry sauce in 1-quart saucepan over medium heat, stirring occasionally, until cranberry sauce is melted. Stir in walnuts. Serve warm. Store covered in refrigerator up to 4 weeks.

1 Tablespoon: Calories 45 (Calories from Fat 0); Fat 0g (Saturated 0g); Cholesterol 0mg; Sodium 0mg; Carbohydrate 10g (Dietary Fiber 0g); Protein 0g
% Daily Value: Vitamin A 0%; Vitamin C 0%; Calcium 0%; Iron 0%
Diet Exchanges: 1/2 Fruit

Holiday Hints

If you have a crowd in for the holidays, wake them up with the aroma of fresh hot waffles! Add dried cranberries, grated orange peel and chopped nuts to your favorite waffle batter, and serve with plenty of creamy butter and Maple-Cranberry Syrup.

HOLIDAY MENU
New Year's Day Brunch

- Assorted juices
- Hot sausage links
- Cheesy Apple-Bacon Strata (page 86)
- Waffles or pancakes with warm Maple-Cranberry Syrup
- Heavenly Fruit Salad (page 102)
- Coffee and tea

Maple-Cranberry Syrup

Spirited Apple Butter

PREP: 20 MIN; COOK: 3 HR; COOL: 1 HR
ABOUT 5 HALF-PINTS BUTTER

1 can (12 ounces) frozen apple juice concentrate

1/2 cup sweet red wine or apple cider

4 pounds cooking apples, peeled and cut into
fourths (about 3 quarts)

3/4 cup packed brown sugar

1 cup apple brandy or apple cider

1 teaspoon ground cinnamon

1 teaspoon ground ginger

1/4 teaspoon ground cloves

Heat apple juice concentrate, wine and apples to boiling
in Dutch oven; reduce heat. Simmer uncovered about
1 hour, stirring occasionally, until apples are very soft.

Mash apples with potato masher if necessary to remove
all lumps. Stir in remaining ingredients. Heat to boiling;
reduce heat. Simmer uncovered about 2 hours, stirring
occasionally, until no liquid separates from pulp.

Immediately pour mixture into hot, sterilized jars, or
freezer containers leaving 1/4-inch headspace. Wipe rims
of jars; seal. Cool on rack 1 hour. Store in refrigerator up
to 2 months.

1 Tablespoon: Calories 40 (Calories from Fat 10); Fat 1g
(Saturated 0g); Cholesterol 0mg; Sodium 0mg; Carbohydrate 8g
(Dietary Fiber 0g); Protein 0g
% Daily Value: Vitamin A 0%; Vitamin C 0%; Calcium 0%; Iron 0%
Diet Exchanges: 1/2 Fruit

SPIRITED PUMPKIN BUTTER: Omit wine. Substitute
3 cans (15 ounces each) pumpkin for the apples. Increase
brown sugar to 1 cup and cinnamon to 1 1/2 teaspoons.
Heat all ingredients to boiling in Dutch oven, stirring
frequently; reduce heat. Simmer uncovered about 1 hour,
stirring frequently. Immediately pour into hot, sterilized
jars, leaving 1/4-inch headspace. Continue as directed.
About 6 half-pints butter.

Holiday Hints

Enjoy this yummy spread on crackers, toasted bread,
English muffins or bagels. For an extra special treat, try
it with mascarpone cheese or cream cheese.

Spirited Apple Butter

Holiday Gifts and Decorations

White Chocolate-Almond Sauce

PREP: 5 MIN; COOK: 10 MIN
ABOUT 2 3/4 CUPS SAUCE

2 tablespoons butter or margarine

1 cup slivered almonds

1 cup whipping (heavy) cream

1 package (12 ounces) white baking chips (2 cups)

1 tablespoon amaretto or 1/4 teaspoon almond extract

Dash of salt

Heat butter and almonds in 3-quart saucepan over medium heat 6 to 8 minutes, stirring frequently, until almonds are medium brown; remove from heat.

Stir in whipping cream until well blended (mixture will spatter). Stir in white baking chips. Heat over low heat, stirring frequently, until chips are melted.

Stir in amaretto and salt. Serve warm or cold. Stir before serving. Store covered in refrigerator up to 4 weeks.

1 Tablespoon: Calories 80 (Calories from Fat 55); Fat 6g (Saturated 3g); Cholesterol 9mg; Sodium 15mg; Carbohydrate 5g (Dietary Fiber 0g); Protein 1g
% Daily Value: Vitamin A 2%; Vitamin C 0%; Calcium 2%; Iron 0%
Diet Exchanges: 1/2 Fruit, 1 Fat

Holiday Hints

Don't limit this sauce to ice cream! Serve it with fresh fruit, Golden Pound Cake (page 136) or warm Gingerbread (page 142).

Gifts for Giving

A tisket, a tasket, why not give a basket? Fill basket with jars with White Chocolate-Almond Sauce, Decadent Fudge Sauce (page 290) and Lemon Curd (page 292). Some gift recipients may like a copy of the recipes; others would prefer a coupon good for a free refill!

Timesaving Tips

Use the microwave to speed up the preparation of this scrumptious sauce. To microwave: Place butter and almonds in 8-cup microwavable measuring cup. Microwave uncovered on High 3 to 4 minutes, stirring every minute, until almonds begin to brown. Stir in whipping cream until well blended. Stir in white baking chips. Microwave uncovered about 1 minute or until chips can be stirred smooth. Stir in amaretto and salt.

Hazelnut-Coffee Caramels (page 291), Decadent Fudge Sauce (page 290) and White Chocolate-Almond Sauce

Decadent Fudge Sauce

PREP: 5 MIN; COOK: 5 MIN
ABOUT 3 CUPS SAUCE

1 can (12 ounces) evaporated milk

1 package (12 ounces) semisweet chocolate chips (2 cups)

1/2 cup sugar

1 tablespoon butter or margarine

2 teaspoons orange-flavored liqueur or 1 teaspoon orange extract, if desired

Heat milk, chocolate chips and sugar to boiling in 2-quart saucepan over medium heat, stirring constantly; remove from heat.

Stir in butter and liqueur until sauce is smooth and creamy. Serve warm over ice cream. Store covered in refrigerator up to 4 weeks.

1 Tablespoon: Calories 60 (Calories from Fat 25); Fat 3g (Saturated 2g); Cholesterol 5mg; Sodium 10mg; Carbohydrate 7g (Dietary Fiber 0g); Protein 1g
% Daily Value: Vitamin A 0%; Vitamin C 0%; Calcium 2%; Iron 0%
Diet Exchanges: 1/2 Fruit, 1/2 Fat

New Twist

Love raspberries and chocolate? Substitute 2 tablespoons raspberry-flavored liqueur for the orange. For classic fudge sauce, omit the liqueur and add 1 teaspoon vanilla.

Gifts for Giving

Looking for that final touch for a gift of chocolate sauce? Surround the filled jar of chocolate sauce with peppermint candy canes and tie with a bright red ribbon.

Hazelnut-Coffee Caramels

PREP: 5 MIN; COOK: 20 MIN

4 DOZEN CANDIES

1/2 cup chopped hazelnuts

3/4 cup butter or margarine

2 cups packed brown sugar

1 cup corn syrup

2 tablespoons instant espresso coffee (dry)

1 tablespoon hazelnut syrup (coffee flavoring)

1 can (14 ounces) sweetened condensed milk

Chocolate-covered coffee beans, if desired

Line square pan, 8 × 8 × 2 inches with aluminum foil, leaving 1 inch of foil overhanging at 2 opposite sides of pan. Butter foil that lines bottom of pan. Sprinkle hazelnuts in pan.

Heat butter, brown sugar, corn syrup, coffee, hazelnut syrup and milk to boiling in heavy 3-quart saucepan. Cook over medium heat, stirring frequently, to 245° on candy thermometer or until small amount of mixture dropped into very cold water forms a firm ball. Pour into pan; cool.

Remove mixture from pan, using foil edges to lift. Cut into 8 rows by 6 rows. Garnish with coffee beans. Wrap pieces individually in waxed paper or cellophane.

1 Candy: Calories 135 (Calories from Fat 45); Fat 5g (Saturated 2g); Cholesterol 10mg; Sodium 45mg; Carbohydrate 21g (Dietary Fiber 0g); Protein 1g
% Daily Value: Vitamin A 2%; Vitamin C 0%; Calcium 4%; Iron 0%
Diet Exchanges: 1 1/2 Fruit, 1 Fat

New Twist

Feeling nutty? Use your favorite nut in this recipe, and use vanilla for the hazelnut syrup.

Gifts for Giving

Oh, what a gift—wonderful to give and even better to receive! Package these treats in holiday cellophane (found in party stores), and place in a clear coffee mug with a small bag of hazelnut coffee. Tie gold ribbons on the mug, and it's ready for a great office gift.

Lemon Curd

PREP: 10 MIN; COOK: 8 MIN
ABOUT 2 CUPS CURD

1 cup sugar

2 teaspoons finely grated lemon peel

1 cup lemon juice (about 5 large lemons)

3 tablespoons firm butter or margarine, cut up

3 eggs, slightly beaten

Mix sugar, lemon peel and lemon juice in heavy 1 1/2-quart saucepan. Stir in butter and eggs. Cook over medium heat about 8 minutes, stirring constantly, until mixture thickens and coats back of spoon (do not boil).

Immediately pour into one 1-pint container or two 1-cup containers. Store covered in refrigerator up to 2 months.

1 Tablespoon: Calories 50 (Calories from Fat 20); Fat 2g (Saturated 1g); Cholesterol 20mg; Sodium 15mg; Carbohydrate 7g (Dietary Fiber 0g); Protein 1g
% Daily Value: Vitamin A 2%; Vitamin C 0%; Calcium 0%; Iron 0%
Diet Exchanges: 1/2 Fruit

Holiday Hints

Try this tart lemon filling spread over:

• Toast or scones

• Golden Pound Cake (page 136)

• Heavenly Cheesecake (page 146)

• Gingerbread (page 142)

• Sugar cookies

New Twist

For a creamy lemon mousse, fold 1 cup whipped cream into lemon curd and use to:

• Fill baked pie shell or miniature tart shells.

• Spoon over angel food cake, sponge cake or sliced strawberries.

Pineapple-Apricot Jam

PREP: 10 MIN; COOK: 12 MIN
ABOUT 5 HALF-PINTS JAM

Flecked with snippets of tropical fruit, this jam is a delight for gift givers and receivers. Once you try a spoonful, you'll agree that the little taste of paradise in every jar makes this jam such a popular present.

1 jar (6 ounces) maraschino cherries, drained and 1/3 cup syrup reserved

1 can (20 ounces) crushed pineapple in syrup, undrained

6 ounces dried apricots, cut into fourths (about 1 cup)

1/4 cup water

3 1/2 cups sugar

2 tablespoons lemon juice

1 pouch (3 ounces) liquid fruit pectin (from 6-ounce package)

Chop cherries; set aside. Heat reserved cherry syrup, the pineapple, apricots and water to boiling in Dutch oven, stirring occasionally; reduce heat. Cover and simmer about 10 minutes, stirring occasionally, until apricots are tender.

Stir in sugar, lemon juice and cherries. Heat to rolling boil over high heat, stirring occasionally. Boil and stir 1 minute; remove from heat. Stir in pectin.

Immediately pour mixture into hot, sterilized jars or freezer containers, leaving 1/2-inch headspace. Wipe rims of jars. Seal immediately; cool. Refrigerate or freeze up to 3 months. Thaw before serving.

1 Tablespoon: Calories 50 (Calories from Fat 0); Fat 0g (Saturated 0g); Cholesterol 0mg; Sodium 0mg; Carbohydrate 13g (Dietary Fiber 0g); Protein 0g
% Daily Value: Vitamin A 2%; Vitamin C 0%; Calcium %; Iron %
Diet Exchanges: 1 Fruit

Gifts for Giving

This brightly colored jam doesn't need much to say Merry Christmas all by itself. Simply:

• Use fancy cut-glass jars and homemade decorative labels to add that holiday sparkle.

• Top it off with a piece of decorative fabric or paper, and tie with a matching ribbon.

• Package it with a holiday tin filled with Apricot Jeweled Scones (page 174).

Apple-Pepper Jelly

PREP: 15 MIN; COOK: 5 MIN
ABOUT 4 HALF-PINTS JELLY

2 cups water

1 can (6 ounces) frozen apple juice concentrate, thawed

1 package (1 3/4 ounces) powdered fruit pectin

3 3/4 cups sugar

Few drops of red food color, if desired

1 to 2 tablespoons crushed red pepper

Mix water, apple juice concentrate and pectin in 3-quart saucepan until pectin is dissolved. Heat to boiling, stirring constantly. Stir in sugar. Heat to rolling boil, stirring constantly; remove from heat. Stir in food color. Quickly skim off foam. Stir in pepper.

Immediately pour into hot, sterilized jars or freezer containers, leaving 1/2-inch headspace. Wipe rims of jars. Seal immediately; cool. Store in refrigerator up to 1 month or in freezer up to 2 months. Thaw before serving.

1 Tablespoon: Calories 55 (Calories from Fat 0); Fat 0g (Saturated 0g); Cholesterol 0mg; Sodium 0mg; Carbohydrate 13g (Dietary Fiber 0g); Protein 1g
% Daily Value: Vitamin A 0%; Vitamin C 0%; Calcium 0%; Iron 0%
Diet Exchanges: 1 Fruit

Apple-Pepper Jelly and Pear-Cranberry Chutney (page 295)

Pear-Cranberry Chutney

PREP: 10 MIN; COOK: 1 HR
ABOUT 2 CUPS CHUTNEY

2 ripe firm medium pears (about 1 pound),
    chopped

1/2 pound cranberries

1 small onion, coarsely chopped (1/4 cup)

1 medium red bell pepper, chopped (1 cup)

3/4 cup packed brown sugar

1/2 cup raisins

1/2 cup white vinegar

1 1/2 teaspoons finely chopped gingerroot

1 clove garlic, crushed

Mix all ingredients in 2-quart saucepan. Heat to boiling, stirring frequently; reduce heat.

Simmer uncovered about 1 hour, stirring frequently, until mixture thickens and fruit is tender. Store covered in nonaluminum container in refrigerator up to 2 weeks.

1 Tablespoon: Calories 35 (Calories from Fat 0); Fat 0g (Saturated 0g); Cholesterol 0mg; Sodium 5mg; Carbohydrate 10g (Dietary Fiber 0g); Protein 0g
% Daily Value: Vitamin A 2%; Vitamin C 6%; Calcium 0%; Iron 0%
Diet Exchanges: 1/2 Fruit

Holiday Hints

For longer storage, pour hot chutney into hot, sterilized jars, leaving 1/4-inch headspace. Wipe rims of jars; seal. Cool on rack 1 hour. Store in refrigerator up to 2 months.

Gifts for Giving

When giving this chutney as a gift, you may like to pass along some serving suggestions:

- Serve chutney over roast turkey, ham or pork.

- Spoon chutney over a block of cream cheese or over a round of Brie cheese. Heat the Brie cheese in the microwave on High for about 1 1/2 minutes. Top with the chutney, and serve with crackers.

- Spread chutney on bagels or savory scones.

Balsamic-Glazed Pearl Onions

PREP: 5 MIN; COOK: 25 MIN

8 SERVINGS

3 tablespoons butter or margarine

2 bags (16 ounces each) frozen small whole onions

1 cup balsamic vinegar

1/4 cup sugar

1 teaspoon salt

1/2 teaspoon pepper

Melt butter in 12-inch skillet over medium heat. Cook frozen onions in butter about 10 minutes, stirring occasionally, until water from onions is reduced and onions begin to soften.

Stir vinegar and sugar into onions. Cook, stirring constantly, until sugar is dissolved; reduce heat. Simmer uncovered about 10 minutes, stirring occasionally, until liquid is reduced to a glaze consistency. Sprinkle with salt and pepper. Store covered in refrigerater up to 2 weeks.

1 Serving: Calories 115 (Calories from Fat 45); Fat 5g (Saturated 3g); Cholesterol 10mg; Sodium 330mg; Carbohydrate 18g (Dietary Fiber 2g); Protein 1g
% Daily Value: Vitamin A 2%; Vitamin C 6%; Calcium 2%; Iron 2%
Diet Exchanges: 3 Vegetables, 1 Fat

Timesaving Tips

- Using frozen onions is a real timesaver, but feel free to substitute fresh small whole onions if you prefer.

- If you're a cook who likes to plan ahead, you'll like this do-ahead recipe. Prepare recipe one day ahead; cover tightly and refrigerate. Rewarm over low heat just before serving.

Balsamic-Glazed Pearl Onions

Citrus-Caraway Mustard

PREP: 10 MIN

1 CUP MUSTARD

1/2 cup mustard seed

2 teaspoons caraway seed

1/2 cup orange marmalade

1/4 cup cider vinegar

1/4 cup water

1 teaspoon salt

Place mustard seed and caraway seed in food processor or blender. Cover and process until finely ground. Add remaining ingredients. Cover and process until smooth.

Pour mustard into jar. Cover and store in refrigerator up to 2 weeks. Flavors mellow after several days.

1 Tablespoon: Calories 60 (Calories from Fat 20); Fat 2g (Saturated 1g); Cholesterol 0mg; Sodium 150mg; Carbohydrate 8g (Dietary Fiber 0g); Protein 2g
% Daily Value: Vitamin A 0%; Vitamin C 2%; Calcium 2%; Iron 2%
Diet Exchanges: 1 Fruit

Holiday Hints

Experiment with gourmet vinegars. You may like to try white wine vinegar, champagne vinegar, balsamic vinegar or a homemade herb vinegar to give this mustard a flavor twist.

Gifts for Giving

Package this mustard in a pretty glass jar and top with fabric or craft paper and ribbon. Tie a wooden ornament or spreader around rim of jar. You won't wait long before the telephone rings and a big thank-you resounds from the other end!

Citrus-Caraway Mustard

Herb Vinegar

PREP: 20 MIN; STAND: 10 DAYS
2 CUPS VINEGAR

2 cups white wine vinegar

1/2 cup firmly packed fresh herb leaves (basil, chives, dill weed, mint, oregano, rosemary or tarragon)

Shake vinegar and herb in tightly covered glass jar or bottle. Let stand in cool, dry place 10 days to flavor vinegar. Strain vinegar. Place 1 sprig of fresh herb in jar to identify if desired.

Gifts for Giving

Surprise your favorite salad lovers with a "vinegar of the month" gift. They will be sure to love these varieties! Or fill a salad bowl with extra-virgin olive oil, gourmet mustard, whole garlic, salad tongs, peppercorns and a pepper grinder, gourmet croutons and several bottles of Herb Vinegar.

1 Tablespoon: Calories 4 (Calories from Fat 0); Fat 0g (Saturated 0g); Cholesterol 0mg; Sodium 0mg; Carbohydrate 1g (Dietary Fiber 0g); Protein 0g
% Daily Value: Vitamin A 0%; Vitamin C 0%; Calcium 0%; Iron 0%
Diet Exchanges: Not recommended

BERRY VINEGAR:
Substitute 2 cups berries, crushed, for the herb.

CRANBERRY-ORANGE VINEGAR:
Substitute peel from 1 orange and 1/2 cup cranberries, crushed, for the herb.

GARLIC VINEGAR:
Substitute 6 cloves garlic, cut in half, for the herb.

GINGER VINEGAR:
Substitute 1/2 cup chopped peeled gingerroot for the herb.

LEMON VINEGAR:
Substitute peel from 2 lemons for the herb.

Herb Vinegar (Garlic and Cranberry-Orange—variations)

Holiday Gifts and Decorations

Spicy Mocha Mix

PREP: 10 MIN
ABOUT 1 CUP MIX (24 SERVINGS)

1/2 cup sugar

1/4 cup instant coffee (dry)

1/4 cup baking cocoa

1 teaspoon ground nutmeg

1/2 teaspoon ground cinnamon

Stir all ingredients until completely mixed. Store in tightly covered container at room temperature up to 6 months.

For each serving: Place 2 to 3 teaspoons mix in cup or mug and fill with 2/3 cup boiling water; stir. Top with whipped cream if desired. For 6 servings, place 1/4 to 1/3 cup mix in heatproof container and add 4 cups boiling water.

1 Serving: Calories 20 (Calories from Fat 0); Fat 0g (Saturated 0g); Cholesterol 0mg; Sodium 0mg; Carbohydrate 5g (Dietary Fiber 0g); Protein 0g
% Daily Value: Vitamin A 0%; Vitamin C 0%; Calcium 0%; Iron 0%
Diet Exchanges: Not recommended

JAVA MIX: Decrease cocoa to 2 tablespoons and omit nutmeg and cinnamon.

ORANGE CAFÉ AU LAIT MIX: Omit cocoa and nutmeg. Add 1/2 cup powdered nondairy creamer and 1 teaspoon grated orange peel.

Gifts for Giving

Any busy friend will love a "pampering package." Fill a basket with a large holiday mug, jars of Spicy Mocha Mix, Java Mix and Orange Café au Lait Mix, a package of biscotti, a relaxation audio tape or a new book off the best-seller list.

Spicy Mocha Mix and Easy Festive Peppermint Marshmallows (page 303)

Easy Festive Peppermint Marshmallows

PREP: 5 MIN; COOK: 10 MIN; STAND: 8 HR
ABOUT 40 MARSHMALLOWS

Powdered sugar

2 1/2 tablespoons unflavored gelatin

1/2 cup cold water

1 1/2 cups granulated sugar

1 cup corn syrup

1/4 teaspoon salt

1/2 cup water

1 teaspoon peppermint extract

Generously dust rectangular baking dish, 11×7 1/2×2 inches, with powdered sugar. Sprinkle gelatin on 1/2 cup cold water in large bowl to soften; set aside.

Heat granulated sugar, corn syrup, salt and 1/2 cup water in 2-quart saucepan over low heat, stirring constantly, until sugar is dissolved. Heat to boiling; cook without stirring to 250° on candy thermometer or until small amount of mixture dropped into very cold water forms a ball that holds its shape but is pliable; remove from heat.

Slowly pour syrup into softened gelatin while beating with electric mixer on high speed. Beat on high speed until mixture is white and has almost tripled in volume. Add peppermint extract; beat on high speed 1 minute. Pour into pan. Sprinkle with powdered sugar, patting lightly with hands. Let stand uncovered at least 8 hours.

Turn pan upside down to remove marshmallow mixture onto board. Cut into shapes with miniature cookie cutters or knife dipped in water to keep from sticking. Store in airtight container at room temperature up to 3 weeks.

1 Marshmallow: Calories 55 (Calories from Fat 0); Fat 0g (Saturated 0g); Cholesterol 0mg; Sodium 25mg; Carbohydrate 14g (Dietary Fiber 0g); Protein 0g
% Daily Value: Vitamin A 0%; Vitamin C 0%; Calcium 0%; Iron 0%
Diet Exchanges: 1 Fruit

Gifts for Giving

Package a collection of marshmallows in a plastic bag, and tie with curly ribbon. Place bags of marshmallows in oversized mugs along with packages of gourmet cocoa.

Holiday Hints

Check out the cookie and canapé cutters in craft and gourmet kitchen stores for fun new shapes. For more holiday flair, drizzle marshmallows with melted vanilla candy coating tinted with paste food color. You may want to let marshmallows air-dry, and then string them on fancy cord as holiday garland.

Sugar-Cube Trees

PREP: 30 MIN

7 DECORATIVE SUGAR-CUBE TREES

119 sugar cubes (about one 1-pound box)

Glue gun and glue sticks or vanilla ready-to-spread frosting

Dragées (nonedible; for decoration only)

Cover cookie sheet with waxed paper. For each tree, attach 5 sugar cubes in a row, using glue or frosting, and make 1 row of 4 cubes, 1 row of 3 cubes and 1 row of 2 cubes. Attach rows in descending order, centering shorter rows on longer rows, in Christmas tree shape.

For tree trunk, attach 2 cubes onto center of 5-cube row. For tree top, attach 1 cube onto center of 2-cube row. Let dry on cookie sheet.

Decorate trees by attaching dragées with glue or frosting. Arrange trees upright on table for centerpiece or place cards.

FOR DECORATION ONLY. NOT EDIBLE.

Holiday Hints

Here are a few ideas to make your Sugar-Cube Trees extra special:

- To make a snow-sparkling tree, brush assembled trees with just enough light corn syrup to cover and sprinkle with white coarse sugar crystals (decorating sugar).

- Personalize trees by piping on decorator frosting from a tube. Guests can take trees home as a Christmas party memento.

- Make a winter "wonderland-scape." Drape cotton batting over table; add trees at different heights.

String miniature battery-powered lights around trees.

- Make holes in tops of trees after assembling, using toothpick, to allow for hanging as decorations in windows or on Christmas trees.

Sugar-Cube Trees

Gingerbread Village

PREP: 1 HR; BAKE: 15 MIN PER PAN; COOL: 30 MIN; STAND: 30 MIN
ONE 4-BUILDING VILLAGE

1/2 cup packed brown sugar

1/4 cup shortening

3/4 cup full-flavor molasses

1/3 cup cold water

3 1/2 cups all-purpose flour

1 teaspoon baking soda

1 teaspoon ground ginger

1/2 teaspoon salt

1/2 teaspoon ground allspice

1/2 teaspoon ground cloves

1/2 teaspoon ground cinnamon

Gingerbread Frosting (right) or Royal Icing
(page 204)

Assorted candies, nuts, cookies, crackers and cereal

Heat oven to 350°. Grease square pan, 9×9×2 inches, and jelly roll pan, 15 1/2×10 1/2×1 inch. Mix brown sugar, shortening and molasses in large bowl. Stir in cold water. Stir in remaining ingredients except Gingerbread Frosting and assorted candies.

Press one-third of dough into square pan. Press remaining dough into jelly roll pan. Bake 1 pan at a time about 15 minutes or until no indentation remains when touched in center. Cool 5 minutes. Turn upside down onto large cutting surface. Immediately cut jelly roll into fourths and then into buildings as shown in illustration. Cut square into braces as shown. Cool completely.

Prepare Gingerbread Frosting. Decorate fronts of buildings as desired, using frosting and assorted candies, nuts, cookies, crackers and cereal. Use frosting to attach braces to backs of buildings. Let stand 30 minutes or until frosting is completely set. Complete by decorating as desired.

Gingerbread Frosting

2 cups powdered sugar

1/3 cup shortening

2 tablespoons light corn syrup

5 to 6 teaspoons milk

Beat all ingredients with spoon until smooth and spreadable.

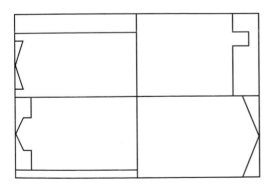

a. *Cut jelly roll into fourths and then into buildings.*

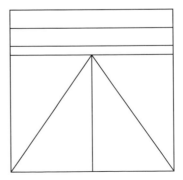

b. *Cut square into braces.*

Gingerbread Village and Miniature Cookie Tree (page 308, variation of Gingerbread Cookie Tree)

Gingerbread Cookie Tree

PREP: 1 HR; CHILL: 2 HR; BAKE: 14 MIN PER SHEET; COOL: 30 MIN; STAND: 30 MIN
1 DECORATIVE COOKIE TREE

3 recipes of dough for Gingerbread Village
  (page 306)

9 cookie cutters, ranging from 2 1/2 inches to
  8 1/2 inches in diameter (increasing by 3/4 inch
  from one size to the next)

Gingerbread Frosting (page 306) or Royal Icing
  (page 204)

Colored glitter sugars

Silver or colored dragées (nonedible; for decoration
  only), if desired

Prepare dough, 1 recipe at a time. Cover and refrigerate about 2 hours or until firm.

Heat oven to 350°. Lightly grease cookie sheet. Roll 1 recipe of dough at a time 1/4 inch thick on lightly floured cloth-covered surface. Cut 3 cookies each with the 3 largest sizes of floured cookie cutters to make 9 cookies. Cut 2 cookies each with the remaining sizes of floured cookie cutters to make 12 cookies. Place about 2 inches apart on cookie sheet. Bake large cookies 12 to 14 minutes, small cookies 10 to 12 minutes, or until no indentation remains when touched. Cool slightly; remove from cookie sheet to wire rack. Cool completely.

Prepare Gingerbread Frosting. Assemble tree on serving plate by stacking unfrosted cookies, starting with largest cookies and stacking in descending sizes, attaching each with a small dab of frosting in center. Let tree stand about 30 minutes or until frosting is completely set, or hold cookies in place with bamboo skewers if necessary. Use remaining frosting to pipe "snow" on the tree, using decorating bag or resealable plastic bag with small tip of corner cut off to allow drizzling. Decorate with glitter sugar and dragées.

FOR DECORATION ONLY. NOT EDIBLE.

Holiday Hints

For a finishing touch, immediately after frosting the tree, sprinkle with coarse decorating sugar to make it glisten like snow. Place a single cookie made from the 2-inch cookie cutter at top of tree. Paint with gold luster dust mixed with a little lemon extract.

If you want to make this an *EDIBLE* centerpiece, use candy decorations instead of the dragées and decorate the treetop star cookie with frosting instead of luster dust.

New Twist

How about a **Miniature Cookie Tree** to complete the landscape of your village? Make the Gingerbread Cookie Tree as directed above, but use just the 5 smallest sizes of cookie cutters to cut out the cookies. Decorate as desired. (See photo on page 307.)

Gingerbread Cookie Tree

Gingerbread Bird Feeder

PREP: 1 HR; BAKE: 12 MIN; COOL: 30 MIN; STAND: 30 MIN
1 DECORATIVE BIRD FEEDER

1 package (14 1/2 ounces) gingerbread cake and cookie mix

1/4 cup hot water

2 tablespoons all-purpose flour

2 tablespoons butter or margarine, melted

1 egg white

1 tablespoon water

1 cup whole almonds

5 cinnamon sticks, about 3 inches long

1 bottle (1 1/4 ounces) whole cloves

Royal Icing (page 204)

Coarse white sugar crystals (decorating sugar)

Heat oven to 375°. Prepare gingerbread mix as directed on package for gingersnaps, using 1/4 cup hot water, flour and butter. Divide dough in half. Roll each half 1/8 inch thick on lightly floured cloth-covered surface.

Cut 3 rectangles, 6 1/2×5 inches, from dough. Place 2 rectangles on ungreased cookie sheet. Beat egg white and 1 tablespoon water in small bowl with fork. Brush 1 rectangle with egg white; press almonds onto rectangle, overlapping slightly, for roof of bird feeder.

Place cinnamon sticks, equally spaced, along one long edge of second rectangle so that they are perpendicular to edge of dough and rest 1 inch on edge of dough (sticks will extend out to form bird perches). Place third rectangle on second rectangle; press lightly to form base of bird feeder.

Roll remaining dough 1/8 inch thick. Cut rectangle, 5× 3 inches, from dough for back of bird feeder; place on cookie sheet. Cut rectangle, 8×3 1/2 inches, from dough. On 8-inch rectangle, measure with ruler 3 inches in from one 8-inch side and mark spot, then measure 3 inches in from opposite end of other 8-inch side and mark spot; cut rectangle diagonally in half from marked spots to make 2 sides of bird feeder (see illustration).

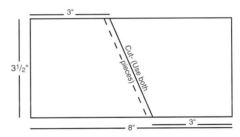

Place on cookie sheet. Brush back and side pieces with egg white; sprinkle with cloves, and press cloves in lightly.

Bake all pieces 8 to 12 minutes or until firm and edges begin to brown. Cool 3 minutes; remove from cookie sheet to wire rack. Cool completely.

Prepare Royal Icing. Attach back and sides of bird feeder to base of feeder at right angle (with perches at front of feeder), using icing as glue. Attach roof, using icing. Let stand about 30 minutes or until icing is completely set. Pipe icing on roof edges to resemble snow; sprinkle with sugar crystals for sparkling effect.

Holiday Hints

Add a final touch to your bird feeder:

• Perch a bird on a cinnamon stick. You can find birds at craft stores, or handcraft one.

• Fill bird feeder with aromatic branches and dried citrus peel or purchased potpourri.

• Surround the feeder with evergreen boughs.

Gingerbread Bird Feeder and Sugar and Spice Bird House (page 312)

Sugar and Spice Birdhouse

PREP: 45 MIN; CHILL: 2 HR; BAKE: 15 MIN; COOL: 30 MIN; STAND: 30 MIN

1 DECORATIVE BIRDHOUSE

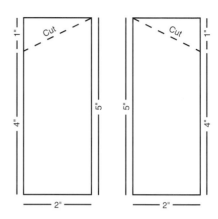

Dough for Gingerbread Village (page 306)

1 egg white

1 tablespoon water

Whole cinnamon sticks

Whole almonds

Whole cloves

Whole star anise

Allspice berries

Royal Icing (page 204)

Coarse white sugar crystals (decorating sugar)

1 craft bird, if desired

Heat oven to 350°. Lightly grease cookie sheet. Prepare dough; divide dough in half. Cover and refrigerate about 2 hours or until firm. Reserve half of dough for another use.

Roll dough slightly less than 1/4 inch thick on lightly floured cloth-covered surface. Cut three 5×4-inch rectangles (front, base and roof), two 5×2-inch rectangles (sides), and one 4-inch square (back) from dough. Place on cookie sheet.

Cut hole in center of one 5×4-inch rectangle with 1 1/2-inch biscuit cutter. On each 5×2-inch rectangle, measure 1 inch down from corner on a long side and cut

from this spot diagonally across rectangle up to opposite corner (see illustration); discard small piece of dough.

Mix egg white and water with fork in small bowl. Brush all dough surfaces except one 5×4-inch rectangle (base) with egg white mixture. Place cinnamon sticks on 4-inch square (roof); press lightly. Place almonds, cloves, anise and allspice on two 5×2-inch rectangles (sides) and on two 5×4-inch rectangles (front and back); press lightly.

Bake about 15 minutes or until no indentation remains when touched in center. Cool 5 minutes; remove from cookie sheet to wire rack. Cool completely.

Prepare Royal Icing. Place undecorated 5×4-inch rectangle (base) on work surface. Attach sides, front (with hole) and back to base at right angle, using icing as glue. Attach roof, using icing. Let stand about 30 minutes or until icing is completely set.

Pipe icing on roof edges to resemble snow; sprinkle with sugar crystals for sparkling effect. Use cinnamon stick for a perch; add craft bird.

Timesaving Tips

If you're looking for an easier way to make this birdhouse or any of the other gingerbread creations, you can use a 14.5-ounce package of gingerbread cake and cookie mix prepared as directed on the package for gingersnaps.

Gingerbread Jewel Box

PREP: 45 MIN; CHILL: 2 HR; BAKE: 15 MIN; COOL: 30 MIN; STAND: 1 HR

1 JEWEL BOX

Dough for Gingerbread Village (page 306)

2 tablespoons luster dust (nonedible; for decoration only)

1/8 teaspoon lemon extract

Royal Icing (page 204)

Assorted jewel candies

Dragées (nonedible; for decoration only), if desired

Heat oven to 350°. Lightly grease cookie sheet. Prepare dough; divide dough in half. Cover and refrigerate about 2 hours or until firm. Reserve half of dough for another use.

Roll dough slightly less than 1/4 inch thick on lightly floured cloth-covered surface. Cut two 5 1/2-or 6-inch circles from dough by tracing pattern of 5 1/2-inch circle or inverting 6-inch-diameter bowl onto dough and cutting around bowl with knife. Cut five 3 × 2 1/2-inch rectangles from dough. Place circles and rectangles on cookie sheet.

Bake about 15 minutes or until no indentation remains when touched in center. Cool 5 minutes; remove from cookie sheet to wire rack. Cool completely.

Place 5 gingerbread rectangles on work surface. Mix luster dust and lemon extract to form a thin paste. Lightly paint on rectangles, using brush. (Mix additional luster dust and lemon extract as needed.) Let stand about 30 minutes or until dry.

Prepare Royal Icing. Place 1 gingerbread circle on work surface to use as bottom of box. Attach rectangles to box bottom at right angle, using icing as glue, to form side of box (see illustration, page 314). Use other gingerbread circle as top of box. Attach candies and dragées to top and sides of box, using icing. Let stand about 30 minutes or until icing is completely set.

FOR DECORATION ONLY. NOT EDIBLE.

Holiday Hints

While colorful luster dusts add vibrant colors and shine, they are not edible and should be used for decoration only.

Button Cookie Box

PREP: 45 MIN; CHILL: 2 HR; BAKE: 15 MIN; COOL: 30 MIN; STAND: 30 MIN

1 COOKIE BOX

Dough for Gingerbread Village (page 306)

Royal Icing (page 204)

Food color, if desired

Red and black shoestring licorice

Shortbread Buttons (page 207)

Heat oven to 350°. Lightly grease cookie sheet. Prepare dough; divide dough in half. Cover and refrigerate about 2 hours or until firm. Reserve half of dough for another use.

Roll dough slightly less than 1/4 inch thick on lightly floured cloth-covered surface. Cut two 6-inch circles from dough by inverting 6-inch-diameter bowl onto dough and cutting around bowl with knife. Cut five 3×2 1/2-inch rectangles from dough. Make 4 holes in center of one of the circles, using end of straw or a toothpick, and use a small bowl to press an indentation inside the circle to create the look of a button. Place circles and rectangles on cookie sheet.

Bake about 15 minutes or until no indentation remains when touched in center. Cool 5 minutes; remove from cookie sheet to wire rack. Cool completely.

Prepare Royal Icing. Place gingerbread circle without holes on work surface to use as bottom of box. Attach rectangles to box bottom at right angle, using icing as glue, to form side of box (see illustration). Let stand about 30 minutes or until icing is completely set.

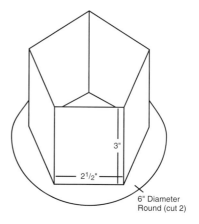

Wind red licorice around body of box to represent thread. Decorate gingerbread circle with holes with icing (tint with food color if desired). Fill box with Shortbread Buttons. String extra shortbread cookies together with black licorice if desired.

Gifts for Giving

Looking for a gift for that favorite Grandma? Surprise her with this gingerbread button box filled with Shortbread Buttons. Include a coupon for a free cookie refill!

Button Cookie Box and Shortbread Buttons (page 207, variation of Sensational Shortbread Cookies)

Santa's Chimney

PREP: 45 MIN; CHILL: 2 HR; BAKE: 15 MIN; COOL: 30 MIN; STAND: 1 HR
1 CHIMNEY

Dough for Gingerbread Village (page 306)

1-quart milk carton

Royal Icing (page 204)

Maple extract or vanilla, if desired

White coarse sugar crystals (decorating sugar)

About 1 yard decorative ribbon

Heat oven to 350°. Lightly grease cookie sheet.

Prepare dough; divide dough in half. Cover and refrigerate about 2 hours or until firm. Reserve half of dough for another use.

Roll dough slightly less than 1/4 inch thick on lightly floured cloth-covered surface. Cut four 3 3/4 × 1-inch rectangles and four 7 × 3-inch rectangles from dough. Place on cookie sheet.

Bake about 15 minutes or until no indentation remains when touched in center. Cool 5 minutes; remove from cookie sheet to wire rack. Cool completely.

Cut off top of milk carton so carton measures 7 inches high. Prepare Royal Icing. Attach 7 × 3-inch rectangles onto sides of milk carton, using icing as glue. Attach 3 3/4 × 1-inch rectangles at top of chimney for flashing (see illustration). Let stand about 30 minutes or until icing is completely set.

Create outline of bricks on chimney with icing (or use white decorating icing from a tube). To tint icing brown, add a few drops of maple extract. Create snow at top of chimney with icing; sprinkle with sugar crystals. Let stand about 30 minutes or until icing is completely set. Tie ribbon around chimney.

Holiday Hints

Fill this chimney with a bag of candy or tiny cookies and include a foil-wrapped chocolate Santa. Or use this fun chimney as a candy or nut dish. Surround with greenery and twinkling battery-powered lights.

Timesaving Tips

If you're looking for an easier way to make this chimney, you can use a 14.5-ounce package of gingerbread cake and cookie mix prepared as directed on the package for gingersnaps. For a super easy no-bake chimney, cut graham crackers to fit milk carton. Using graham crackers may require more frosting for gluing pieces together.

Salt Dough Decorations

PREP: 30 MIN; BAKE: 2 HR PER SHEET; COOL: 30 MIN
ABOUT 5 DOZEN 2 1/2-INCH DECORATIONS

4 cups all-purpose flour

2 cups salt

1 1/2 cups water

1 teaspoon powdered alum

Clear sealing spray for crafts, if desired

Mix all ingredients thoroughly with hands. (If dough is too dry, work in 1 tablespoon water.) If desired, tint dough by dividing into several parts and kneading desired food color into each part. Roll or mold dough as directed below. Cover and refrigerate dough up to 2 weeks

To roll: Roll dough 1/8 inch thick on lightly floured surface. Cut with cookie cutters. If making ornaments to be hung, make a hole in each 1/4 inch from top with end of plastic straw.

To mold: Shape dough, no more than 1/2 inch thick, into figures such as flowers, fruits, vegetables or animals. If making ornaments to be hung, insert fine wire in each.

Heat oven to 250°. Place decorations on ungreased cookie sheet. Bake 30 minutes. Remove from oven; turn decorations over (if possible). Bake about 1 1/2 hours longer or until completely hard and dry. Remove from cookie sheet to wire rack; cool completely.

Lightly sand flat surfaces of decorations with fine sandpaper until smooth. Outline desired designs on decorations with pencil. Paint with plastic-based poster or acrylic paint. (Paint sides and backs of ornaments, too.) Let stand until paint is dry. Place decorations on waxed paper. Spray with sealing spray.

FOR DECORATION ONLY. NOT EDIBLE.

Holiday Hints

Kids will have fun using this easy-to-make dough to create place cards, ornaments or tabletop decorations. Here are a few tips to help with your merry making:

- Use whole wheat flour for the all-purpose flour to craft teddy bears, mice and natural-colored decorations.

- Press dough through a garlic press to produce textures for hair, animal fur, grass and greenery for wreaths and trees.

- Brush dough with slightly beaten egg white before baking for a glossy surface.

- Brush dough with milk before baking for a golden brown color.

Cranberry Kissing Ball

PREP: 45 MIN
1 DECORATION

12 inches 20-gauge wire

1 plastic foam ball, 3 inches in diameter

Round toothpicks

1/2 pound fresh cranberries

1 small bunch (about 5 sprigs) fresh eucalyptus

1 package craft straight pins

1 yard decorative ribbon

Wrap wire tightly around diameter of foam ball once. Twist wire at top of ball to secure. Tuck ends into ball.

Break toothpicks in half. Push cranberry onto broken end of toothpick; push other end of toothpick into foam ball. Continue until ball is well filled with cranberries.

Fill in open spaces on ball with 1 1/2- to 2-inch cuts of eucalyptus, securing with pins.

Slip ribbon through wire twist at top; tie ribbon to make loop for hanging ball. The cranberries will stay plump and pretty for about three to four days. To extend its life, hang the ball in a cool spot, such as in an entryway or on a porch.

New Twist

Hanging in an entryway, a kissing ball welcomes guests with a romantic touch. Instead of eucalyptus, you may like to add mistletoe or holly for a hint of Christmas past or, if you're not fond of eucalyptus, use popped popcorn to fill in the open spaces between cranberries.

Holiday Hints

Having trouble finding craft straight pins? Look for them in the notions department of sewing and fabric stores.

Cranberry Kissing Ball

Fill a Vase

PREP: 20 MIN
1 CENTERPIECE

1 bag (16 ounces) fresh cranberries

Clear glass vase

1 medium orange, cut into 1/4-inch slices

1 medium lemon or lime, cut into 1/4-inch slices

Bouquet of fresh flowers

Place cranberries in vase. Fill vase 3/4 full with water. Place orange and lemon slices in vase between cranberries and side of vase. Arrange flowers in vase.

Holiday Hints

If you plan on using this vase for a centerpiece for a table, keep the stems of the flowers short, so your guests can see across the table.

New Twist

• Use lemon slices for the oranges, and fill the vase with lemon branches and pepperberries.

• Skip filling the vase with water. Instead of using cranberries and oranges, fill the vase with coffee beans and pecan halves, and add dried flowers.

• Skip the orange and lemon slices, and fill the vase with an elegant bouquet of deep red or white roses.

Fill a Vase

Frosty Fruit Bowl

PREP: 30 MIN; STAND: 15 MIN
1 CENTERPIECE

10 Bartlett pears

1 egg white, beaten

Granulated sugar or white coarse sugar crystals
  (decorating sugar)

12-inch cake platter or serving bowl

13 to 15 kumquats

1 stem blueberry juniper, cut into 6-inch sprigs

Fresh lemon leaves, if desired

Brush half of each pear with egg white; sprinkle with sugar. Let stand about 15 minutes or until dry.

Arrange pears on platter. Arrange kumquats among pears. Fill in spaces with juniper and lemon leaves.

New Twist

These frosted pears mimic the look of winter frost, but don't limit your "snow-covered" fruit to pears. Apples, grapes, mangoes, cranberries and citrus fruits can look just as frosty. Consider adding greenery, bay leaves and lemon leaves that are frosted as well to complete your look.

Holiday Hints

As tempting as these frosty fruits appear, make sure you wash all decorated fruit thoroughly because raw egg white should not be eaten.

Frosty Fruit Bowl

Christmas Ball Bowl

PREP: 30 MIN
1 CENTERPIECE

Large serving bowl

Sugar

Christmas ball ornaments with removable tops

Small funnel

Florist glue

Fresh flowers

Fresh evergreen sprigs, if desired

Fill bowl about 1/3 full with sugar. Arrange 1 layer of ornaments in bowl, pressing lightly into sugar to position.

Remove tops from additional ornaments; fill ornaments about 1/2 full with water, using funnel (water may cause outside surface of ornament to crack). Apply small amount of florist glue to bottoms and sides of water-filled ornaments. Arrange on first layer of ornaments, attaching with glue. For ornaments at side of bowl, attach to bowl with small amount of glue. Place flowers and evergreen sprigs in water-filled ornaments.

Holiday Hints

Christmas ball ornaments also make charming place settings. Write the name of each guest on an ornament with a metallic marking pen. Set one ornament at each place setting and steady it on a vinyl hose washer—that's right, the kind you find at your local hardware store. The washers work great for making the ornaments stay put, and you can spray paint them to match. Remove the tops from the ornaments, and fill about half full with water. Place flowers in ornaments and tie with a decorative ribbon.

Christmas Ball Bowl

Kumquat and Bay Leaf Tree

PREP: 1 HR
1 CENTERPIECE

About 3 pounds kumquats

Round toothpicks

1 package (1/2 ounce) fresh bay leaves

Green floral foam in pyramid shape, 12×4 inches

Push each kumquat onto end of toothpick; spear bay leaf
with other end of toothpick. Push toothpicks into foam
pyramid (with bay leaves against pyramid), starting at
top and working downward in spiral fashion, until
pyramid is completely filled.

Holiday Hints

Display your kumquat and bay leaf tree on a cake stand,
and surround it with votive candles, citrus- and gold-
colored ribbons and other citrus fruits.

New Twist

You may like to make a collection of trees of various
sizes. A glue gun or long straight pins may be helpful for
securing items to the foam. Instead of using bay leaves
and kumquats, try one of these combinations:

- **Chocolate-Apricot Tree:** Dried apricots
  with ends dipped in melted white
  chocolate for a snow-tipped effect.

- **Nuts and Spice Tree:** Miniature
  pinecones, whole almonds, star anise
  and stick cinnamon. A glue gun may
  be helpful for securing these natural
  ingredients.

- **Rosemary-Cranberry Tree:** Fresh
  rosemary sprigs and cranberries.

- **Beads and Baubles Tree:** Wrap a
  plastic foam pyramid with prestrung beads or wire by coiling
  from top to bottom. Top with a
  purchased gold star decoration.

Chocolate-Apricot
Tree (variation)

Kumquat and Bay Leaf Tree (Rosemary-Cranberry Tree, variation)

Noel Napkin Rings

PREP: 25 MIN
4 NAPKIN RINGS

12 brass screw eyes

12 whole chestnuts

Gold metallic marking pen

Four 12-inch lengths decorative ribbon

Twist 1 screw eye into each chestnut. Decorate as desired using metallic pen. Group 3 chestnuts together and string ribbon through screw eyes; tie ribbon. Tie around napkins.

New Twist

Looking for some holiday ideas to jazz up your place settings?

• Tie raffia ribbon around a rolled napkin, and tuck in sprigs of fresh rosemary.

• Coil prestrung beads around napkins; tuck in ends.

• Fold napkins to make a pocket, and fill pocket with a holly sprig and a personal wish for each guest.

• Wrap a piece of gourmet candy in a miniature plastic bag, secure with curly gold ribbons and tie around napkin.

Festive Garnish Plate

PREP: 15 MIN
1 SERVING PLATE

Poinsettia leaves or fresh flower petals

Serving plate

Clear plastic wrap (cling type)

Sliced fruit or cheese

Arrange leaves or petals on plate. Stretch plastic wrap over plate, making sure surface is tight and flat.

Arrange fruit or cheese on surface of plastic wrap so leaves or petals show through.

New Twist

Use a plate or platter that's slightly deep and check out these ideas:

- Fill with prestrung tiny beads or miniature ornaments.
- Fill with cranberries and greenery.
- Fill with coffee beans and whole almonds.

Fireside Tray

1 TRAY

1 picture frame, about 11×14 inches

Paper (card-stock weight), to fit picture frame

Christmas cards or photographs

About 1 yard decorative ribbon

Screw-on handles, if desired

Remove back from frame. Place paper on back of frame. Arrange cards and ribbon on paper.

Place glass and frame on top of design. Carefully turn over frame, glass and back. Close frame. Turn right side up.

To carry platter as a serving tray, drill 2 small holes on short sides of frame, and attach handles.

New Twist

Let your imagination run wild when you make your own trays. Here are some ideas to get you going:

- Place assorted dried or fresh flowers or flat dried fruit in frame. Add small boughs of evergreen or holly.

- Use decorative ribbon to create a colorful design.

- Show off antique needlework or handkerchiefs without running the risk of getting it ruined.

- Using tiny strung beads, spell out "Merry Christmas" or another holiday greeting. If you have another language in your heritage, you may like to add it as well.

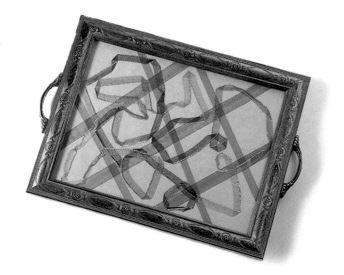

Betty Crocker's Best Christmas Cookbook

Fireside Tray

Holiday Gifts and Decorations

Candles, Coffee and More

PREP: 15 MIN
1 CENTERPIECE

5 pillar candles of various heights and diameters

1 platter, about 12 inches in diameter

1 pound coffee beans

1 pound whole hazelnuts (in the shell)

1 yard decorative ribbon, if desired

Arrange candles on platter. Arrange coffee beans and hazelnuts around candles. Decorate with ribbon.

New Twist

This attractive holiday centerpiece is easily adapted using items found around the house. Instead of coffee beans and hazelnuts, try some of these items:

- Tiny Christmas ball ornaments in any color
- Gilded pinecones and fresh evergreen sprigs
- Seasonal red and green candies
- Fresh cranberries
- Coarse decorating sugar or salt, which will glisten like snow
- Wrapped candies and ribbon
- Red and green pistachios
- Red and green dried pasta in various shapes

Candles, Coffee and More

Golden Glow Candy Wreath

PREP: 45 MIN
1 WREATH

1 coat hanger

Wire cutters

Cloth tape (duct tape)

Embroidery floss or thin all-purpose string, about
 3 1/2 yards

2 pounds butterscotch or gold-foil wrapped hard
 candies

String of small battery-powered lights

Gold ribbon, if desired

Gold pearl beads or charms, if desired

Snip coat hanger at base of hook, using wire cutters, leaving approximately 3 feet of wire. Shape wire into 8-inch circle, twisting ends of wire back around circle. Secure ends to circle with tape.

Tie a 6-inch piece of floss to wire circle. Place ends of 3 candy wrappers on wire; tie knot in floss to secure candies to circle. Continue in this manner, arranging candy to the inside and outside of the circle.

Weave string of lights in wreath to create a glowing golden halo of candy. Decorate wreath with gold ribbon and beads.

Holiday Hints

Adapt this wreath to your holiday color scheme. If it's metallic silver, use silver wrapped candies, silver beads and silver ribbons. If you prefer a red color scheme, scan the candy section for red wrapped candies, and use red holiday balls, beads and ribbons.

Golden Glow Candy Wreath

Decorator Wreath

PREP: 1 HR; BAKE: 3 1/2 HR; STAND: 8 HR
1 WREATH

6 small bright-red apples (such as Rome Beauty or
Red Rome), 2 1/2 inches in diameter

Lemon juice or lemon-lime soda pop

Wire racks

Waxed paper

Spray varnish, if desired

6 cinnamon sticks, 10 inches long

Florist wire

Straw wreath, 10 inches in diameter

2 yards 3/4-inch ribbon

Hot-glue gun with glue sticks

5 cinnamon sticks, 3 1/2 inches long

Fresh bay leaves or silk leaves

Wire hanger, if desired

Heat oven to 200°. Cut apples lengthwise from stem end through core into 1/4-inch slices. Dip apples into lemon juice to prevent browning; place on wire racks. Carefully place wire racks on oven rack. Bake 3 1/2 hours. Turn off oven; leave apples in oven 8 hours or overnight.

Place dried apples on waxed paper. Coat each side with 2 light coats of spray varnish, following manufacturer's directions.

Tie 10-inch cinnamon sticks together with florist wire. Attach to front of wreath with 6 inches of the ribbon. Glue dried apple slices and 3 1/2-inch cinnamon sticks to front and side of wreath, using glue gun. Attach leaves to ribbon on 10-inch cinnamon sticks. Make a bow with remaining ribbon, and attach to wreath. Attach wire hanger.

New Twist

Personalize wreaths to represent your heritage, living locale or personal interests. Scan craft shops, garden stores and Grandma's attic to find unique items to enhance your wreath. You may want to use a glue gun found at craft stores to secure objects. Try these fun ideas:

- Gilded leaves and pinecones

- Strung beads and white feathers or seashells

- Ornamental birds, pinecones

- Tree ornaments, such as snowshoes, miniature bird houses and birch bark canoes

- Miniature flags and orna-ments of a specific country

Decorator Wreath

Holiday Garland

PREP: 1HR; BAKE: 3 1/2 HR; STAND: 8 HR

1 GARLAND

3 bright-red small apples (such as Rome Beauty or Red Rome)

Lemon juice or lemon-lime soda pop

Wire racks

Waxed paper

Spray varnish, if desired

Hot-glue gun with glue sticks

About 1 pound mixed nuts in shells

12 cinnamon sticks, 3 1/2 inches long (about 1 1/2 one-ounce jars)

20 whole bay leaves (about one 0.18-ounce jar)

Purchased garland, about 6 feet long

Heat oven to 200°. Cut apples lengthwise from stem end through core into 1/4-inch slices. Dip apples into lemon juice to prevent browning; place on wire racks. Carefully place wire racks on oven rack. Bake 3 1/2 hours. Turn off oven; leave apples in oven 8 hours or overnight.

Remove wire racks from oven. Place dried apples on waxed paper. Coat each side with 2 light coats of spray varnish, following manufacturer's directions. Glue dried apples, nuts, cinnamon and bay leaves to garland, using glue gun. Let dry.

Holiday Hints

To add your own personal touch, you may like to use one of these garland suggestions:

- String colored holiday dried pasta to use as a simple garland or to intertwine in purchased green garland.

- String or tie purchased wrapped candies, using brightly colored cording and intertwine in garland. Candy canes, lollipops and foil-wrapped candies are especially fun choices if you have kids around.

- Tie jingle bells on prestrung beads, using tiny ribbons.

Holiday Garland

Holiday Gifts and Decorations

Helpful Nutrition and Cooking Information

Nutrition Guidelines

We provide nutrition information for each recipe that includes calories, fat, cholesterol, sodium, carbohydrate, fiber and protein. Individual food choices can be based on this information

Recommended intake for a daily diet of 2,000 calories as set by the Food and Drug Administration:

Total Fat	Less than 65g
Saturated Fat	Less than 20g
Cholesterol	Less than 300mg
Sodium	Less than 2,400mg
Total Carbohydrate	300g
Dietary Fiber	25g

Criteria Used for Calculating Nutrition Information

- The first ingredient was used wherever a choice is given (such as 1/3 cup sour cream or plain yogurt).

- The first ingredient amount was used wherever a range is given (such as 3 to 3 1/2 pound cut-up broiler-fryer chicken).

- The first serving number was used wherever a range is given (such as 4 to 6 servings).

- "If desired" ingredients (such as sprinkle with brown sugar if desired) and recipe variations were *not* included .

- Only the amount of a marinade or frying oil that is estimated to be absorbed by the food during preparation or cooking was calculated.

Ingredients Used in Recipe Testing and Nutrition Calculations

- Ingredients used for testing represent those that the majority of consumers use in their homes: large eggs, 2% milk, 80% lean ground beef, canned ready-to-use chicken broth, and vegetable oil spread containing *not less than 65 percent fat.*

- Fat-free, low-fat or low-sodium products are not used, unless otherwise indicated.

- Solid vegetable shortening (not butter, margarine, non-stick cooking sprays or vegetable oil spread as they can cause sticking problems) is used to grease pans, unless otherwise indicated.

Equipment Used in Recipe Testing

We use equipment for testing that the majority of consumers use in their homes. If a specific piece of equipment (such as a wire whisk) is necessary for recipe success, it will be listed in the recipe.

- Cookware and bakeware **without** nonstick coatings were used, unless otherwise indicated.

- No dark colored, black or insulated bakeware was used.

- When a baking *pan* is specified in a recipe, a *metal* pan was used; a baking *dish* or pie *plate* means oven-proof glass was used.

- An electric hand mixer was used for mixing *only when mixer speeds are specified* in the recipe directions. When a mixer speed is not given, a spoon or fork was used.

Cooking Terms Glossary

Beat: Mix ingredients vigorously with spoon, fork, wire whisk, hand beater or electric mixer until smooth and uniform.

Boil: Heat liquid until bubbles rise continuously and break on the surface and steam is given off. For rolling boil, the bubbles form rapidly.

Chop: Cut into coarse or fine irregular pieces with a knife, food chopper, blender or food processor.

Cube: Cut into squares 1/2 inch or larger.

Dice: Cut into squares smaller than 1/2 inch.

Grate: Cut into tiny particles using small rough holes of grater (citrus peel or chocolate).

Grease: Rub the inside surface of a pan with shortening, using pastry brush, piece of waxed paper or paper towel, to prevent food from sticking during baking (as for some casseroles).

Julienne: Cut into thin, matchlike strips, using knife or food processor (vegetables, fruits, meats).

Mix: Combine ingredients in any way that distributes them evenly.

Sauté: Cook foods in hot oil or margarine over medium-high heat with frequent tossing and turning motion.

Shred: Cut into long thin pieces by rubbing food across the holes of a shredder, as for cheese, or by using a knife to slice very thinly, as for cabbage.

Simmer: Cook in liquid just below the boiling point on top of the stove; usually after reducing heat from a boil. Bubbles will rise slowly and break just below the surface.

Stir: Mix ingredients until uniform consistency. Stir once in a while for stirring occasionally, often for stirring frequently and continuously for stirring constantly.

Toss: Tumble ingredients lightly with a lifting motion (such as green salad), usually to coat evenly or mix with another food.

Metric Conversion Guide

Volume

U.S. Units	Canadian Metric	Australian Metric
1/4 teaspoon	1 mL	1 ml
1/2 teaspoon	2 mL	2 ml
1 teaspoon	5 mL	5 ml
1 tablespoon	15 mL	20 ml
1/4 cup	50 mL	60 ml
1/3 cup	75 mL	80 ml
1/2 cup	125 mL	125 ml
2/3 cup	150 mL	170 ml
3/4 cup	175 mL	190 ml
1 cup	250 mL	250 ml
1 quart	1 liter	1 liter
1 1/2 quarts	1.5 liters	1.5 liters
2 quarts	2 liters	2 liters
2 1/2 quarts	2.5 liters	2.5 liters
3 quarts	3 liters	3 liters
4 quarts	4 liters	4 liters

Weight

U.S. Units	Canadian Metric	Australian Metric
1 ounce	30 grams	30 grams
2 ounces	55 grams	60 grams
3 ounces	85 grams	90 grams
4 ounces (1/4 pound)	115 grams	125 grams
8 ounces (1/2 pound)	225 grams	225 grams
16 ounces (1 pound)	455 grams	500 grams
1 pound	455 grams	1/2 kilogram

Measurements

Inches	Centimeters
1	2.5
2	5.0
3	7.5
4	10.0
5	12.5
6	15.0
7	17.5
8	20.5
9	23.0
10	25.5
11	28.0
12	30.5
13	33.0

Temperatures

Fahrenheit	Celsius
32°	0°
212°	100°
250°	120°
275°	140°
300°	150°
325°	160°
350°	180°
375°	190°
400°	200°
425°	220°
450°	230°
475°	240°
500°	260°

Note: The recipes in this cookbook have not been developed or tested using metric measures. When converting recipes to metric, some variations in quality may be noted.

INDEX

NOTE: Page numbers in *italics* indicate a photograph.

Almond
  Bonbons, 214, *215*
  Pound Cake, 136
  -Toffee Triangles, 230, *231*; varia-
    tions: Coffee-Hazelnut Bars;
    Maple-Praline Bars, 230
  -White Chocolate Sauce, 288,
    289
  White, Fondue, 152, *153*; dip-
    pers for, 152
Angel Meringue Torte, *126*, 148;
    Cranberries Jubilee for, 148
Appetizer, 20–43
  Basil Brie in Pastry, 34, *35*; top-
    pings for, 34
  Bruschetta Romana, 32, *37*; top-
    pings for, 32, variations,
    Pesto-Brie; Portabella-
    Parmesan; Star, 33
  Caramelized Onion Tartlets, 40,
    41; variations, 40
  Cheese Fondue Dip, 25, *25*; dip-
    pers for, 25
  Cheese Trees, 20, *21*; variation,
    Snowman, 20
  Cheesy Apple-Polenta Bites, *42*,
    43
  Chicken Cheesecake, Savory, 31,
    31
  Crab Dip, Hot, 26, *27*
  Cream Cheese Penguins, 22, *22*
  Cucumbers, Carrots and Smoked
    Salmon Crudités, *6*, 23
  Ginger Shrimp Kabobs, 28, *29*
  Gorgonzola and Rosemary Cream
    Puffs, 38, *39*
  last minute suggestions for (moz-
    zarella and tomatoes, baked
    Brie), 38

Meatball Merriment, *6*, 30; varia-
    tions, Burgundy; Cranberry;
    Spicy Apricot; Swedish, Sweet-
    and-Sour, 30
party, red and green (menu), 36
Pesto Pinwheels, 36, *37*
Sun-Dried Tomato Dip, 24, *37*;
    dippers for, 24
Apple(s)
  Applesauce-Sweet Potato Bake,
    116, *117*
  -Bacon Strata, Cheesy, 86, *87*
  Butter, Spirited, 286, *287*; varia-
    tion, Pumpkin, 286
  -Caramel Oven Caramel Corn,
    253
  -Cinnamon Muffins, 172
  -Cran Glaze (turkey), 64
  -Cranberry Dumplings with
    Crimson Sauce, 154, 155
  -Cranberry Stuffing (turkey), 106
  Gems, No-Bake (cookies), 223
  -Leek-Yam Gratin, 118, *119*
  -Orange Stuffing (turkey), 106,
    107
  -Pepper Jelly, 294, *294*
  -Polenta Bites, Cheesy, *42*, 43
  Red Cabbage with, 122, *122*
  Stuffing, Roast Goose with, 72,
    73
Applesauce-Sweet Potato Bake, 116,
    117
Apricot
  -Chocolate Tree (decoration),
    326, *326*
  Gems, No-Bake, 223, *229*; varia-
    tions: Apple; Cherry;
    Cranberry, 223
  -Ginger Muffins, 172

Jeweled Scones, 174, *175*; varia-
    tions, 174
  Meatballs, Spicy, 30
  -Pineapple Jam, 293, *293*
  -Pistachio Rolled Pork, 56, *57*
Asian Cabbage Salad, Frozen, 94, *95*

Bacon-Apple Strata, Cheesy, 86, *87*
Baked Ham, Glazed, 58, *59*; carv-
    ing, 58; sauces for, 59
Ball Bowl, Christmas (decoration),
    324, *325*
Balsamic-Glazed Pearl Onions, 296,
    297
Bar Cookies, Ribbon, 222
Basil
  Brie in Pastry, 34, *35*; toppings
    for, 34
  Butter, 189
Beads and Baubles Tree (decoration),
    326
Bean(s)
  Red, White and Green, *57*, 123
  and Rice Roll-Ups, 80, *81*
  Three- Christmas Chili, 79, *79*
Beef
  carving, 46
  Curried Coconut, with Winter
    Vegetables, 50, *51*
  Gravy, 46
  Marinated Tenderloin of, 48, *49*
  Rib Roast with Herb Rub, 46,
    47
  Stew, Burgundy, 52, *53*
Berry
  Merry, Frozen Soufflé, *164*, 165;
    Candied Cranberries for, 165
  Vinegar, 300
Beverage, 8–19. *See also* Drink

Bird Feeder
     Gingerbread, 310, *311*
     Treat, P B (peanut butter) and
          "Jay", 281, *281*; Cranberry
          Heart for, 281
Birdhouse, Sugar and Spice, *311*, 312
Biscotti, Cashew-Rum, 226, *227*;
          variations: Merry Cherry;
          Pistachio, 226
Biscuits. *See also* Rolls
     Pesto, 196, *197*
Bonbons
     Almond, 214, *215*
     Peanut Butter, 262
Bourbon Balls (candies), 244
Brandy-Pecan Pie, 130
Bread, Holiday, 168–201. *See also*
          Coffee Cake; Muffins;
          Popovers; Rolls; Scones
     Bruschetta Romana, 32, *37*; top-
          pings for, 32; variations:
          Pesto-Brie; Portabella-
          Parmesan; Star, 33
     Cheesy Roasted Red Pepper, 194,
          195
     Eggnog, Spirited, with Rum
          Glaze, 170, *171*
     Focaccia, Festive, 192, *193*
     Garlic Wreath, 189, *189*; Basil
          Butter for, Sun-Dried Tomato
          Butter for, 189
     Julekake (with mixed candied
          fruit), 184, *185*; variation,
          using bread machine, 184
     Onion Twist, Savory, 190, *191*;
          Easy Refrigerator Dough for,
          190
     Poppy Seed, 169, *169*
     Puff Twists, Easy, 199, *199*; varia-
          tions, 199
     Pumpkin-Marmalade, 168, *169*;
          Marmalade Glaze for, 168
     Whole Wheat-Cranberry, 186,
          187; using bread machine for,
          186; fancy butters for, 186
Bread Pudding, Peanut Brittle, 149,
          149; Hot Buttered Rum Sauce
          for, 149
Breakfast. *See also* Brunch
     Santa's (menu), 272

Brie
     Basil, in Pastry, 34, *35*; toppings
          for, 34
     -Pesto Bruschetta, 33, *33*
Broccoli
     -Corn Casserole, *124*, 125
     -Tortellini Salad, 97, *97*
Brownies
     Layered, 234
     Tom-and-Jerry, 232, *233*; varia-
          tions: Chocolate-Covered
          Cherry; Cinnamon-Spiced;
          Creamy Cappuccino, 232
Brunch. *See also* Breakfast
     Cheesy Apple-Bacon Strata, 86,
          87
     Easy (menu), 86
     French Toast, Morning Glory
          Oven, 88, 89
     New Year's Day (menu), 284
Bruschetta Romana, 32, *37*; top-
          pings for, 32; variations:
          Pesto-Brie; Portabella-
          Parmesan; Star, 33
Buns, Saint Lucia, 180, *181*
Burgundy
     Beef Stew, 52, *53*
     Meatballs, 30
Butter
     Apple, Spirited, 286, *287*; varia-
          tion, Pumpkin, 286
     Basil, 189
     Cranberry-Orange, 186
     Maple-Peanut Butter Spread, 186
     Pecan, 186, *187*
     Strawberry, 186
     Sun-Dried Tomato, 189
Butternut Squash Soup, *47*, 78
Button Cookie Box (decoration),
          314, *315*

Cabbage
     Red, with Apples, 122, *122*
     Salad, Asian, Frozen, 94, *95*
Cake, 136–48. *See also* Coffee Cake;
          Torte
     Angel Meringue Torte, *126*, 148;
          Cranberries Jubilee for, 148
     Cheesecake, Heavenly, 146, *146*,
          decorations for, 147

Fruitcake, Jeweled, 140, *141*;
          variations, 140
     Gingerbread with Lemon Sauce,
          142, *143*
     Meringue-Swirled Chocolate,
          144, *145*
     Pound, Cassata, Christmas, *126*,
          138
     Pound, Golden, 136, *136*; varia-
          tions: Almond; Lemon;
          Orange-Coconut; Triple
          Ginger, 136; toppings for,
          137
     Pound, Tiramisu Dessert, Easy,
          158, *159*
     Wild Rice-Nut (bundt cake),
          139, *139*
Candied Cranberries, 165
Candles, Coffee (beans) and More
          (decoration), 332, 333
Candy(ies), 234–53. *See also*
          Cookies
     Cappuccino-Pecan Nuggets, 240,
          241
     Caramel Corn, Oven, *252*, 253;
          variations: Caramel-Apple;
          Hawaiian; Red and White
          Christmas, 253
     Chocolate-Covered Peanut
          Butter, 238, *239*
     Chocolate Marble Fudge,
          Creamy, 234, *237*
     Chocolate Spoons, 268, *269*
     Chocolate-Wine Balls, 244, *245*;
          variations: Bourbon; Rum;
          White Wine, 244
     Divinity, 250, *251*; variations:
          Cherry-Almond; Chocolate-
          Mint; Peppermint, 250
     Fudge, Deluxe Christmas, 236,
          237
     Hazelnut-Coffee Caramels, *289*,
          291
     Maple-Nut Brittle, 246, *247*
     Peppermint Bark, 242, *242*; vari-
          ations, 242
     Peppermint Wands (candy canes),
          270, *269*
     Praline Truffle Cups, 248, *249*;
          variations: Cherry;

Crème de Menthe; Raspberry, 248
  Toffee, 243, *247*
  Truffles, *202*, 235
Candy Cane Coffee Cake, 178, *179*
Candy Wreath, Golden Glow (decoration), 334, 335
Cappuccino
  Brownies, Creamy, 232
  Eggnog, Hot, 14
  -Pecan Nuggets, 240, *241*
Caramel(s)
  -Apple Oven Caramel Corn, 253
  Corn, Oven, *252*, 253; variations: Caramel-Apple; Hawaiian; Red and White Christmas, 253
  Hazelnut-Coffee, *289*, 291
Caramelized Onion Tartlets, 40, *41*; variations, 40
carrot cookie press, 259
Carrots, Cucumbers and Smoked Salmon Crudités, *6*, 23
carving beef, 46; ham, 58; lamb, 60
Cashew-Rum Biscotti, 226, *227*; variations: Merry Cherry; Pistachio, 226
Cassata, Christmas, *126*, 138
Casserole
  Applesauce-Sweet Potato Bake, 116, *117*
  Baked Polenta and Peperonata, 84, *85*
  Broccoli-Corn, *124*, 125
  Cheesy Apple-Bacon Strata, 86, *87*
  Cheesy Potatoes, 112, *113*
  Chicken Dijon, 63, *63*
  Leek-Apple-Yam Gratin, 118, *119*
  Mashed Potatoes, Do-Ahead, 109; variations, 109
  Old-Fashioned Stuffing, *44*, 106, *107*; variations, 106
  Parmesan-Shrimp Pasta Bake, 74, 75
  Turkey-Wild Rice, 66, *67*
Castle, Winter Wonderland, *254*, 278; Critters for, 279–80

Cheese. *See also* Brie; Cream Cheese; Gorgonzola; Parmesan
  Cheesecake, Savory Chicken, 31, *31*
  Fondue Dip, 25, *25*; dippers for, 25
  Trees, Appetizer, 20, *21*; variation, Snowman, 20
Cheesecake
  Heavenly, 145, *146*, decorations for, 147
  Savory Chicken, 31, *31*
Cheesy
  Apple-Bacon Strata, 86, *87*
  Apple-Polenta Bites, *42*, 43
  Potatoes, 112, *113*
  Roasted Red Pepper Bread, 194, *195*
Cherry
  -Almond Divinity (candies), 250
  Biscotti, Merry, 226, *227*
  Chocolate-Covered Brownies, 232, 233
  Gems, No-Bake (cookies), 223
  Swirl Coffee Cake, 176, *176*
  Truffle Cups (candies), 248
Chestnut Stuffing (turkey), 106
Chicken
  Cheesecake, Savory, 31, *31*
  Dijon Casserole, 63, *63*
  with Orange-Pecan Rice, 62, *62*
Chili, Three-Bean Christmas, 79, *79*
Chocolate. *See also* Fudge
  -Apricot Tree (decoration), 326, *326*
  Brownies, Tom-and-Jerry, 232, *233*; variations: Chocolate-Covered Cherry; Cinnamon-Spiced; Creamy Cappuccino, 232
  Cake, Meringue-Swirled, 144, *145*
  Cappuccino-Pecan Nuggets, 240, *241*
  Chip-Peanut Pie, 130
  -Covered Peanut Butter Candies, 238, *239*
  Crinkles, 224, *225*
  Fudge, Deluxe Christmas, 236, *237*
  Fudge Sauce, Decadent, 289, 290

Fudge Truffle Tart, 134, *135*; decorations for, 135
  Marble Fudge, Creamy, 234, *237*
  -Marshmallow Dip, 271, *271*; dippers for, 271
  -Mint Divinity (candies), 250
  Mousse in Chocolate Cups, 160, *161*
  -Pecan Pie, 130
  Sandwich Cookies, Double-Frosted, 266, *267*
  Spoons, 268, *269*
  Spritz, 210
  Truffles, *202*, 235
  White, -Almond Sauce, 288, *289*
  -Wine Balls, 244, *245*; variations: Bourbon; Rum; White Wine, 244
Christmas. *See* Individual Categories (Cookies, Decorations, Gifts, Menus, etc)
Chutney, Pear-Cranberry, *294*, 295
Cider, Cinnamon, *15*, 18
Cinnamon
  -Apple Muffins, 172
  Cider, *15*, 18
  -Nut Popovers, 200
  -Spiced Brownies, 232
  Squash Rings, 120, *120*
Citrus
  -Caraway Mustard, 298, *299*
  Punch, Frosty, 10, *11*
Coconut
  Beef, Curried, with Winter Vegetables, 50, 51
  -Orange Pound Cake, 136
Coffee. *See also* Mocha
  (beans), Candles and More (decoration), 332, 333
  -Hazelnut Bars (cookies), 230
  -Hazelnut Caramels, *289*, 291
Coffee Cake
  Candy Cane, 178, *179*
  Cherry Swirl, 176, *176*
  Lemon-Glazed Coffee Wreath, *166*, 177
  Raspberry and Cream Cheese, 182, 183
  Saint Lucia Crown (with dried fruit), 180, *181*; Buns, 180

conversion guide, metric, 342
Cookie
Crust, 132
Tree, Gingerbread (decoration), 308, *309*
Cookies, 204–32, 256–63, 266. *See also* Candy
Almond Bonbons, 214, *215*
Almond-Toffee Triangles, 230, *231*; variations: Coffee-Hazelnut Bars; Maple-Praline Bars, 230
Brownies, Layered, 234
Brownies, Tom-and-Jerry, 232, *233*; variations: Chocolate-Covered Cherry; Cinnamon-Spiced; Creamy Cappuccino, 232
Chocolate Crinkles, 224, *225*
Chocolate Sandwich Cookies, Double-Frosted, 266, *267*
Fruit Drops, Heirloom Holiday, 228, *229*
Fudgy No-Bakes, 260, *261*
Gingersnaps, 220, *221*; variations: Black-and-White; Ginger Cut-outs; Laced, Snowcapped, 220
Hidden Treasure, 258, *258*; variations, 258
Lemon Stampers, 259, *259*; carrot cookie press for, 259
Melting Moments, Holiday, 218, *219*
Minty Middle Treasures, 216, *217*
No-Bake Apricot Gems, 223, *229*; variations: Apple; Cherry; Cranberry, 223
Peanut Butter Squares, 262, *262*; variation, Bonbons, 262
Rum-Cashew Biscotti, 226, *227*; variations: Merry Cherry; Pistachio, 226
Shortbread, Christmas Mice, 263, *263*
Shortbread, Sensational, 207, *208*; variations, 209
Slice-It-Easy, 222, *222*; variations: Christmas Trees;

Holiday Tarts; Peppermint Pinwheels; Ribbon Bars; Sugar-Coated Slices, 222
Snowballs, 212, *213*; variations: Lemon; Peppermint, 212
Spritz, Holiday, 210, *211*; variations: Chocolate; Rum Butter; Spicy, 210
Sugar, Melt-in-Your-Mouth, 204, *205*; variations, 206
Sugar, No-Roll, 256, *257*; Rainbow Dust (Colored Sugar) for, 256
cooking and nutrition information, 340
cooking terms glossary, 341
Corn
-Broccoli Casserole, *124*, 125
Bread Stuffing (turkey), 106
Cornish Hens, Herbed, 70, *71*
Couscous Salad, Christmas, 98, *98*
Crab Dip, Hot, 26, *27*
Cran-Apple Glaze (turkey), 64
Cranberry(ies)
-Apple Dumplings with Crimson Sauce, 154, *155*
-Apple Glaze (turkey), 64
-Apple Stuffing (turkey), 106
Candied, 165
Gems, No-Bake (cookies), 223, *229*
-Hoisin-Turkey Wraps, 68, *69*
-Honey-Wine Tart, 132, *133*; Cookie Crust for, 132
Jubilee, 148
Kissing Ball (decoration), 318, *319*
-Maple Syrup, 284, 285
Meatballs, 30
Merry Muffins, *166*, 172; variations: Apricot-Ginger; Apple-Cinnamon; Date-Nut, 172
Mold, Classic, 104, *105*
-Orange Butter, 186
Orange Slush Cocktail, *6*, 12
-Orange Vinegar, 300
-Pear Chutney, *294*, 295
-Pecan Pie, 130
-Pistachio Salad with Champagne Vinaigrette, 92, *92*

Punch, Quick, 8, *9*
-Rosemary Tree (decoration), 326, *327*
-Whole Wheat Bread, 186, *187*; using bread machine for, 186; fancy butters for, 186
-Wild Rice Bake, *71*, 108
Cream Cheese
Honey-Walnut, for popovers, 200
Penguins, 22, *22*
and Raspberry Coffee Rounds, 182, *183*
Cream Puffs, Gorgonzola and Rosemary, 38, *39*
Creamy Sauce (steamed pudding), 150
Crème de Menthe Truffle Cups (candies), 248
Crown Roast of Pork with Stuffing, 54, *55*
Crudités, Cucumbers, Carrots and Smoked Salmon, *6*, 23
Cucumbers, Carrots and Smoked Salmon Crudités, *6*, 23
Curd, Lemon, 292, *292*
Curried Coconut Beef with Winter Vegetables, 50, *51*

Date-Nut Muffins, 172
Decorations, 304–38. *See also* Gifts
Birdhouse, Sugar and Spice, *311*, 312
Candles, Coffee (beans) and More, 332, 333
Candy Wreath, Golden Glow, 334, 335
Christmas Ball Bowl, 324, *325*
Cranberry, Kissing Ball, 318, *319*
Edible (for the birds), 281
Festive Garnish Plate, 329, *329*
Fill a Vase (fruit and flowers), 320, *321*
Fireside Tray, 330, *331*
Fruit Bowl, Frosty, 322, *323*
Gingerbread Cookie Tree, 308, *309*
Gingerbread Village, 306, *307*
Holiday Garland, 338, *339*
Jewel Box, Gingerbread, 313, *313*

Kumquat Bay Leaf Tree, 326, *327*; variations: Beads and Baubles; Chocolate-Apricot; Nuts and Spice; Rosemary-Cranberry, 326

Noel Napkin Rings, 328, *328*

Salt Dough, 317, *317*

Santa's Chimney, *283*, 316

Sugar-Cube Trees, 304, *305*

Table, *73*

Wreath, Decorator, 336, *337*

Dessert, 128–65. *See also* Cake; Chocolate; Dumplings; Fondue; Name of Fruit; Pie; Pudding; Soufflé; Trifle; Tortoni

Dijon Chicken Casserole, 63, *63*

Dinner Party Menus
    Christmas Celebration, 48
    Christmas Eve, Memorable, 57
    for Friends, 62; Holiday, 78

Dinner Rolls, *57*, 188; using bread machine, 188

Dip
    Cheese Fondue, 25, *25*; dippers for, 25
    Chocolate-Marshmallow, 271, *271*; dippers for, 271
    Hot Crab, 26, *27*
    Sun-Dried Tomato, 24, *37*; dippers for, 24

Divinity, 250, *251*; variations: Cherry-Almond; Chocolate-Mint; Peppermint, 250

Do-Ahead Mashed Potatoes, 109; variations, 109

Double-Frosted Chocolate Sandwich Cookies, 266, *267*

Dough, Easy Refrigerator (for onion twist), 190

Drink, 8–19
    Cinnamon Cider, 18, *15*
    Citrus Punch, Frosty, 10, *11*
    Cranberry-Orange Slush Cocktail, *6*, 12
    Cranberry Punch, Quick, 8, *9*
    Eggnog, Holiday, 14, *15*; variation, Hot Cappuccino, 14
    Hot Buttered Rum, 16, *17*
    Hot Spiced Wine, 19, *81*

Strawberry Margaritas, Frozen, 13, *13*; variation, Raspberry, 13

Strawberry Smoothie, North Pole, 272, *273*

Dumplings, Cranberry-Apple, with Crimson Sauce, 154, *155*

Edible Decorations (for the birds), 281

Eggnog
    Bread, Spirited, with Rum Glaze, 170, *171*
    Holiday, 14, *15*; variation, Hot Cappuccino, 14

Eggs
    French Toast, Morning Glory Oven, *88*, 89
    Strata, Cheesy Apple-Bacon, 86, *87*

equipment used in recipes, 341

Fill a Vase (fruit and flowers), 320, *321*

Fireside Tray (decoration), 330, *331*

Fish. *See* Smoked Salmon

Focaccia, Festive, 192, *193*

Fondue
    Cheese Dip, 25, *25*, dippers for, 25
    Peanut Butter, Christmas Vacation, 274, *275*; dippers for, 274
    White Almond, 152, 153; dippers for, 152

French Toast, Morning Glory Oven, *88*, 89

Frosty
    Citrus Punch, 10, *11*
    Fruit Bowl (decoration), 322, *323*

Frozen
    Asian Cabbage Salad, 94, *95*
    Soufflé, Merry Berry, *164*, 165; Candied Cranberries for, 165
    Strawberry Margaritas, 13, *13*; variation, Raspberry, 13

Fruit. *See also* Name of Fruit
    Bowl, Frosty (decoration), 322, *323*

Drops, Heirloom Holiday, 228, *229*

Salad, Heavenly, 102, *103*

Fruitcake, Jeweled, 140, *141*; variations, 140

Fudge. *See also* Chocolate
    Creamy Chocolate Marble, 234, *237*
    Deluxe Christmas, 236, *237*
    Fudgy No-Bakes (cookies), 260, *261*
    Sauce, Decadent, *289*, 290
    Truffle Tart, 134, *135*; decorations for, 135

Fudgy No-Bakes (cookies), 260, *261*

Garlic
    Bread Wreath, 189, *189*
    Mashed Potatoes, 109
    Vinegar, 300

Garnish Plate, Festive (decoration), 329, *329*

Gifts. *See also* Decorations
    Bird Feeder Treat (for the birds), P B and "Jay", *281*
    Biscotti (Italian cookies), 226
    Brownies, Layered, ingredients for, 234
    Candy Cane Coffee Cake, 178
    Caramels, Hazelnut-Coffee, 291
    casserole dish filled with special recipe, 125
    Chocolate Spoons, 268, *269*
    colander filled with pasta and other good things, 96
    "dessert of the month," 138
    Dessert Sauce, 288, 290
    drink mix assortment, 302
    dry snacks, 264
    Eggnog Bread in holiday basket, 170
    Fudge, in cookie-cutter shapes, 236
    fudgy no-bakes, from the family, 260
    Gingerbread Button Box, 314
    Gingerbread Drum filled with treats, 276
    Homemade Cookie Dough, ready to bake, 224

Gifts *(cont.)*
    Jam, Pineapple-Apricot, 293
    marshmallow collection, 303
    Mustard, Citrus-Caraway, 298
    packaging for, 243
    petite fruitcakes or mini-loaves, 140, *141*
    quick bread wrapped in holiday dish towel, 169
    Reindeer Snack (for santa's reindeer), 265
    Savory Scones, 198; with Apple-Pepper Jelly, 294
    Truffles, wrapped in cellophane, 235
    "vinegar of the month", 300
    Winter Wonderland Castle, 278; critters for, 279–80
Ginger
    Shrimp Kabobs, 28, *29*
    Triple, Pound Cake, 136
    Vinegar, 300
Gingerbread
    Bird Feeder (decoration), 310, *311*
    Birdhouse, Sugar and Spice, *311*, 312
    Button Cookie Box (decoration), 314, *315*
    Cookie Tree (decoration), 308, *309*
    Drum, 276, *277*
    Jewel Box, 313, *313*
    with Lemon Sauce, 142, *143*
    Muffins, 173, *173*
    Santa's Chimney, *283*, 316
    Village, 306, *307*
Gingersnaps, 220, *221*; variations: Black-and-White; Ginger Cookie Cut-outs; Laced; Snowcapped, 220
Glazed Baked Ham, 58, *59*; carving, 58; sauces for, 59
glossary of cooking terms, 341
Golden Pound Cake, 136, *136*; variations: Almond; Lemon; Orange-Coconut; Triple Ginger, 136; toppings for, 137
Goose, Roast, with Apple Stuffing, 72, *73*

Gorgonzola and Rosemary Cream Puffs, 38, *39*
grains, how to measure, 100
Gravy, Beef, 46; Lamb, 60; Turkey, 64
Green Beans, Red and White, *57*, 123

Ham. *See also* Pork
    Glazed Baked, 58, *59*; carving, 58; sauces for, 59
    Hash Browns, Holiday, 114, *115*; toppings for, 114
Hawaiian Oven Caramel Corn, 253
Hazelnut-Coffee
    Bars (cookies), 230
    Caramels, *289*, 291
Heirloom Holiday Fruit Drops, 228, *229*
Herb
    Rub, Rib Roast with, 46, *47*
    Vinegar, 300, *301*; variations: Berry; Cranberry-Orange; Garlic; Ginger; Lemon, 300
Herbed Cornish Hens, 70, *71*
Hidden Treasure Cookies, 258, *258*; variations, 258
Hoisin-Cranberry-Turkey Wraps, 68, *69*
Holiday Garland (decoration), 338, *339*
Holiday Menu
    Appetizer Party, Red and Green, 36
    Breakfast, Santa's, 272
    Brunch, Easy, 86
    Brunch, New Year's Day, 284
    Dinner, Christmas Celebration, 48
    Dinner, Christmas Eve, Memorable, 57
    Dinner Party, for Friends, 62, 78
    Office Bash, 23
    Supper, Candlelight, Christmas Eve, 77
    Supper, Fireside, 70
    Supper, Winter Cozy, 50
Honey
    Pecan Pie, 130
    -Walnut Cream Cheese, for popovers, 200

-Wine-Cranberry Tart, 132, *133*; Cookie Crust for, 132
Horseradish Sauce (roast beef), 46
Hot Buttered Rum Sauce, 149
Hot Dips
    Cheese Fondue, 25, *25*; dippers for, 25
    Crab, 26, *27*
Hot Drinks
    Buttered Rum, 16, *17*
    Cappuccino Eggnog, 14
    Spiced Wine, 19, *81*

Ice Cream, Tortoni, Christmas, 162, *162*
ice-ring, frosty, making, 8
ingredients used in recipes, 341

Jam. *See also* Butter; Chutney; Jelly Pineapple-Apricot 293, *293*
Java Mix (drink), 302
Jelly, Apple-Pepper, 294, *294*
Jeweled Fruitcake, 140, *141*; variations, 140
Julekake (with mixed candied fruit), 184, *185*; variation, using bread machine, 184

Kabobs, Ginger Shrimp, 28, *29*
Kissing Ball, Cranberry (decoration), 318, *319*
Kumquat Bay Leaf Tree (decoration), 326, *327*; variations: Beads and Baubles; Chocolate-Apricot; Nuts and Spice; Rosemary-Cranberry, 326

Lamb
    Gravy, 60
    Minted Leg of, 60, *61*; carving, 60
Lasagna, Roasted Vegetable, 82, *83*
Leek-Apple-Yam Gratin, 118, *119*
Leg of Lamb, Minted, 60, *61*; carving, 60
Lemon
    Curd, 292, *292*
    -Glazed Coffee Wreath, *166*, 177
    -Poppy Seed Popovers, 200
    Pound Cake, 136

Sauce, Gingerbread with, 142,
143
Snowballs, 212
Stampers (cookies), 259, *259*;
carrot cookie press for, 259
Vinegar, 300
Lobster Bisque, *49*, 76; variation,
with fish, 76

Main Dishes, 46–89. *See also*
Individual Category
Maple
-Cranberry Syrup, 284, *285*
-Nut Brittle, 246, *247*
-Peanut Butter Spread, 186
-Praline Bars (cookies), 230
Margaritas, Frozen Strawberry, 13,
13, variation: Raspberry, 13
Marinated
Tenderloin of Beef, 48, *49*
Vegetables, Holiday, 93, *93*
Marshmallow(s)
-Chocolate Dip, 271, *271*; dip-
pers for, 271
Peppermint, Easy Festive, 303
Meatball Merriment, *6*, 30; varia-
tions: Burgundy; Cranberry;
Spicy Apricot; Swedish; Sweet-
and-Sour, 30
Melt-in-Your-Mouth Sugar Cookies,
204, *205*; variations, 206
Melting Moments, Holiday, 218,
219
menus. *See* Holiday Menus
Meringue
-Swirled Chocolate Cake, 144,
145
Torte, Angel, *126*, 148;
Cranberries Jubilee for, 148
Merry
Berry Frozen Soufflé, *164*, 165;
Candied Cranberries for,
165
Cherry Biscotti, 226, *227*
Muffins (cranberry), *166*, 172;
variations: Apricot-Ginger;
Apple-Cinnamon; Date-Nut,
172
metric conversion guide, 342
Mincemeat-Pear Pie, 131, *131*
mini-loaves (fruitcake), 140

Minted Leg of Lamb, 60, *61*; carv-
ing, 60
Minty Middle Treasures, 216, *217*
Mocha. *See also* Coffee
Mix, Spicy, 302, *302*; variations:
Java; Orange Café au Lait,
302
Morning Glory Oven French Toast,
88, 89
Mousse, Chocolate, in Chocolate
Cups, 160, *161*
Muffins. *See also* Popovers; Scones
Gingerbread, 173, *173*
Merry (cranberry), *166*, 172;
variations: Apricot-Ginger;
Apple-Cinnamon; Date-Nut, 172
Petite Fruitcakes, 140
Mushroom(s)
Portabella-Parmesan Bruschetta,
33, *33*
Stuffing (turkey), 106
Mustard, Citrus-Caraway, 298, *299*

Napkin Rings, Noel (decoration),
328, *328*
Nibbles, Savory, 20–43. *See also*
Appetizer
No-Bake Cookies
Apricot Gems, 223, *229*; varia-
tions: Apple; Cherry;
Cranberry, 223
Fudgy, 260, *261*
North Pole Strawberry Smoothie,
272, *273*
Nut(s). *See also* Almond; Cashew;
Hazelnut; Peanut; Pecan;
Pistachio
-Date Muffins, 172
-Maple Brittle, 246, *247*
and Spice Tree (decoration), 326
-Wild Rice Cake, 139, *139*
nutrition and cooking information,
340

Office Bash (menu), 23
Onion(s)
Balsamic-Glazed Pearl, 296, *297*
Tartlets, Caramelized, 40, *41*;
variations, 40
Twist, Savory, 190, *191*; Easy
Refrigerator Dough for, 190

Orange
-Apple Stuffing (turkey), 106,
107
Café au Lait Mix (drink), 302
-Coconut Pound Cake, 136
-Cranberry Butter, 186
-Cranberry Slush Cocktail, *6*, 12
-Cranberry Vinegar, 300
-Pecan Pie, 130
-Pecan Rice, Chicken with, 62,
62
Oven Caramel Corn, *252*, 253; vari-
ations: Caramel-Apple;
Hawaiian; Red and White
Christmas, 253
Oyster
Stew, 77, *77*
Stuffing (turkey), 106

Parmesan
Portabella Bruschetta, 33, *33*
-Shrimp Pasta Bake, 74, *75*
Party Pointers (ideas for parties)
appetizers, 36
aprés-ski, 80
brunch, planning, 89
buffet bash, 23
congestion, avoiding, 16
cookie swap, 216
luminaria candles, using, 10
progressive dinner, 74
slow cooker, using, 18
table decorations, 73
tree-trimming, 79
Pasta
Bake, Parmesan-Shrimp, 74, *75*
Chicken Dijon Casserole, 63, *63*
Lasagna, Roasted Vegetable, 82,
83
Salad, Zesty, 96, *96*
Tortellini-Broccoli Salad, 97, *97*
Pastry
Basil Brie in, 34, *35*; toppings
for, 34
Cookie Crust, 132
Pie, 128
Peanut
Brittle Bread Pudding, 149, *149*;
Hot Buttered Rum Sauce for,
149
-Chocolate Chip Pie, 130

Peanut Butter
    Candies, Chocolate-Covered,
        238, *239*
    Fondue, Christmas Vacation,
        274, *275*; dippers for, 274
    -Maple Spread, 186
    P B and "Jay" Bird Feeder Treat,
        281, *281*
    Squares, 262, *262*; variation,
        Bonbons, 262
Pear(s)
    -Cranberry Chutney, *294*, 295
    -Mincemeat Pie, 131, *131*
    Poached, Winter, 156, *156*
Pecan
    Butter, 186, *187*
    -Cappuccino Nuggets, 240, *241*
    Maple-Praline Bars (cookies), 230
    Pie, *129*, 130; variations: Brandy-;
        Chocolate-; Cranberry-;
        Honey-; Orange-; Peanut-
        Chocolate Chip, 130
Peperonata and Baked Polenta
        Casserole, 84, *85*
Pepper-Apple Jelly, 294, *294*
Peppermint
    Bark, 242, *242*; variations, 242
    Divinity (candies), 250
    Marshmallows, Easy Festive, 303
    Pie, Fluffy, *162*, 163
    Pinwheels (cookies), 222
    Snowballs, 212
    Wands (candy canes), 270, *269*
Pesto
    Biscuits, 196, *197*
    -Brie Bruschetta, 33, *33*
    Pinwheels, 36, *37*
Pie, 128–34
    Cookie Crust for, 132
    Fudge Truffle Tart, 134, *135*;
        decorations for, 135
    Honey-Wine-Cranberry Tart,
        132, *133*; Cookie Crust for,
        132
    Mincemeat-Pear, 131, *131*
    Pastry for, 128
    Pecan, *129*, 130; variations:
        Brandy-; Chocolate-;
        Cranberry-; Honey-; Orange-;
        Peanut-Chocolate Chip, 130

Peppermint, Fluffy, *162*, 163
    Pumpkin, 128, *129*
Pineapple-Apricot Jam, 293, *293*
Pistachio
    -Apricot Rolled Pork, 56, *57*
    Biscotti, 226, *227*
    -Cranberry Salad with
        Champagne Vinaigrette, 92,
        92
Plate, Garnish, Festive (decoration),
        329, *329*
Polenta
    -Apple Bites, Cheesy, *42*, 43
    Baked, and Peperonata Casserole,
        84, *85*
pomegranate seeds, adding to salad,
        102
Popcorn, Oven Caramel Corn, *252*,
        253; variations: Caramel-
        Apple; Hawaiian; Red and
        White Christmas, 253
Popovers, 200, *201*; Honey-Walnut
        Cream Cheese for, 200; varia-
        tions: Cinnamon-Nut;
        Lemon-Poppy Seed, 200
Poppy Seed Bread, 169, *169*
Pork
    Apricot-Pistachio Rolled, 56, *57*
    Crown Roast of, with Stuffing,
        54, *55*
    Ham, Glazed Baked, 58, *59*;
        carving, 58; sauces for, 59
Portabella-Parmesan Bruschetta, 33,
        33
Potato(es). *See also* Sweet Potato;
        Yam
    Cheesy, 112, *113*
    Hash Browns, Holiday, 114, *115*;
        toppings for, 114
    Mashed, Do-Ahead, 109; varia-
        tions, 109
    Twice-Baked, 110, *111*; micro-
        waving, 110
Pound Cake
    Cassata, Christmas, *126*, 138
    Golden, 136, *136*; variations:
        Almond; Lemon; Orange-
        Coconut; Triple Ginger, 136;
        toppings for, 137
    Tiramisu Dessert, Easy, 158, *159*

Praline
    -Maple Bars (cookies), 230
    Truffle Cups, 248, *249*; varia-
        tions: Cherry; Crème de
        Menthe; Raspberry, 248
Pudding
    Bread, Peanut Brittle, 149, *149*;
        Hot Buttered Rum Sauce for,
        149
    Steamed, Christmas, 150, *151*;
        Creamy Sauce for, 150; Rum
        Hard Sauce for, 150
Puff Twists, Easy, 199, *199*; varia-
        tions, 199
Pumpkin
    Butter, 286
    -Marmalade Bread, 168, *169*;
        Marmalade Glaze for, 168
    Pie, 128, *129*; Pastry for, 129
Punch
    Citrus, Frosty, 10, *11*
    Cranberry, Quick, 8, *9*

Rainbow Dust (Colored Sugar) for
        No-Roll Sugar Cookies, 256
Raspberry
    and Cream Cheese Coffee
        Rounds, 182, *183*
    Margaritas, Frozen, 13
    Trifle, 157, *157*
    Truffle Cups (candies), 248
Red
    Cabbage with Apples, 122, *122*
    Pepper Bread, Cheesy Roasted,
        194, *195*
    and White Christmas Oven
        Caramel Corn, 253
    White and Green Beans, *57*,
        123
Reindeer Snack (popcorn, potatoes,
        pretzels, etc), 265
Rib Roast with Herb Rub, 46, *47*
Rice
    and Bean Roll-Ups, 80, *81*
    Orange-Pecan, Chicken with, 62,
        62
    Wild, Turkey- Casserole, 66, *67*
Roast(ed)
    Goose with Apple Stuffing, 72,
        73

Turkey, *44*, 64; Cran-Apple
    Glaze, 64; Traditional Gravy,
    44, 64
Vegetable Lasagna, 82, *83*
Vegetable Medley, 121, *121*
Rock Cornish Hens. *See* Cornish
    Hens
Rolls. *See also* Biscuits
    Dinner, *57*, 188; using bread
        machine, 188
Rosemary
    -Cranberry Tree (decoration),
        326, *327*
    and Gorgonzola Cream Puffs, 38,
        39
Rum
    Balls (candies), 244
    Butter Spritz (cookies), 210
    -Cashew Biscotti, 226, *227*; vari-
        ations: Merry Cherry;
        Pistachio, 226
    Glaze, Spirited Eggnog Bread
        with, 170, *171*
    Hard Sauce (steamed pudding),
        150
    Hot Buttered, 16, *17*; Sauce, 149

Saint Lucia Crown (coffee cake with
    dried fruit), 180, *181*; Buns,
    180
Salad, 92–104
    Cabbage, Frozen Asian, 94, *95*
    Couscous, Christmas, 98, *98*
    Cranberry Mold, Classic, 104,
        105
    Cranberry-Pistachio, with
        Champagne Vinaigrette, 92,
        92
    Fruit, Heavenly, 102, *103*
    Pasta, Zesty, 96, *96*
    Spinach, Christmas, 99, *99*; vari-
        ations, 99
    Tortellini-Broccoli, 97, *97*
    Vegetables, Holiday Marinated,
        93, *93*
    Winter Wheat Berry, 100, *101*
Salt Dough Decorations, 317, *317*
Salmon. *See* Smoked Salmon
Sandwich, Hoisin-Cranberry-Turkey
    Wraps, 68, *69*

Santa's Chimney, *283*, 316
Sauce. *See also* Butter; Syrup
    for Baked Ham, 59
    Creamy (steamed pudding), 150
    Fudge, Decadent, *289*, 290
    Horseradish (roast beef), 46
    Hot Buttered Rum, 149
    Lemon (gingerbread), 142
    Lemon Curd, 292, *292*
    Rum Hard (steamed pudding),
        150
    White Chocolate-Almond, 288,
        289
Sausage Stuffing (turkey), 106
Savory
    Chicken Cheesecake, 31, *31*
    Mini-Scones, *77*, 198
    Nibbles, 20–43. *See also* Appetizer
    Onion Twist, 190, *191*; Easy
        Refrigerator Dough for, 190
Scones
    Apricot Jeweled, 174, *175*; varia-
        tions, 174
    Mini-, Savory, *77*, 198
Seafood. *See* Crab; Lobster; Oyster;
    Shrimp
Shortbread Cookies
    Christmas Mice, 263, *263*
    Sensational, 207, *208*; variations,
        209
Shrimp
    Kabobs, Ginger, 28, *29*
    -Parmesan Pasta Bake, 74, *75*
Side Dishes, 106–25. *See also* Name
    of Vegetable; Salad; Stuffing;
    Wild Rice
Slice-It-Easy Cookies, 222, *222*;
    variations: Christmas Trees;
    Holiday Cookie Tarts;
    Peppermint Pinwheels;
    Ribbon Bar Cookies; Sugar-
    Coated Slices, 222
slush, freezing (for drinks), 12
Smoked Salmon, Cucumbers and
    Carrots Crudités, *6*, 23
Smoothie, Strawberry, North Pole,
    272, *273*
Snack
    Reindeer (popcorn, potatoes,
        pretzels, etc), 265

Toss, Teddy Bear (graham crack-
    ers, peanuts, etc), 264, *264*
Snowballs, 212, *213*; variations:
    Lemon; Peppermint, 212
Snowman Cheese Ball, 20, *21*
Soufflé, Frozen, Merry Berry, *164*,
    165; Candied Cranberries for,
    165
Soup. *See also* Stew
    Butternut Squash, *47*, 78
    Lobster Bisque, *49*, 76; variation,
        with fish, 76
Spiced Wine, Hot, 19, *81*
Spicy
    Apricot Meat Balls, 30
    Spritz (cookies), 210
Spinach Salad, Christmas, 99, *99*;
    variations, 99
Spritz (cookies), Holiday, 210, *211*;
    variations: Chocolate; Rum
    Butter; Spicy, 210
Squash
    Cinnamon Rings, 120, *120*
    Soup, Butternut, *47*, 78
Star Bruschetta, 33, *33*
Steamed Pudding, Christmas, 150,
    151; Creamy Sauce for, 150;
    Rum Hard Sauce for, 150
Stew. *See also* Soup
    Beef, Burgundy, 52, *53*
    Oyster, *77*, *77*
Strata, Cheesy Apple-Bacon, 86, *87*
Strawberry
    Butter, 186
    Margaritas, Frozen, 13, *13*; varia-
        tion, Raspberry, 13
    Smoothie, North Pole, 272, *273*

Stuffing
  Apple, Roast Goose with, 72, *73*
  Old-Fashioned for Turkey, *44*,
    106, *107*; variations: Apple-
    Cranberry; Chestnut; Corn
    Bread; Mushroom; Orange-
    Apple; Oyster; Sausage, 106
Sugar
  -Coated Slices (cookies), 222
  -Cube Trees (decoration), 304,
    305
  and Spice Birdhouse (decoration),
    311, 312
Sugar Cookies
  Melt-in-Your-Mouth, 204, *205*;
    variations, 206
  No-Roll, 256, 257; Rainbow
    Dust (Colored Sugar) for, 256
Sun-Dried Tomato. *See* Tomato
Supper (menu)
  Christmas Eve Candlelight, 77
  Fireside, 70
  Winter, Cozy, 50
Swedish Meatballs, 30
Sweet Potato. *See also* Yam
  -Applesauce Bake, 116, *117*
Sweet-and-Sour Meatballs, 30
Syrup, Maple-Cranberry, 284, *285*

table decorations, 73
Tart
  Fudge Truffle, 134, *135*; decora-
    tions for, 135
  Honey-Wine-Cranberry, 132,
    133; Cookie Crust for, 132
Tartlets, Caramelized Onion, 40, *41*;
    variations, 40

Teddy Bear Snack Toss (graham
    crackers, peanuts, etc), 264,
    264
Tenderloin of Beef, Marinated, 48,
    49
Three-Bean Christmas Chili, 79, *79*
Tiramisu Dessert, Easy, 158, *159*
toasting nuts (in microwave, oven,
    skillet), 31
Toffee, 243, *247*
  -Almond Triangles, 230, *231*;
    variations: Coffee-Hazelnut
    Bars; Maple-Praline Bars, 230
Tom-and-Jerry Brownies, 232, *233*;
    variations: Chocolate-Covered
    Cherry; Cinnamon-Spiced;
    Creamy Cappuccino, 232
Tomato, Sun-Dried
  Butter, 189
  Dip, 24, *37*; dippers for, 24
Torte, Angel Meringue, *126*, 148;
    Cranberries Jubilee for, 148
Tortellini-Broccoli Salad, 97, *97*
Tortilla Roll-Ups, Rice and Bean,
    80, *81*
Tortoni, Christmas, 162, *162*
Tortoni, Christmas, 162, *162*
Tray, Fireside (decoration), 330, *331*
Trees, Sugar-Cube (decoration), 304,
    305
Trifle, Raspberry, 157, *157*
Truffle(s), *202*, 235
  Cups, Praline, 248, *249*; varia-
    tions: Cherry; Crème de
    Menthe; Raspberry, 248
Turkey
  -Hoisin-Cranberry Wraps, 68, *69*
  Old-Fashioned Stuffing for, *44*,
    106, *107*; variations: Apple-
    Cranberry; Chestnut; Corn
    Bread; Mushroom; Orange-
    Apple; Oyster; Sausage, 106
  Roast, *44*, 64; Cran-Apple Glaze
    for, 64; Traditional Gravy for,
    44, 64
  roasting timetable for, 65
  tips for, 65
  -Wild Rice Casserole, 66, *67*
Twice-Baked Potatoes, 110, *111*
Twists, Puff, Easy, 199, *199*; varia-
    tions, 199

Vegetable(s)
  Marinated, Holiday, 93, *93*
  Medley, Roasted, 121, *121*
  Roasted, Lasagna, 82, *83*
  Winter, Curried Coconut Beef
    with, 50, *51*
Vinegar, Herb, 300, *301*; varia-
    tions: Berry; Cranberry-
    Orange; Garlic; Ginger;
    Lemon, 300

Wheat Berry, Winter, Salad, 100,
    101
White
  Almond Fondue, 152, *153*; dip-
    pers for, 152
  Chocolate-Almond Sauce, 288,
    289
  Wine Balls (candies), 244,
    245
Whole Wheat-Cranberry Bread,
    186, *187*; using bread
    machine for, 186; fancy but-
    ters for, 186
Wild Rice
  -Cranberry Bake, *71*, 108
  -Nut Cake, 139, *139*
  Orange-Pecan, Chicken with, 62,
    62
  -Turkey Casserole, 66, *67*
Wine
  -Chocolate Balls (candies), 244,
    245; variations: Rum or
    Bourbon; White Wine, 244
  Hot Spiced, 19, *81*
Winter
  Poached Pears, 156, *156*
  Vegetables, Curried Coconut Beef
    with, 50, *51*
  Wheat Berry Salad, 100, *101*
  Wonderland Castle, *254*, 278;
    critters for, 279–80
Wreath
  Candy, Golden Glow (decora-
    tion), 334, *335*
  Decorator, 336, *337*
  Holiday Garland, 338, *339*

Yam. *See also* Sweet Potato
  -Leek-Apple Gratin, 118, *119*